BIOETHICS

BRIDGE TO THE FUTURE

PRENTICE-HALL BIOLOGICAL SCIENCE SERIES

Carl P. Swanson, *editor*

PRENTICE-HALL INTERNATIONAL, INC., *London*
PRENTICE-HALL OF AUSTRALIA, PTY. LTD., *Sydney*
PRENTICE-HALL OF CANADA, LTD, *Toronto*
PRENTICE-HALL OF INDIA PRIVATE LIMITED, *New Delhi*
PRENTICE-HALL OF JAPAN, INC., *Tokyo*

BIOETHICS
BRIDGE TO THE FUTURE

Van Rensselaer Potter

Professor of Oncology and Assistant Director
McArdle Laboratory for Cancer Research
Medical School, University of Wisconsin

PRENTICE-HALL, INC., *Englewood Cliffs, New Jersey*

Current printing (last digit):

10   9   8   7   6   5   4   3   2

C—13-076513-9
P—13-076505-8

Library of Congress Catalog Card Number 72-149060

Printed in the United States of America

This book is dedicated to the memory of
ALDO LEOPOLD,
who anticipated the extension of ethics to Bioethics:

The first ethics dealt with the relation between individuals; the Mosaic Decalogue is an example. Later accretions dealt with the relation between the individual and society. The Golden Rule tries to integrate the individual to society; democracy to integrate social organization to the individual.

There is as yet no ethic dealing with man's relation to land and to the animals and plants which grow upon it. Land, like Odysseus' slavegirls, is still property. The land-relation is still strictly economic, entailing privileges but not obligations.

The extension of ethics to this third element in human environment is, if I read the evidence correctly, an evolutionary possibility and an ecological necessity. It is the third step in a sequence. The first two have already been taken. Individual thinkers since the days of Ezekiel and Isaiah have asserted that the despoliation of land is not only inexpedient but wrong. Society, however, has not yet affirmed their belief. I regard the present conservation movement as the embryo of such an affirmation.

An ethic may be regarded as a mode of guidance for meeting ecological situations so new or intricate, or involving such deferred reactions, that the path of social expediency is not discernible to the average individual. Animal instincts are modes of guidance for the individual in meeting such situations. Ethics are possibly a kind of community instinct in-the-making.

Preface

The purpose of this book is to contribute to the future of the human species by promoting the formation of a new discipline, the discipline of *Bioethics*. If there are "two cultures" that seem unable to speak to each other—science and the humanities—and if this is part of the reason that the future seems in doubt, then possibly, we might build a "bridge to the future" by building the discipline of Bioethics as a bridge between the two cultures.

This book is not such a bridge; it is merely a plea that such a bridge be built. In the past *ethics* has been considered the special province of the humanities in a liberal arts college curriculum. It has been taught along with logic, esthetics, and metaphysics as a branch of Philosophy. Ethics constitutes the study of human values, the ideal human character, morals, actions, and goals in largely historical terms, but above all *ethics implies action* according to moral standards. What we must now face up to is the fact that human ethics cannot be separated from a realistic understanding of ecology in the broadest sense. *Ethical values* cannot be separated from *biological facts*. We are in great need of a Land Ethic, a Wildlife Ethic, a Population Ethic, a Consumption Ethic, an Urban Ethic, an International Ethic, a Geriatric Ethic, and so on. All of these problems call for actions that are based on values *and* biological facts. All of them involve Bioethics, and survival of the total ecosystem is the test of the value system. In this perspective, the phrase "survival of the fittest" is simplistic and parochial.

This book is a by-product of 30 years of cancer research—years that might be considered successful from the standpoint of career, publications, promotions, awards, and personal day-to-day satisfaction of intellectual curiosity, but years which must be considered to have fallen far short of the goal of eliminating the scourge of cancer from man's horizon. Progress has been made in prevention and cure, but the conviction has grown that we must be content with small victories and not expect the type of breakthrough that was achieved in the case of poliomyelitis.

During these 30 years a growing philosophical concern about the future, about the concept of human progress, and about the fundamental nature of disorder was a constant thread of unity in my extra-curricular activities. The obsession with the cancer problem is an obvious explanation for the digression into these clearly related issues. The motivation to find "ordered disorder" at the cosmic level to explain the "disorder" seen in the practical aspects of the cancer problem must be the subconscious drive that resulted in the various thoughts that led to this small volume.

Certain isolated publications and personal contacts must be credited as milestones in the development of the interwoven themes of this book. These themes are (a) the relation between order and disorder, (b) the concept of dangerous knowledge, (c) human progress and human survival, (d) the obligation to the future, (e) the control of technology, and (f) the need for interdisciplinary effort. Although I have always been interested in philosophy, it was not until I read "Toward More Vivid Utopias" by Margaret Mead (*Science* **126:**957–961, 1957) that I became activated in a well-defined effort outside my discipline. Margaret Mead has written extensively and well, and with impressive bibliographies on the general subject of the present book. In 1957 she issued a call that struck a responsive chord in me: ". . . we need in our universities . . . Chairs of The Future. . . ." I organized a local group of faculty members as the Interdisciplinary Seminar on the Future of Man and soon afterward was asked to help plan a conference for the American Academy of Arts and Sciences (Hudson Hoagland and Ralph W. Burhoe, issue editors, "Evolution and Man's Progress," *Daedalus,* 1961). At that conference

I met and was further impressed by Dr. Mead, as well as by Dr. Hoagland and Dr. Burhoe. Through Ralph Burhoe, I was introduced to the 1961 paper by Anthony F. C. Wallace entitled "Religious Revitalization," later included in his book *Religion: An Anthropological View* (1966). Wallace alerted me to the idea that both religion and science attempt in characteristic ways to distinguish order and disorder through "a process of maximizing the quantity of organization in the matrix of perceived human experience." By 1962 the Interdisciplinary Studies Committee on the Future of Man was an official faculty committee at the University of Wisconsin. We were privileged to meet in dialogue Anthony Wallace, Don Price, John R. Platt, and others. In 1964 an invitation to participate in a symposium on Teilhard de Chardin caused me to examine his work more closely and to see his contribution as an attempt to bridge the gap between science and humanistic religion. Earlier invitations to participate in symposia, to lecture or to write in the broad area of science and society led to the separate publication of nine of the chapters in the present volume. These have now been collected and arranged in what is hoped to be a logical order. They have been supplemented by an introductory chapter, a chapter on order and disorder in human thought and action (Chapter 7), and two closing chapters.

The discussions in this book on the concept of dangerous knowledge, the fallacy of "more and better," and the problem of controlling the technology were published as early as 1962, but they could accomplish little in the hands of a very restricted group of readers. Today, thanks to the efforts of men like Congressman Emilio Daddario and Senator Gaylord Nelson, technology is receiving careful scrutiny and the environment may possibly be reclaimed. The obligation to the future has been recognized, and the need for combining science with the talents of concerned individuals in the humanities is being met with new legislation calling for an Office of Technology Assessment. The National Science Foundation is sponsoring interdisciplinary programs. Thousands of college students have suddenly realized that the future is at stake.

When I first visualized this volume, I intended to prepare a new chapter entitled "Man's Uncertain Future." In the past six months there have been so many books on various aspects of this subject that an additional projection of statistics into the year 2000 would surely be skipped by most readers. Nevertheless, those who haven't already done so should certainly read *Population, Resources, Environment, Issues in Human Ecology* by Paul R. Ehrlich and Anne

H. Ehrlich and *The Environmental Handbook* by Garrett de Bell. The latter is a collection of over 50 previous articles or excerpts and includes an extensive bibliography organized into about a dozen categories.

Bibliographies and references are important. I have great respect for a writer who includes references, and I dislike the journalistic technique in which the writer seems to disclaim any debt to the sources that in many cases he simply transcribed. The bibliography in the present volume is limited, but I have tried to acknowledge my sources and to give the reader an opportunity to read further in an organized way. No doubt some ideas have been separated from their sources and given without suitable credit, but in no case was this intentional and any instances will be corrected as promptly as possible after they are noted. An interesting final thought has to do with the uniqueness of the human individual, both biologically and culturally. One kind of cultural uniqueness is expressed by the list of books and articles one has read. The narrower the specialization, the more our book list overlaps with other specialists in the same field until the point is reached at which we become so specialized that we read only what we write. But if we begin to read both in science and in the humanities, it is unlikely that anyone else in the world has read the same books that we have. Should we not then try to draw some conclusions from the reading that no one else has done? Or if there are others who have read the same collection, should we not ask whether they derived the same message?

Madison, Wisconsin   VAN RENSSELAER POTTER

Acknowledgments

The following chapters have appeared previously in the journals or books indicated and are reprinted by permission of the editors, publishers, and copyright owners.

Teilhard de Chardin and The Concept of Purpose (Chapter 2).
Zygon, Journal of Religion and Science, **3:**367–376, December, 1968.
© The University of Chicago.

Bridge to the Future: The Concept of Human Progress (Chapter 3).
J. of Land Economics, **38:**1–8, February, 1962.
© The Regents of The University of Wisconsin.

Society and Science (Chapter 4).
Science, **146:**1018–1022, November 20, 1964.
© The American Association for the Advancement of Science.

Dangerous Knowledge: The Dilemma of Modern Science (Chapter 5).
The Capital Times, 50th Anniversary, December 13, 1967.
© The Capital Times, Madison, Wisconsin.

Council on the Future: A Proposal to Cope with the Gulf between Scientific Knowledge and Political Direction (Chapter 6).
  The Nation, February 8, 1965, pages 133–136.
  © The Nation.

The Role of the Individual in Modern Society (Chapter 8).
  From *Changing Concepts of Productive Living,* Robert B. Boyd, Editor. University Extension, Madison, Wisconsin, 1967.
  © The Regents of the University of Wisconsin.

Intracellular Responses to Environmental Change: The Quest for Optimum Environment (Chapter 9).
  Environmental Research, **3:**176–186, 1970.
  © Academic Press, Inc.

How is an Optimum Environment Defined? (Chapter 10).
  Environmental Research, **2:**476–487, 1969.
  © Academic Press, Inc.

Science and Biological Man (Chapter 11).
  From the Dedication Symposium on Sciences and the Future of Man, by permission of the University of Wisconsin, Marathon County Campus, Madison, Wisconsin.

   The author also acknowledges with thanks permission from the following sources to quote copyrighted material:

In Chapters 2 and 7, from *The Phenomenon of Man* by Pierre Teilhard de Chardin, Copyright 1955 by Editions du Seuil, Paris, Copyright © 1959 in the English translation by Wm. Collins Sons & Co. Ltd., London and Harper and Row, Publishers, New York. By permission of the publishers. In Chapter 7, from *The Greeks and The Irrational* by E. R. Dodds, with permission of the author, and The University of California Press. From *The Ghost in the Machine* by Arthur Koestler, with permission of the author and The Macmillan Company. From "Erratic Displays as a Device Against Predators," *Science* **156:**1767 (1967) by P. M. Driver and D. A. Humphries with permission of the authors and the American Association for the Advancement of Science. From manuscript on *Protean Behavior* with permission from the authors P. M. Driver and D. A. Humphries. From *Religion: An Anthropological View* by A. F. C. Wallace, with permission of the author and Random House. From an article on Arthur Schlesinger, Jr. dated December 17, 1965, with permission from TIME, The Weekly Newsmagazine, Copyright Time, Inc., 1965. From *Doubt and Certainty in Science: A Biologist's Reflections on the Brain* with permission from the author, J. Z. Young, and The Clarendon Press.

The author also gratefully acknowledges the accurate typing of the manuscript made possible by the cooperation of Helen Iverson and Karen Pond and the availability of the Magnetic Tape Selectric Typewriter manufactured by International Business Machines.

V.R.P.

Contents

1   **Bioethics, The Science of Survival**   1

Biology and Wisdom in Action ☐ *Reductionism versus Holism in Biology* ☐ *Mechanism versus Vitalism* ☐ *Man as an Error-Prone Cybernetic Machine* ☐ *Twelve Categories and Paradigms in Mechanistic Biology* ☐ *Physiological Adaptation as the Key to Biology* ☐ *Biology, Philosophy, and Cultural Adaptation*

2   **Teilhard de Chardin and the Concept of Purpose**   30

Teilhard and Science ☐ *Teilhard as an Evolutionist* ☐ *Teilhard's Use of the Evolutionary Picture to Understand Religious Values* ☐ *The Cybernetics of Human Values* ☐ *The Role of Knowledge, Ignorance, and Natural Selection in Further Evolution of Values* ☐ *Summation*

3   **Bridge to the Future: The Concept of Human Progress**   42

The Idea of Progress ☐ *Three Concepts of Progress* ☐ *The Religious Concept of Progress* ☐ *The Materialistic Concept of Progress* ☐ *Darwin and Spencer* ☐ *Spengler and Toynbee* ☐ *Survival or Extinction?* ☐ *More and Better?* ☐ *The Scientific-Philosophic Concept of Progress*

4   Society and Science   **55**

*Science and Disorder □ The Quest for Order □ Rise of Un-
manageable Knowledge □ Upsurge in Molecular Biology □
The Living Machine □ Chemical Control of Life Processes
□ Specific Suggestions □ Conclusion*

**5   Dangerous Knowledge: The Dilemma of
    Modern Science**   **69**

6   Council on the Future   **75**

*Dangerous Knowledge □ Knowers and Doers □ A Council
on the Future □ The Tree of Knowledge □ Value Systems in
Peril □ A Journal for Mankind □ Conclusion*

7   The Role of Disorder in Human Activity and Thought   **83**

*The Essence of the Religious Process □ Categories of Religious
Viewpoints □ Disorder, Chaos, Randomicity and Chance □
Teilhard de Chardin and Disorder □ Beyond Teilhard: The
Next Step □ Disorder in Human Affairs □ The Greeks and
Disorder □ Confusion Theory □ Protean Behavior □ Vari-
able Behavior □ The Human Brain □ Rationalizing the Ir-
rational*

8   The Role of the Individual in Modern Society   **103**

*The Individual and His Environment □ The Nature of Man
and His Ideas □ Application □ Adaptation □ Human Welfare
□ Conclusion*

**9   Intracellular Responses to Environmental Change: The
    Quest for Optimum Environment**   **118**

*The Wisdom of the Body □ Changes in Enzyme Amount □
Three Kinds of Adaptation □ Systematic Oscillations in
Animals on Controlled Feeding Schedules □ The Quest for
Optimum Environment □ Conclusion*

10 How Is an Optimum Environment Defined? 133

Optimum Stress □ Culture as Environment □ Physiologic Adaptation □ Enzyme Adaptation to Toxic Hazards □ Enzyme Adaptation to Daily Regimens □ Enzyme Adaptation to Fasting □ Definition of Optimum Environment

11 Science and Biological Man 149

Society and the Specialist □ The Priority Problems of Our Time □ The Role of Biology □ Biology for the Future □ Nature or Nurture? □ Summary

12 Biocybernetics—The Key to Environmental Science 162

E-Day □ Ecology or Economics □ Technology Assessment □ Feedback Loops from Effect to Cause □ Atomic Reactors as Black Boxes □ Living Systems as Black Boxes □ Population, Feedback, and Ecosystems □ Studies on Populations of Small Mammals □ Zero Population Growth

13 Survival as a Goal for Wisdom 183

Wisdom: The Discipline for Action □ Societal Competence as a Function of Wisdom and Knowledge □ Toward a Common Value System □ A Bioethical Creed for Individuals □ Future Action

Author Index 197

Subject Index 201

CHAPTER ONE

Bioethics, The Science of Survival

Abstract Man's natural environment is not limitless. Education should be designed to help people understand the nature of man and his relation to the world. The subject matter should include both the reductionist view and the holistic view of biology and should be broader than both together. Man is considered as an error-prone cybernetic machine, and 12 categories of relevant knowledge and their corresponding paradigms are presented. Man's survival may depend on ethics based on biological knowledge; hence Bioethics.

Biology and Wisdom in Action

Mankind is urgently in need of new wisdom that will provide the "knowledge of how to use knowledge" for man's survival and for improvement in the quality of life. This concept of wisdom as a guide for action—the knowledge of how to use knowledge for the social good—might be called *Science of Survival*, surely the prerequisite to improvement in the quality of life. I take the position that the science of survival must be built on the science of biology and enlarged beyond the traditional boundaries to include the most essential elements of the social sciences and the humanities with emphasis

1

on philosophy in the strict sense, meaning "love of wisdom." A science of survival must be more than science alone, and I therefore propose the term *Bioethics* in order to emphasize the two most important ingredients in achieving the new wisdom that is so desperately needed: biological knowledge and human values.

In this age of specialization we seem to have lost contact with the daily reminders that must have driven home the truth to our ancestors: man cannot live without harvesting plants or killing animals. If plants wither and die and animals fail to reproduce, man will sicken and die and fail to maintain his kind. As individuals we cannot afford to leave our destiny in the hands of scientists, engineers, technologists, and politicians who have forgotten or who never knew these simple truths. In our modern world we have botanists who study plants and zoologists who study animals, but most of them are specialists who do not deal with the ramifications of their limited knowledge. Today we need biologists who respect the fragile web of life and who can broaden their knowledge to include the nature of man and his relation to the biological and physical worlds. We need biologists who can tell us what we can and must do to survive and what we cannot and must not do if we hope to maintain and improve the quality of life during the next three decades. The fate of the world rests on the integration, preservation, and extension of the knowledge that is possessed by a relatively small number of men who are only just beginning to realize how inadequate their strength, how enormous the task. Every college student owes it to himself and his children to learn as much as possible of what these men have to offer, to challenge them, to meld biological knowledge with whatever additional ingredient they are able to master, and to become, if their talents are adequate, the leaders of tomorrow. From such a pooling of knowledge and values may come a new kind of scholar or statesman who has mastered what I have referred to as Bioethics. No individual could possibly master all of the components of this branch of knowledge, just as no one today knows all of zoology or all of chemistry. What is needed is a new discipline to provide models of life styles for people who can communicate with each other and propose and explain the new public policies that could provide a "bridge to the future." The new disciplines will be forged in the heat of today's crisis problems, all of which require some kind of a mix between basic biology, social sciences, and the humanities.

Biology is more than botany and zoology. It is the foundation on which we build *ecology*, which is the relation among plants, animals, man, and the physical environment. Biology includes the science of genetics, which has to do with all aspects of heredity, and physiology, which deals with the function of individuals. For thousands of years men have lived on this earth with no generally disseminated knowledge of their chemical nature. Man's dependence upon his natural environment was widely understood, but Nature's bounty was considered to be limitless and Nature's capacity to recover from exploitation was considered to be ample. Eventually it was realized that man was exploiting the earth to an extent that required the use of more and more science and technology as the richest sources of iron and copper, for example, were used up. From the biological standpoint man has progressively taken over the planet's resources by decreasing the numbers and kinds of other species of life and by increasing only those species that were useful to man, such as wheat, beef cattle, and other consumables. As a cancer specialist, I was naturally impressed with Norman Berrill's statement, which has been repeated in various forms by others without citation since his publication of *Man's Emerging Mind* in 1955 (1). He observed that "So far as the rest of nature is concerned, we are like a cancer whose strange cells multiply without restraint, ruthlessly demanding the nourishment that all of the body has need of. The analogy is not far fetched for cancer cells no more than whole organisms know when to stop multiplying, and sooner or later the body of the community is starved of support and dies." In other words, we can ask the question, is it man's fate to be to the living Earth what cancer is to Man?

In 1955 these words could go largely unheeded, despite the fact that Berrill's book is one of the biological classics of our time. It was widely assumed that science could produce "more and better" of everything that man needed and that progress could be equated with growthmanship (see Chapter 3). The end of that era came suddenly and dramatically at a moment that in retrospect is easy to pinpoint. It came with the publication of *Silent Spring* in 1962 by Rachel Carson (2), who was soon to feel the fury of the interests who were stung by her indictment. Now we can see that the issue is no longer whether she overstated the case against pesticides, and she must be credited with starting the tide of questions that have now reached the flood stage. We now are no longer assuming that science can produce the technology to feed man's increasing numbers (3, 4). We have been told that without the pesticides and herbicides the job would be impossible, and now we are beginning to hear that man may be endangered by some of the very chemicals that were said to be his salvation (5). From many uninformed quarters we now hear demands for a moratorium on science, when what we need is more and better science. We need to combine biology with humanistic knowledge from diverse sources and forge a science of survival that will be able to set a system of priorities. We need to start action in the areas where knowledge is already available, and we need to reorient our research effort to get the necessary knowledge if it is not available.

The age-old questions about the nature of man and his relation to the world become increasingly important as we approach the remaining three decades in this century, when political decisions made in ignorance of biological knowledge, or in defiance of it, may jeopardize man's future and indeed the future of earth's biological resources for human needs. As individuals we speak of the "instinct for survival," but the sum total of all our individual instincts for survival is not enough to guarantee the survival of the human race in a form that any of us would willingly accept. An *instinct* for survival is not enough. We must develop the *science* of survival, and it must start with a new kind of ethics—bioethics. The new ethics might be called *interdisciplinary ethics*, defining interdisciplinary in a special way to include both the sciences and the humanities. This term is rejected, however, because the meaning is not self-evident.

As a discipline, traditional biology has reached the stage where it can be taught in terms of principles, recognizing that it is impossible for any individual to become familiar with all the available examples that illustrate the principles. Bioethics can serve no useful ends if it is to be merely a watered-down version of contemporary biology. Therefore, I will present in this chapter 12 fundamental biological concepts that seem important to me as a mechanistic biologist, because of my conviction that Bioethics must be based on modern concepts of biology and not on unsupported introspection.

Before presenting the mechanistic concepts it may be desirable to first mention the nature of the scientific revolution and some of the major historical polarizing views of *mechanism versus vitalism* and *reductionism versus holism*, which in my opinion have delayed the development of a broad and unified biologically-oriented value system. Reductionism and mechanism are the aspects of biology that push the dissection of the living organism to the smallest possible units, inquiring at each stage how the units interact. As the dissection has proceeded to the level of atoms and molecules, the new biologists have become chemists, taking the name *molecular* biologists, and have given the impression that they are not concerned with the organism but only with the parts. These biologists frequently present the popular image of *scientist* as opposed to *humanist*, and their contribution to Bioethics is the reductionist knowledge that comes from the laboratory. Meanwhile the biologists concerned with the *whole* organism, the *holists*, tend toward the humanistic side of the balance, but not as far as the *vitalists*, who in most cases today are not professional biologists. The vitalists are frequently people in the humanities or people whose religious convictions affect their introspective attempts to understand biology. Some highly respected biologists of earlier times were vitalists for historical reasons; that is, they were unable to explain their observations without invoking the idea that mysterious or supernatural ("vital") forces guided all living organisms. Hence the concept of *vitalism*. I hope to make clear my own viewpoint that Bioethics should attempt to integrate the reductionistic and mechanistic principles with the holistic principles. Moreover, Bioethics should examine the nature of human knowledge and its limitations because, in my opinion, it is in this area that the only valid residue of vitalism makes its stand. Bioethics should develop a realistic understanding of biological knowledge and its limitations in order to make recommendations in the field of public policy.

The Scientific Revolution

In order to understand where contemporary biology stands, we need to look upon biological science as one of the consequences of the scientific revolution. Biological knowledge is not something that can be gained by introspection alone. The reason for doubting the validity of unsupported introspection is based on cumulative knowledge about human behavior: we all have built-in instincts for self- and ego-preservation, and we have passions, emotions, and irrational moments. Moreover, we are built in such a way that each new idea appears to solve some problem and creates in us a glow of euphoria. We feel that we have the answer to whatever it was that stimulated us, however transient the feeling may be. Each of the great advances in biology, such as Mendelian genetics and Darwinian evolution, was based on years of experimentation and observation. Nevertheless, these advances had to overcome the previous and persisting ideas that had been arrived at by men whose ideas came from within and were reenforced by a euphoria that was personally convincing. Many of the deep-rooted ideas remaining in the world today—not only in science but in all fields—were originated by individual men who were convinced that they knew truth from within (or by a proclaimed revelation from an outside source) and who by strength of personality were able to gain momentum enough to silence their possible critics. Obviously some ideas have been helpful, while others (for example, those of Hitler) have been the source of much trouble in the world.

The chief feature which distinguishes the scientific approach to a problem from the nonscientific approach (whatever that is called) is the realization than an idea is not necessarily valid just because it seems right to its possessor and makes him feel good. When a scientist gets an idea, he, too, has a pleasant reaction, but he starts looking for a way to test the idea, charging with it into his peer group, suggesting an experiment, referring to previous work (called "the literature"), and occasionally crossing the disciplinary boundaries. In suggesting a new discipline called Bioethics and specifying that we look outside the traditional sciences, I am not suggesting that we abandon the traditional treatment for a new idea, but rather that we cross the disciplinary boundaries on a somewhat broader scope and look for ideas that are susceptible to objective verification in terms of the future survival of man and improvement in the quality of life for future generations (6). In general we can only learn by hindsight, but even this is impossible if we do not keep adequate records and if we rely only on our individual impressions. In the humanities the only test of an idea is its acceptance by society, and if society chooses on the basis of conventional but ill-founded wisdom or on individual short-term gratifications, it may perpetuate an idea that might better have been buried. We need to reexamine our premises and look for better ways to reach a consensus among disciplines, based as far as possible on objective verification and adequate monitoring of the trends in environmental quality.

One of the most important aspects of the scientific revolution is the recognition that ideas can no longer be based on introspection or logic alone. Furthermore, as a general proposition, they cannot be based on a single proof, though they can be rejected on the basis of a single experimentally valid disproof (7, 8). Instead of the word *idea* as used above, T. S. Kuhn (9) has employed the term *paradigm* to describe the basic ideas or concepts in what he refers to as "normal science," which in turn appears to mean the research activities of specialists working within accepted disciplines. These paradigms are the ideas, concepts, hypotheses, or models that provide convenient packages or labels for the basic propositions on which the particular field is constructed. They should be clear enough to be understood by the specialists, yet open-ended enough to provide for further effort. Kuhn emphasizes the resistance displayed by scientists toward any threatened change in the paradigms that characterize their specialty. As I understand his message, a paradigm is much more than a widely accepted hypothesis or postulate; it is a statement that *no one among the experts expects to see disproved*. Thus the concepts to be presented later in this chapter are 12 paradigms in the Kuhn sense (9), covering major aspects of biochemistry and molecular biology, on the assumption that these information capsules may be helpful for those who wish to work in the field of Bioethics by gaining some appreciation of working assumptions that contemporary biologists do not expect to see disproved.

Reductionism versus Holism in Biology

In advocating a new branch of biology I am aware of an existing schism in present biology making for more specialization rather than less. The molecular biologists, whose specialty is unquestionably symbolized by the DNA double helix of Watson and Crick (10), are often accused of being ignorant of "real" biology; their discipline is equated with reductionism. "Real" biology is said to be holistic biology—that is, it is concerned with the whole animal and the whole situation. The trouble with the separation into reductionism and holism is that in considering the whole animal and the whole situation we now have to consider the intimate reductionist details of molecular biology, because these are the *targets* of our environmental hazards, as will be noted. This discussion is therefore a defense of reductionism and molecular biology as stages in the evolution of the new holistic biology that I refer to as Bioethics.

The molecular biologists have their own paradigms; the one best known is called the Central Dogma, which has been remarkably productive. It simply states that biological information passes from nucleic acids to protein. In more detail, it holds that the linear sequence of DNA information bits (base pairs) specifies not only the template for its own replication but also the template for the linear sequence of RNA information bits, which in turn specifies the linear sequence of protein building blocks, which in turn determines the 3-dimensional folding. No exceptions have been established up to now, and there is nothing in the Dogma that denies the possibility that the information in one DNA subsection may be modulated by products from some other subsection of DNA. Nor is it implied that DNA molecules replicate themselves or transcribe themselves to RNA as some critics have charged. The replications and transcriptions are brought about by proteins whose structure is specified by a particular subsection of the DNA complement. It is not assumed that these details can be understood without considerable chemical background and preparation.

But these details of the Central Dogma do not exhaust the possibilities for its continued articulation by molecular biologists. The Central Dogma has been paralleled by another paradigm that has been described by Platt as epitomizing the approach of the molecular biologists. This is the method of strong inference and multiple alternative hypotheses (7). According to this approach even the Central Dogma cannot be proved; it can only survive by failing to be disproved, and like the whole of science in this era, conclusions must be considered as tentative and subject to disproof. What is meant is that a theory can only encompass the available facts, and the possible dimensions of future experiments cannot be foreseen. A theory is not necessarily disproved but frequently may be enlarged or modified to accomodate new knowledge. The acceptance of this new paradigm of the uncertainty of human knowledge has led to a new breed of scientists who enjoy science as a game of wits in which parry and thrust are the order of the day. Students are conditioned to challenge their mentors and to be able to relinquish their fondest beliefs. While it is conceivable that a whole generation could be misled into accepting the Central Dogma as a universal truth rather than as an expedient operating premise, there are enough rewards for dissent to insure that minority views will be heard.

Of all the dissenting views elicited by molecular biology one of the most frequent is the complaint that the new biologists are reductionists who believe that cells can be explained solely in terms of molecules, that animals and man can be explained solely in terms of cells, and so on. But the people who voice the complaints are usually leaping to the conclusion that the enthusiasm and brashness of the new biologists means that they believe that cells can be explained in terms of molecules *and nothing else.* It would be more accurate to say that they believe that cells must be explained in terms of molecules, and men in

terms of cells, and that principles of higher organization will emerge as
the lower levels become understood. Indeed, these principles are now
emerging in terms of feedback loops between the component molecules. The idea that all of biology can be explained in terms of chemistry and physics *and nothing else that is not available to the minds of
men* is a proposition that can be acted upon even if it remains to be
proved, and its chief drawback has been the lack of humility and ordinary prudence that it has encouraged in the application of limited biological knowledge to environmental problems of heroic proportions.
While it is perfectly conceivable that eventually all of biology, including ecology and environmental hazards, can be explained and predicted in terms that are available to the minds of men, I for one do not
believe that the information can ever be contained in the mind of a
single man, and I have serious doubts as to whether it can be computer-
ized or otherwise managed so as to be available to a single man or group
of men for purposes of infallible prediction of side-effects. Although
earlier in this chapter I defined wisdom as the knowledge of how to use
knowledge, that is, how to balance science with other knowledge for
social good (see also Chapter 3) I am here reminded of the ancient
psalmist who said "The fear of the Lord is the beginning of wisdom."
In contemporary terms this can be taken to mean that the forces of
Nature cannot easily be manipulated to man's short-range demands
without society's incurring many long-range consequences that cannot
always be foreseen. Thus in many cases we learn by hindsight, but what
is more tragic is our frequent *failure* to learn by hindsight. The beginning of wisdom in the sense of the psalmist and in contemporary terms
may invoke in us a decent respect for the far-flung web of life and a
humility as to our limited ability to comprehend all of the repercussions of our technological arrogance. I think that it is one thing to
accumulate knowledge at the molecular level and to proceed on the
assumption that it will be manageable, and it is quite another to operate
at the management level and to deal with the application of knowledge
that is always incomplete. Yet this is the predicament of the Federal
Food and Drug Administration and many other government agencies,
who can scarcely avoid a charge of under-reaction or over-reaction in
many instances that are judged with the benefit of hindsight. There can
be no doubt that neither our medical experts nor the administrative
officers with whom they must cooperate can possibly have as much
information and insight as they need for decisions on any given occasion, or as much public understanding of their predicament as they
deserve.

It is clear that in the face of our actual needs, the arguments of reductionism versus holism become absurd. The intact organism is more than a simple sum of its parts, but the organism arises by virtue of the communication between cells. This communication is in terms of molecules and is best understood by the reductionists, but at the same time it forms the feedback network and structural integration that makes holistic mechanisms a reality. Thus each hierarchical level is formed by the feedback connections that link its subunits into a higher organization. We must combine biological reductionism and holism and then proceed to an ecological and ethical holism if man is to survive and prosper. But this integration may be impeded by a tendency to equate reductionism with the mechanistic view of life and holism with the vitalistic view of life; this tendency will now be discussed.

Mechanism versus Vitalism

A number of years ago I made the statement that man is a machine, and I took the position that this was no longer a debatable point, noting that we should direct our attention to the question "What kind of a machine is man?" (Chapter 4). More recently I had the opportunity to review (11) the book by Reiner, *The Organism As An Adaptive Control System*, (12) and to observe that his description is a more meaningful description of life than the simple term *machine,* which is immediately alienating to some and is misunderstood by many others. Nonetheless the concept of life as an adaptive control system is still on the side of mechanism in the old argument between the mechanistic and vitalistic concepts of life and of man. From time to time we see statements that the mechanistic concept of man is outmoded, no longer held, invalidated by new knowledge, and so on, but these statements mean nothing as unsupported opinions. We really are obliged to ask what mechanists believe, what vitalists believe, and if man is a machine, what kind of a machine is man?

Here I must identify myself as a mechanist and place myself in opposition to all who wish to challenge that view. As a matter of opinion, I would go along with the words of Nobel prizewinner Francis Crick who said " . . . And so to those of you who may be vitalists I would make this prophecy: What everyone believed yesterday and you believe today, only cranks will believe tomorrow" (13).

If we examine the opposing views more closely, we find that they are really matters of belief, i.e., of opposing kinds of faith. In essence the mechanist says "life is explainable in terms of chemistry and physics and nothing more that is not available to the minds of men" while the vitalist says "life is not explainable in terms of chemistry and physics alone, and the added ingredients transcend the realm of knowledge that is available to the minds of men." The mechanist has faith that even if all the facts are not known today, some day they will be known. I suspect that the vitalist fears the advent of such a day, and probably hopes (perhaps rightly) that it will never arrive. Meanwhile the world is in danger of going down the drain while we argue the question "to tamper or not to tamper" because in many respects this is what the argument between mechanists and vitalists is all about. There is ample evidence that much of the opposition to science and to environmental planning comes from people who believe that the world operates according to an already established plan and that any attempts to dissect, understand mechanistically, or manipulate are simply getting off on the wrong foot and certain to fail in the long run. My own view as a pragmatic mechanist is that the question of success or failure still hangs in the balance, but the question to tamper or not to tamper has already been answered. Cultural evolution has decided that man *will* tamper with his environment and with his own biology. Man has tampered on a colossal scale, and we cannot revert to a hands-off policy at this point in history. Henceforth we can only plead for more intelligent, more conservative, and more responsible tampering. We must plead not for a moratorium on new knowledge but for a coupling of biological knowledge and human values, i.e., an interdisciplinary or biologically-based ethics.

I have already indicated that I am not convinced of the validity of the mechanistic view in its extreme form that all knowledge is theoretically available, and I have a lurking suspicion that the minds of men may not achieve the societal wisdom that is needed. But as a professional biochemist trying to "solve" the cancer problem, and having become interested in the dilemma of science and technology —to tamper or not to tamper—I have concluded that we have to proceed on the basis of the mechanistic premise, but we must bring in greater emphasis on human values and ethics. We have to proceed *as if* we believed that the solution to man's major problems includes nothing that isn't "available to the minds of men," with just the added ingredient of humility ("fear of the Lord") that admits the possibility that natural forces may elude our attempts to build the kind of Utopia we can imagine. Whether a belief in a Deity is required or not is less important to me than the question of whether we proceed with humility or with arrogance, whether we respect the forces of Nature or whether we assume that science can do anything, whether we look at our ethical heritage or whether we ignore it.

It seems to me we have no choice other than to try to deal with dangerous knowledge by seeking more knowledge (Chapter 5). We have already decided to tamper with the system, now we can do no less than to proceed with humility, respect the forces of Nature, and with respect to our ethical heritage, "prove all things; hold fast that which is good." The situation is urgent. In the opinion of many some aspects of our ecological problem may already have reached a point of "no return" as far as man's purposes are concerned. We need to rather quickly discover the weakest links in our environmental complex and begin to correct our past mistakes.

Man as an Error-Prone Cybernetic Machine

The concept of life as a cybernetic machine has been admirably discussed by Reiner in the publication (12) referred to earlier, and if this is a correct image, the humanistic biologist will have to adjust to it. I have only to add one more ingredient that was not stressed by Reiner, namely, the quality of disorder (Chapter 7). I would agree with Reiner that man can be described as an adaptive control system, but I would insist that it is not enough to assume that the quality of disorder is implicit in that definition. I would insist that it be explicit. Thus I would postulate that *man is an adaptive control system with elements of disorder built into every hierarchial level.* Reiner has emphasized the description of machines or control devices in terms of the "mode of operation" and the "mode of control," each of which may be *fixed* or *variable.* By this approach we come up with the following categories and my own modification:

Device	Mode of Operation	Mode of Control	Reference
Simple machine	Fixed	Fixed	Reiner (12)
Simple control system	Variable	Fixed	Reiner (12)
Adaptive control system	Variable	Variable	Reiner (12)
Living system	Variable + disorder	Variable + disorder	Potter (11)

The modification that I have proposed can be illustrated by Reiner's description (12) of the variable modes of operation and control typified by a man running toward the trajectory of a ball that he is trying to catch, when he suddenly discovers that it is not what he had assumed but something dangerous (Reiner mentioned a concrete block or a rattlesnake), whereupon the man rationally changes his attitude from wanting-to-catch to not-wanting-to-catch (as any good adaptive control mechanism should). I pointed out (11) that we all know of situations where the human machine for inexplicable reasons changes back from the rational move (not-wanting to catch) to the irrational move (wanting to catch the rattlesnake) in a split second, and sometimes gets away with it and thereby establishes a new behavioral pattern (cf. Chapter 7).

It is not possible to discuss details of living systems as adaptive systems with built-in disorder without looking into the molecular levels of life. I have rather arbitrarily set up 12 categories of biological knowledge which can be used to organize the detailed knowledge in the field, and I will follow each category with a brief statement which will be an accepted postulate, or paradigm in the sense employed by Kuhn (9), that is, an accepted postulate that is not doubted by experts in the field.

Twelve Categories and Paradigms in Mechanistic Biology

1. Molecular Structure, Interconversion, and Interaction

Paradigm   *Every living system is a community of molecules, maintained in organized configurations and relationships by undergoing continual syntheses and degradations through successive small changes that take up or give off energy in the form of heat or work (14, 15).*

There are no texts, references, or encyclopedias that attempt to list the total number of kinds of molecules required for even the simplest form of life, probably because the task has been considered impossible to fulfill. It is possible to hazard a guess that the number is not less than 1000 but whether it is 3000 or 10,000 or greater is anyone's guess. It was formerly thought that cells with simple nutritive requirements (so-called autotrophs) were simple cells; but with the discovery that these cells contained all the compounds most characteristic of higher forms of life, it was realized that all cells have a long list of substances that are required for their on-going life processes, called *essential metabolites.* Some cells make these substances themselves and do not need them as nutrients. Other cells are unable to make some of the compounds, and for such cells we can draw up a list of *essential nutrients.* For man the list of essential nutrients is fairly long and includes a number of vitamins, amino acids, minerals, and additional substances (see reference 16).

2. Catalysis, More Specifically, the Chemistry of Enzyme Action

Paradigm *The majority of chemical reactions in living cells are too slow and too improbable to occur in the absence of a catalyst, and the cells have mechanisms for increasing or decreasing the amount and the activity of the proteinaceous catalysts (enzymes) that make the necessary reactions occur at an appropriate rate. All specialized functions and all general organismic functions depend on catalysis.*

Chemical reactions cannot be catalyzed unless they are energetically possible, and it is often said that an enzyme cannot bring about a conversion that would not occur spontaneously at a slower rate. This statement is true, but it sometimes gives the misleading impression that life without enzymes would be possible though sluggish. This does not follow, for reasons that will become apparent below (also see reference 17).

3. Energy-Coupling Mechanisms

Paradigm *Life is maintained by a continual input of energy which must be available to convert building blocks to more complicated essential metabolites, to provide heat, and to do electrical, mechanical, and chemical work. The essential trick of using energy-yielding reactions to drive energy-requiring reactions is called energy-coupling, and without it life would be impossible.*

The energy is obtained by the combustion of fuel that can be obtained from the environment and oxidized with atmospheric oxygen or by means of cleavages and reactions with other electron acceptors. A compound frequently mentioned as an energy coupler is ATP (adenosine triphosphate) because it is frequently a common denominator, being formed by energy-yielding reactions and dissipated by energy-requiring reactions (18).

4. Alternative Metabolic Pathways

Paradigm   *Individual molecules of nearly every essential nutrient and essential metabolite and most intermediary metabolites are not predestined to be used either as fuel or as building blocks for energy-requiring reactions but collectively may be used in varying proportions for alternative divergent pathways, the balance of which is determined by the amount and activity of the several enzymes that compete with each other for any given molecule (16). Similarly, alternative converging pathways provide for multiple routes of synthesis for many essential metabolites.*

It is the existence of alternative pathways and competing enzyme systems that makes the possibility of "sluggish" life without enzymes completely impossible. Thus the idea of enzymes doing nothing but speeding up reactions is absurd. If a metabolite A can go to either B or C, and these in turn can go to D or E and F or G, respectively, the proportion of A that ends up as D, E, F, and G will in fact be determined by the amount and activity of the six competing enzymes (catalyzing A to B, A to C, B to D, B to E, C to F, and C to G, respectively), and the proportions will vary widely in different cells at the same time and in the same cells at different times. It is the competition between alternative divergent and convergent pathways that determines the course and duration of life (and, I might add, the presence or absence of cancer, and the difficulties of cancer chemotherapy). See Fig 1.1.

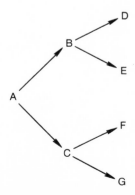

Fig. 1.1   Alternative pathways of metabolism illustrating competition between enzymes. See text.

5. Energy Storage, Gauging, and Replenishment

Paradigm *Every cell and every hierarchy of cells has a limited amount of reserve energy in the form of compounds immediately available and in the form of back-up reservoirs that can be used to replenish the working reserves. In addition the inventory of reserves must be constantly known and warning signals must be activated to demand replenishment of the energy reserves from outside sources, whenever the internal reserves are threatened.*

This is probably the key piece of information that vitalists seem not to have understood. Vitalists usually emphasize the idea of a guiding purposeful drive in living organisms, sometimes referred to as the *élan vital*. In the absence of detailed understanding of the built-in mechanisms by which even the simplest organism can judge the status of its energy reserves and mechanistically take action when these reserves are threatened, it is easy to imagine some mysterious vitalistic principle as the explanation. But obviously a rather simple machine could be devised to do the job of sensing energy status and acting appropriately. The point is that any cell that could not perform in this way never survived to be observed by us, so all successful living organisms behave purposefully in terms of their own or their species' survival.

6. Information Storage

Paradigm *All living organisms at all hierarchical levels must cope with their environment and, having survived, be able to store and retrieve the vital know-how, using relatively stable molecules like DNA (deoxyribonucleic acid) (19) or relatively stable associations of communicating cells, as in brain and nerve networks, or organs that communicate by means of special chemicals via blood and body fluids. The stored information is part of the machinery that provides for both the formation of the catalysts (enzymes) and their structural and humoral organization.*

I have estimated the number of DNA molecules in a human cell at 450,000 based on actual analyses and assuming a molecular weight and the possible number of informational bits (base pairs) at about 5.8 billion. The sum total of the information in the DNA molecules in an organism constitutes the *genotype*, and biological scientists are eager to learn whether DNA molecules are the only form of biological information storage. Four nucleotides in a sequence of 2 can be arranged in 4^2 or 16 different ways, and a sequence of 10 can be arranged in 4^{10} or about a million different ways. Thus, the possible total of sequences for 5.8 billion base pairs is for practical purposes infinite (20).

Similarly, if the number of central neurons in the brain system is 10 billion (Chapter 8), the number of possible connections is practically infinite. It is inconceivable that we will ever have all the possible details of the stored information mastered, and we have to ask ourselves the practical question of how much to tamper? when? and how? As indicated earlier, we have already tampered with Nature a great deal, and to do nothing at this time is also a form of tampering with the system.

7. Information Replication

Paradigm   *A cell or a hierarchy of cells that has the ability to cope with its environment must pass this information on to its progeny if life is to persist, and it does so by replicating the necessary information in ultramicro-packages, apportioning the duplicated material to progeny cells partly by Mendelian genetics (21) and partly by other mechanisms.*

When the basic structure of the DNA double helix (cf. model, reference 22) was first proposed by Watson and Crick (10), they stated at once, "It has not escaped our notice that the specific pairing we have postulated immediately suggests a possible copying mechanism for the genetic material." Whether all of the nontransient information in a fertilized egg is contained in its nuclear and extranuclear DNA molecules is still not known, but the process of differentiation and development that leads to an adult in organisms with or without brains is in any case encoded. The information that is thus programmed is not a fixed program but a program of unfolding capacities for physiological and psychological adaptation. We are programmed to respond in a variable way to a certain range of environmental contingencies. As men we are not built to respond in the best possible way to any possible environment, but to respond in a satisfactory way to the environment in which we evolved to *Homo sapiens*. It is my contention that this response included the preservation of a built-in tendency toward irrational or erratic behavior, if the unplanned or irrational behavior led to desirable results. Man would then *learn* to repeat this behavior (Chapter 7). Thus, we are not robots but are capable of learning by unplanned experience (i.e., by hindsight) in addition to learning by planned experience (e.g., from traditions in the cultural heritage). Information gathering capacity in single cells can be passed to the progeny by means of DNA and possibly unknown mechanisms. Information gathering capacity in man is replicated and passed through the germ line in a similar way. In addition information is replicated in the culture by word of mouth, by recorded language and symbols, and by example.

8. Imperfection in the Information System

Paradigm *There is a finite probability of error in the course of information replication. Novelty may be introduced by a built-in tendency toward spontaneous copy-error or by increased copy-error from environmental hazards. The errors may then be replicated and subjected to the test of survival. This paradigm is the basis for Darwinian evolution by natural selection (23), which of course acts on the whole animal.*

If the first DNA molecule had been replicated without error and novelty had depended on the spontaneous formation of additional and different molecules, evolution probably never would have occurred. But with a tendency in the molecule toward a nearly but not quite perfect replication ability, novelty (mutation: copy-errors) was guaranteed while gains were conservatively maintained. Similarly, cultural evolution would have been very slow were it not for the tendency of man to introduce novelty by sheer inability to learn exactly what he is taught. This is not to say that the trick of creativity cannot be accomplished deliberately once we get the significance of it. Man undoubtedly has a higher capacity for storing abstract information than any other form of life, but this fact is inevitably accompanied by the fact that man has a greater tendency to introduce error or deliberate variance into his memory bank than any other form of life and hence the greatest opportunity to introduce novelty into his life. This set of opinions is highly relevant to the ancient problem of determinism versus free will. Because man can make mistakes or deliberately introduce novelty into his life and in either case learn by hindsight, his behavior can never be automated; he is less determined by fate and has more opportunity to depart from the established norm. To this extent he has more opportunity for the exercise of individual free will than other life forms.

9. Feedback Mechanisms

Paradigm *Every form of life has built-in mechanisms by which it constantly reads its own performance in relation to its environment and automatically regulates its physiological and psychological behavior within the limits set by its inherited and genetically established feedback components (12).*

The product of a chemical reaction catalyzed by an enzyme constitutes information that can be used to decide whether the immediate reaction or some other reaction should be speeded up or slowed down. This product not only provides information, but it may actually be the effector and thereby directly regulate enzyme synthesis or enzyme activity. The feedback concept is probably the most important biological idea to be introduced into biology since the concept of the gene and Mendelian heredity. Whereas Mendel's work was done in the 1860's and the gene was rediscovered in the early 1900's (21), the feedback concept at the level of enzyme activity and enzyme synthesis was not clearly enunciated until 1956 and the years that followed the papers by Umbarger, Pardee, and Vogel. The process of physiological adaptation has as one of its principal ingredients feedback from enzyme products on enzyme activity or synthesis (cf. references in Chapter 9).

10. Cellular and Organismic Structure

Paradigm *Three-dimensional structure and compartmentation of cell activities within and among cells and separate from the environment is the basis of morphology and provides the means by which all of the preceding biological categories can be linked to the classical characteristics of life such as reproduction, irritability, motility, and so on.*

The cell remains the most important link between inanimate molecules and all the higher forms of life. Certainly no virus possesses all the qualities of life included above in items 1–10. The compartmentation of cells into nucleus, cytoplasm, membranes, and the organelles within these compartments, has been studied to great advantage by means of the electron microscope as shown by Swanson's book entitled *The Cell* (24). The diversity in form, color, and behavior in multicellular organisms is so great that no biologist is considered an expert on all the available genera. The variety is so great and the "purposefulness" so uniquely displayed in some forms that the late Raymond Nogar, O.P., was led to comment in *The Lord of the Absurd* [(25), p. 143], that "No one can contemplate the beak of the Brazilian caw-caw, the horn of the rhino, or the buck teeth of the wild boar without concluding the Creator is a clown." We are led finally to conclude that any change in the genetic code, any reaction, and any morphological structure will be permitted if the property can pass the hurdles: Will it survive? Will it do a job? Will it confer no disadvantage that will be too great? Will the organism reproduce? Will the organism adapt to its environment or force its environment to adapt to its own needs?

11. Environmental Hazards

Paradigm *The natural as well as the man-made environment contains many small molecules that resemble essential metabolites sufficiently to interact with and damage specific enzymes, information systems, or structures and thereby produce malfunction in the living system. In addition, many nonspecific damaging chemicals and agents such as radiation occur in the environment.*

Although enzymes are highly specific in their interaction with the compounds in living tissue, they are not completley specific, that is, they cannot discriminate between substances Nature patterned them to act upon and substances that are very similar but toxic for them. It is one of the tenets of modern chemotherapy that if an enzyme exists and its specific substrate is known, organic chemists can build a molecule that will inhibit the enzyme, albeit not on the first try as a rule. Various forms of life also produce substances that are toxic to other forms of life, and it is widely accepted that by suitable tests plant extracts and fermentation liquors can be assayed for their ability to kill infectious bacteria or to kill cancer cells. Thus the sulfa drugs were made by organic chemists, while penicillin was isolated from mold cultures. More recently, powerful agents have been synthesized for the purpose of acting as nerve gases, insecticides, pesticides, or herbicides (weed-killers or crop-killers). Just as cancer-killing drugs are not without action on normal cells, the insecticides and the plant killers are not totally innocuous to other forms of life, and the complete range of their biological activity can obviously never be checked out on every species in advance. Yet they have been deliberately disseminated in the natural environment on the basis of tests on what were felt to be representative species. Especially in cases where agents are toxic in very small quantities, it is axiomatic that they act by combining with a special type of enzyme or with hereditary material. In addition to the environmental hazards that act more or less specifically, there are of course many that act nonspecifically. Among these, the radiations, including X-rays, radioactive fallout, cosmic radiation, and even sunlight, all have the capacity to produce mutations in the hereditary substance and to damage cells in other ways.

12. Physiological Adaptation

Paradigm   *Every living organism possesses a genotype that determines its ability to alter its physiological mechanisms in response to changes in the environment, which may include various kinds and amounts of environmental hazards.*

The phenotype was originally defined by geneticists in terms of outward expressions of the genotype such as color of eyes and hair, structural markings or forms, skin color, and other features that are more or less permanent. Later the discovery of "inborn errors of metabolism" led to considerations of metabolic pathways and enzymes that appeared to be present or absent. More recently metabolic pathways and enzyme levels have been shown to vary widely in a matter of hours in normal metabolism as well as in the response to various insults in the form of toxic substances that are environmental hazards (Chapters 9 and 10). Many toxic compounds lead to the formation of enzymes that destroy the compounds, but sometimes the compounds are made more toxic. Little is known about any disadvantages accruing from an adaptive increase in the amount of drug-detoxifying enzymes, but in the case of the peregrine falcon it appears that enzyme changes include increased breakdown of steroid sex hormones, interference in calcium metabolism resulting in weaker eggshells, and resulting failure to produce young birds (5).

The genotype can be shown to determine adaptability to environment in many ways. The genetically-determined property of skin pigmentation permits some humans to tolerate extreme exposure to sunlight while others are simply incapable of developing a protective darkening of the skin in response to sunlight. Some individuals can increase their tolerance to high altitudes, while others cannot. Thus the hereditary apparatus determines not only the more obvious phenotypic characters but also the more subtle variable characters that delimit the range of environmental extremes that can be tolerated. These environmental extremes probably include noise, pyschological pressure, and many other environmental hazards that are still poorly understood. Studies on adaptation are needed not only in connection with environmental hazards but also in connection with the concept of optimal stressor levels that would help human individuals approach the optimum phenotypic expression permitted by their genotype (Chapters 9 and 10).

Physiological Adaptation as the Key to Biology

Of all the things we need to know about biology, adaptation is the phenomenon that we can least afford to ignore. We ought to begin with adaptation and use it to bring into focus all the other facets of biological knowledge, which have been briefly touched upon above. Although we cannot hope to master all the detailed information and interactions that are possible and that actually occur, we can reasonably be expected to know that we as individuals can do something about adaptation. It is the handle on biology, the rudder by which we can steer a course between boredom and weakness on the one hand and information overload and exhaustion on the other.

The genetic basis of life is usually given much more emphasis than adaptation in the teaching of biology, although an individual's heredity is presently fixed by acts beyond his control in contrast to his adaptive level. Heredity sets limits on our powers of adaptation and the special kinds of adaptation that we are best suited for. But few people ever develop their adaptive powers to the fullest, and we still have much to learn about the benefits and costs of adaptation. What we do know is that adaptation can best be understood by combining the inputs from both the reductionist and holistic points of view.

The adaptation that I have been referring to is adaptation by individuals, which is properly called *physiological adaptation*. It involves a variety of hormones and a realignment of many cellular processes in all parts of the body. Physiological adaptation occurs in every one of us every day. The shifts in body chemistry may be minimal or they may approach the limits of our capacity in response to the stressors that we encounter. Each of us is forced to make some adaptations every time we get out of bed in the morning, and as we proceed through the day we may encounter heat or cold outside the limits that we prefer. We may need to run to catch a bus, we may climb a flight of stairs, breathe some automobile exhaust, take a tranquilizer, smoke a cigarette, drink a cocktail, eat an unusually large meal (or one that is high in protein, carbohydrate, or fat), go hungry, travel to a higher altitude, face darkness or bright lights, shiver in silence or cringe at loud noises, and so on. Most of the stressors are not continuous. They wax and wane, they occur in cycles, they are repetitive in some kind of a daily, weekly, or seasonal rhythm, and we are able to cope with them because they do not all occur at once nor do they occur continuously. We do not know the optimum level and optimum cycle frequency for the various stressors that we are exposed to, and we know too little about the physiological cost of making an adaptation to any given stressor. *Nor do we know enough about the cost of having no adaptational demands.* But it is clear that this is the part of biology that each of us needs to know more about because it affects us personally. As individuals we can do something about adaptation, given a little more knowledge from our school system and accepting the task of acquiring more knowledge as a lifetime process. Moreover, knowledge about adaptation is something that will affect the way we choose to bring our offspring through childhood and adolescence. How much should we shield and how much should we expose our children?

Another kind of adaptation is *evolutionary adaptation*. This applies to populations and occurs by mutations (copy errors) in the genetic material. The change in the hereditary material may be an improvement, a disadvantage, or it may be neutral, and the neutral changes may persist until some future generation in which they are helpful or harmful. Thus, the hereditary makeup keeps changing from generation to generation, always being challenged in terms of reproduction and survival in the current environment. One of the characteristics toward which evolutionary adaptation moves is the capability for physiological adaptation, but it also moves toward a closer fit to the environment, a fit which will require less physiological adaptation. Since evolutionary trends are not reversible, a species that is becoming better and better fitted to its environment can become extinct if the environment changes more rapidly than the species can undergo evolutionary adaptation. But the message that I wish to convey is that, from the standpoint of human society, the problems of the next 30 years cannot be solved by attempting to direct human evolution, and by the same token, inattention to human evolution *for this period* can do little harm. Adaptation by evolution is a slow process, it occurs over many generations, and it is inherently difficult to direct in man for many reasons, including our inability to decide on positive goals. On the contrary, physiological adaptation is something that individuals can accomplish and, moreover, they can choose to alter their course from time to time.

A third kind of adaptation is *cultural adaptation*, a process that occurs in both individuals and populations. Cultural adaptation involves psychological and behavioral changes that are affected by the underlying physiological and cellular biology. We are rapidly approaching an era in which it will be impossible to deal with the problems of behavioral change induced by a cultural adaptation to an overwhelming and widespread use of drugs that modify behavior unless we simultaneously learn more about the nature of biological man and the molecular targets of the new drugs. If we can establish which drugs produce dangerous and irreversible changes, for example, we can take firmer steps to prevent their acceptance. A desirable cultural adaptation would be the wider acceptance of the available knowledge in cancer prevention and health improvement. Other types of cultural adaptations with far-reaching consequences would be the decisions to accept population control by encouraging the use of contraceptive measures or by facilitating the ease with which women can secure medically safe and competent abortions. Cultural adaptation seems to impinge on evolutionary adaptation and physiological adaptation in virtually every instance that can be imagined.

Biology, Philosophy and Cultural Adaptation

The idea that disorder is built into biological and cultural systems at all levels came to my attention most forcibly from two different sources at about the time that I was beginning to ask myself, "Why cancer?" One source was Professor A. F. C. Wallace, who is quoted elsewhere in this book (Chapters 4 and 7). Almost simultaneously (1961), *Darwin and the Modern World View* by John C. Greene (23) appeared. Greene quotes many conflicting views on chance versus design in the purposefulness of Nature. I was especially impressed with his citation of a passage by Nogar whose later work (25) has

already been cited above. Nogar observed [(23), p. 66] that philosophers tend to fail to understand that " . . . when the Darwinist asserts openly that chance is the sufficient reason for the organization
of the world, and denies outright the existence of intrinsic finality
among organisms" or asserts "that organic agents simply do not act
for any purpose or end, he is calmly saying what is intrinsic to his
biological theory of the evolution of species. This is not an unwar-
ranted extrapolation, an inferential extension of Darwinian theory; it
is inherent in the very theory itself and has been all along."

In a curriculum designed around Bioethics, the ideas of Wallace
and of Greene ought to be included among readings in *philosophical
biology*, and the role of disorder in biological and cultural evolution
should be fully explored. Disorder is a force to be utilized, the raw
material for creativity. The problem is to harness it and keep it
within the bounds of reason, that is, to be rational about irrationality. A thorough study of biological disorder would reveal that it is
normal, not pathological, although it can appear in the form of pathology when extreme. The study of the nature and role of disorder
in biology and in cultural evolution would do much to help interpret
the supposed conflict between "humanism" and "science" as illustrated by the collection of 18 essays entitled *The Scientist vs The
Humanist* (26). The editors comment that "Among the classic de-
bates of history, none has more relevance to our age than that between the scientist and the humanist. No debate is more central to
society's definition of an educated man; no debate is more important
to the student faced with the choice of a career. And no debate more
clearly focuses the long-standing antagonism between those who see
the meaning of life in terms of material progress and increased
knowledge of the natural world and those who see it only in the
personal fulfillment of every man's 'humanity'—of his moral, intellectual, and aesthetic capacities." They further ask, as I have asked
in this chapter, "How can the advances of science and the heritage
of humanities be combined to the benefit of the individual and of
society?" I have taken the position that biology is the science that
can most fruitfully be combined with the humanities and that both
are necessary for our survival.

The assumption that the students who take one semester of
biology are automatically able to think in terms of Bioethics because
of their other exposures would be a serious mistake, yet they may
be closer to that goal than those who specialize in some present
phase of biology. It would not be possible to build a suitable interdis-

ciplinary course in biology and humanistic subjects by combining a variety of existing courses unless each of the courses in the curriculum were directed to the purpose of training and inspiring students who could be called properly qualified in Bioethics.

Somehow the idea has to be promulgated that the future of man is not something that we can take for granted (6). Human progress is not guaranteed nor is it a natural consequence of Darwinian evolution. The natural world cannot be depended upon to withstand our insults and support our offspring in limitless numbers. Science cannot substitute for Nature's bounty when Nature's bounty has been raped and despoiled. The idea that man's survival is a problem in economics and political science is a myth that assumes that man is free or could be free from the forces of Nature (27). These disciplines help to tell us what men want, but it may require biology to tell what man can have, i.e., what constraints operate in the relationship between mankind and the natural world. Bioethics would attempt to balance cultural appetites against physiological needs in terms of public policy. A desirable cultural adaptation in our society would be a more widespread knowledge of the nature and limitations of all kinds of adaptation.

Bioethics, as I envision it, would attempt to generate wisdom, the knowledge of how to use knowledge for social good from a realistic knowledge of man's biological nature and of the biological world. To me, a realistic knowledge of man is a knowledge that includes his role as an adaptive control system with built-in error tendencies. This mechanistic view, which combines reductionist and holistic elements, would be totally incapable of generating wisdom unless supplemented with both a humanistic and an ecological outlook (28). The concepts and viewpoints expressed in this chapter may be examined in relation to the books by Teilhard de Chardin, especially *The Phenomenon of Man* and *The Future of Man*, which were written nearly 30 years ago (29). Although he differs in approach, his aim is the same: to combine the science of biology with a preservation of human values and to strive to make man's future come up to what it could conceivably be. The present world is dominated by military policy and by an overemphasis on production of material goods. Neither of these enterprises have given any thought to the basic facts of biology. An urgent task for Bioethics is to seek biological agreements at the international level.

REFERENCES AND NOTES

1. N. J. Berrill, *Man's Emerging Mind* (New York: Dodd, Mead and Co., 1955). Man's progress through time—trees, ice, flood, atoms, and the universe. Citation from p. 210.

2. Rachel Carson, *Silent Spring* (Boston: Houghton Mifflin Company, 1962). When a local radio announcer arranged a book review panel discussion, his job was actually put in jeopardy, though he did not lose it.

3. William and Paul Paddock, *Famine—1975!* (Boston: Little, Brown and Company, 1967).

4. Durward L. Allen, *Population, Resources, and the Great Complexity*, PRB Selection No. 29, The Population Reference Bureau, Washington, D. C., August, 1969, 6 pp.

5. Joseph J. Hickey, ed., *Peregrine Falcon Populations. Their biology and Decline*, a conference, Madison, Wis., 1965 (Madison: University of Wisconsin Press, 1969). Reviewed by G. H. Lowery, Jr. under the title, "An Examination of a Worldwide Disaster," *Science* **166:**591, 1969.

6. V. R. Potter, D. A. Baerreis, R. A. Bryson, J. W. Curvin, G. Johansen, J. McLeod, J. Rankin, and K. R. Symon, "The Purpose and Function of the University," *Science* **167:**1590-1593, 1970.

7. John R. Platt, "Strong Inference," *Science* **146:**347–353, 1964. (See the following reference.)

8. E. M. Hafner and S. Presswood, "Strong Inference and Weak Interactions," *Science* **149:**503–510, 1965. [This article was written specifically to present counter-arguments, drawn from research in physics on the universal Fermi interactions, against the idea of strong inference (7) as a universally applicable approach in research.]

9. T. S. Kuhn, *The Structure of Scientific Revolutions* (Chicago: University of Chicago Press, 1962).

10. J. D. Watson and F. H. C. Crick, "Molecular Structure of Nucleic Acids: A Structure for Deoxyribose Nucleic Acid," *Nature* **171:**737–738, 1953; and "Genetical Implications of the Structure of Deoxyribonucleic Acid," *Nature* **171:**964–967, 1953.

11. V. R. Potter, "What Is a Living Organism?" (book review), *Science* **160:**651–652, 1968.

12. J. M. Reiner, *The Organism as an Adaptive Control System* (Englewood Cliffs, N.J.: Prentice-Hall, Inc., 1968).

13. F. H. C. Crick, *Of Molecules and Men* (Seattle: University of Washington Press, 1966).

14. W. D. McElroy, *Cell Physiology and Biochemistry*, 3rd Ed., in the Foundations of Modern Biology Series (Englewood Cliffs, N. J.: Prentice-Hall, Inc., 1971).

15. E. H. White, *Chemical Background for the Biological Sciences*, 2nd Ed., in the Foundations of Modern Biology Series (Englewood Cliffs, N. J.: Prentice-Hall, Inc., 1970).

16. V. R. Potter and C. Heidelberger, "Alternative Metabolic Pathways," *Physiol. Rev.* **30:**487–512, 1950.

17. V. R. Potter, *Enzymes, Growth and Cancer* (Springfield, Ill.: Charles C. Thomas, Publisher, 1950).

18. V. R. Potter, "Biological Energy Transformations and the Cancer Problem," in F. F. Nord and C. H. Werkman, eds., *Advances in Enzymology, Vol. 4* (New York: Interscience Publishers, Inc., 1944), pp. 201–256.

19. J. D. Watson, *Molecular Biology of the Gene* (New York: W. A. Benjamin, 1965).

20. V. R. Potter, *Nucleic Acid Outlines* (Minneapolis, Minn.: Burgess Publishing Co., 1960).

21. J. M. Barry, *Molecular Biology: Genes and the Chemical Control of Living Cells* (Englewood Cliffs, N. J.: Prentice-Hall, Inc., 1964).

22. V. R. Potter, *DNA Model Kit* (Minneapolis, Minn.: Burgess Publishing Co., 1959).

23. John C. Greene, *Darwin and the Modern World View* (Baton Rouge: Louisiana State University Press, 1961).

24. C. P. Swanson, *The Cell*, 3rd Ed., in the Foundations of Modern Biology Series (Englewood Cliffs, N. J.: Prentice-Hall, Inc., 1969).

25. Raymond Nogar, *The Lord of the Absurd* (New York: Herder and Herder, 1966).

26. George Levine and Owen Thomas eds., *The Scientist vs The Humanist* (New York: W. W. Norton and Co., Inc., 1963). A collection of 18 essays by as many authors.

27. G. A. Harrison, J. S. Weiner, J. M. Tanner, and N. A. Barricot, *Human Biology: An Introduction to Human Evolution, Variation and Growth* (New York and London: Oxford University Press, 1964). The foreword to this book, by Sir Peter B. Medawar, describes and defines "human biology" and makes the point that biologists have much to learn from this field of study, especially that the biologists' tendency

to draw a distinction between Nature, on the one hand, and Man and his works on the other, "is one that damages his understanding of both."

28. Julian Huxley, ed., *The Humanistic Frame* (New York: Harper and Row, Publishers, 1961). A collection of essays by 26 authors on the general theme that the traditional antithesis between science and the humanities is artificial and in need of resolution. Sir Julian Huxley also wrote the introduction to *The Phenomenon of Man*, the subject of Chapter 2, this volume.

29. In subsequent chapters we will adopt the viewpoint that a world goal of zero population growth is mandatory for the preservation of human values. If Père Teilhard de Chardin were alive and writing books today, it would be no more unlikely that he would adopt a similar view than it was for him to champion evolution in his day (see Chapter 2).

Additional references not mentioned in text

30. E. Mendelson, D. Shapere, and G. E. Allen, Conference on Explanation in Biology: Historical, Philosophical, and Scientific Aspects, *J. Hist. Biol.* **2**:No. 1, 1–281, Spring, 1969 (special issue). A collection of 21 papers and comments which bear on the problems of reductionism versus holism, molecular biology versus organismic biology, the problem of the definition of life, and many other problems in greater philosophical depth than has been possible in this chapter.

CHAPTER TWO

Teilhard de Chardin and the Concept of Purpose

Abstract Teilhard was an evolutionist who foresaw a future when human research would take charge of human evolution. He sought to channel the new powers into a unified worldwide cultural community, but he did not clearly distinguish between biological and cultural evolution nor did he consider the desirability of multiple alternative evolutionary pathways.

Teilhard and Science

Teilhard de Chardin devoted his entire life to the reconciliation of science and religion. At the very outset I wish to make clear that he felt no obligation to limit himself to science. He was an advocate using all the means at his disposal. Because of his strong religious training during his formative years plus his experience as a stretcher bearer in World War I, he could never turn his back on the crying need of his fellow men for spiritual support. Yet his early interest in geology and mineralogy evolved into a study of fossils and human paleontology and inexorably led him into the area of human evolution and finally into an over-all philosophy of the evolutionary process. While many other men have trod a similar path and found it incompatible with the ancient religious beliefs, Teilhard believed that he had a vision that was grand enough to embrace the best parts of Christian humanism and science. It is clear that there were many aspects of Christian theology that Teilhard simply did not wish to write about, and it is his steadfast attempt to come to grips with the issue of human progress that makes me so interested in his attempts to rationalize science and religion. For Teilhard, human progress is the goal of the universe. In other words, the whole evolutionary process operates with a purpose of bringing mankind slowly and inexorably up to a point just short of the divine, which he refers to as the Omega Point (1).

Anything negative that I have to say about Teilhard is said with considerable reluctance. I wish I could report that other evolutionists like George Gaylord Simpson (2), Ernest Mayr (3), and Theodosius Dobzhansky (4) could agree with Teilhard that a divine purpose could be fulfilled and human progress could be assured if only his indicated path were to be taken. I wish that I could avoid the role of the critic and be satisfied with the great humanistic creed that Teilhard has attempted to outline, since he has come so far from the ideas that must have prevailed during his childhood, and since I am convinced that he is correct in saying that man must make a conscious choice to build a better future.

But I must play out my role as a representative of the intellectual background from which I arise and hope that we can begin a dialogue out of which a further insight into the human purpose may emerge. For if Teilhard is basically correct in his beliefs, they will improve with discussion; and if he is in any way in error, it behooves us to sift and winnow his wisdom and separate the wheat from the chaff.

I will begin by calling your attention to certain passages that illustrate just how far Teilhard moved in the direction of the position I shall represent. Indeed, frequently he is more optimistic about science than I am. I will then discuss some of the information that was not available to him and conclude with a view that hopefully some future idealist will be able to incorporate science into a humanistic philosophy with as much imagination and poetry as Teilhard brought to bear on the concept of Darwinian evolution.

Teilhard as an Evolutionist

Teilhard was an evolutionist without reservation. As Dr. George Beadle, former president of the University of Chicago, once said, "The trouble with evolution is that if you believe in a little of it, you have to believe in all of it." Dr. Beadle was willing to believe in evolution all the way from protons and electrons to molecules, cells, and man, admitting perhaps a divine plan in the protons and electrons whose origin he could not account for (5).

Teilhard was not far behind. In *The Phenomenon of Man* he said:

> Blind indeed are those who do not see the sweep of a movement whose orbit infinitely transcends the natural sciences and has successively invaded and conquered the surrounding territory—chemistry, physics, sociology and even mathematics and the history of religions. One after the other all the fields of human knowledge have been shaken and carried away by the same current in the direction of the study of some development. Is evolution a theory, a system or a hypothesis? It is much more: it is a general condition to which all theories, all hypotheses, all systems must bow and which they must satisfy henceforward if they are to be thinkable and true. Evolution is a light illuminating all facts, a curve that all lines must follow. (6)

Teilhard had a correct understanding of the biology of man when he said: "Zoologically speaking, mankind offers us the unique spectacle of a 'species' capable of achieving something in which all previous species had failed. It has succeeded, not only in becoming cosmopolitan, but in stretching a single organized membrane over the earth without breaking it" (7). This single sentence epitomizes the message in Carleton Coon's new volume, *The Origin of Races*, which has been exquisitely reviewed by Ernst Mayr (3).

Teilhard was aware of the latest developments in molecular biology, and he fully appreciated the role of chance variations in organic evolution. His words were as follows:

> Of old, the forerunners of our chemists strove to find the philosopher's stone. Our ambition has grown since then. It is no longer to find gold but life; and in view of all that has happened in the last fifty years, who would dare to say that this is a mere mirage? With our knowledge of hormones we appear to be on the eve of having a hand in the development of our bodies and even of our brains. With the discovery of genes it appears that we shall soon be able to control the mechanism of organic heredity. And with the synthesis of proteins imminent, we may well one

day be capable of producing what the earth, left to itself, seems no longer able to produce: a new wave of organisms, an artifically provoked neo-life. Immense and prolonged as the universal groping has been since the beginning, many possible combinations have been able to slip through the fingers of chance and have had to await man's calculated measures in order to appear. Thought artificially perfects the thinking instrument itself; life rebounds forward under the collective effect of its reflection. The dream which human research obscurely fosters is fundamentally that of mastering, beyond all atomic or molecular affinities, the ultimate energy of which all other energies are merely servants; and thus grasping the very mainspring of evolution, seizing the tiller of the world. (8)

Here Teilhard seems to be outsciencing the scientists, none of whom are fully prepared to seize the tiller of the world. What he is discussing I have referred to elsewhere as potentially dangerous knowledge, or knowledge without wisdom (9).

Teilhard's Use of the Evolutionary Picture to Understand Religious Values

I am in complete agreement with Teilhard when he says: " ... modern thought is at last getting acclimatized once more to the idea of the creative value of synthesis in the evolutionary sense. It is beginning to see that there is definitely *more* in the molecule than in the atom, *more* in the cell than in the molecule, [more in the organism than in the cell] *more* in society than in the individual" (10). He later says, in effect, that there is more in the Omega Point than in Society as we know it.

If we think of the Omega Point in terms of a scientifically and philosophically oriented ideal society, which Teilhard simply rationalized in terms of his own religious background, we can remove the veil of mystery and come to terms with means and ends. He says: "Mankind, the spirit of the earth, the synthesis of individuals and peoples, the paradoxical conciliation of the element with the whole, and of unity with multitude—all these are called Utopian and yet they are biologically necessary. And for them to be incarnated in the world, all we may well need is to imagine our power of loving developing until it embraces the total of men and of the earth" (11).

He continues:

It may be said that this is the precise point at which we are invoking the impossible. Man's capacity, it may seem, is confined to giving his affection to one human being or to very few. [They say that] beyond that radius the heart does not carry, and there is only room for cold justice and cold reason. [They say that] to love all and everyone is a contradictory and false gesture which only leads in the end to loving no one.

To that I would answer that if, as you claim, a universal love is impossible, how can we account for that irresistible instinct in our hearts which leads us towards unity whenever and in whatever direction our passions are stirred? A sense of the universe, a sense of the All, the nostalgia which seizes us when confronted by nature, beauty, music—these seem to be an expectation and awareness of a Great Presence. The "mystics" and their commentators apart, how has psychology been able consistently to ignore this fundamental vibration whose ring can be heard by every practised ear at the basis, or rather at the summit, of every great emotion? Resonance to the All—the keynote of pure poetry and pure religion. Once again: what does this phenomenon, which is born with thought and grows with it, reveal if not a deep accord between two realities which seek each other; the severed particle which trembles at the approach of "the rest"? (12)

Speaking of the intellect, he says: "It may well be that in its individual capacities and penetrations our brain has reached its organic limits. But the movement does not stop there. From west to east, evolution is henceforth occupied elsewhere, in a richer and more complex domain, constructing, with all minds joined together, mind. Beyond all nations and races, the inevitable taking-as-a-whole of mankind has already begun" (13).

Here, obviously, he is speaking of the evolution of a world culture. At this point a footnote takes us back to a quotation from the biochemist J. B. S. Haldane: "Now, if the co-operation of some thousands of millions of cells in our brain can produce our consciousness, the idea becomes vastly more plausible that the co-operation of humanity, or some sections of it, may determine what Comte calls a Great Being" (14).

Teilhard's Omega Point is a cultural concept, a world in which the *minds of men* have attained a common language of scientific humanism, just as long ago the *genes of men* were encompassed in a common gene pool, as a single species. Just as the genes form "a membrane that stretches over all the earth," so the minds of men, he believes, will form a continuous network of communication around the world. Teilhard's Omega Point is thus the birth of a new

God or Great Being in the form of a world culture, and it is only in his Epilogue that he equates the Omega Point with the already existing Christian God (15). But earlier he said:

> The truth is that, as children of a transition period, we are neither fully conscious of, nor in full control of, the new powers that have been unleashed. Clinging to outworn habit, we still see in science only a new means of providing more easily the same old things. We put Pegasus [in harness.] And Pegasus languishes—unless he bolts with the band-wagon! But the moment will come—it is bound to—when man will be forced by the disparity of the equipage to admit that science is not an accessory occupation for him but an essential activity, a natural deriva-tive of the overspill of energy constantly liberated by mechanisation.
>
> We can envisage a world whose constantly increasing "leisure" and heightened interest would find vital issue in fathoming everything, try-ing everything, extending everything; a world in which giant telescopes and atom smashers would absorb more money and excite more spon-taneous admiration than all the bombs and cannons put together; a world in which, not only for the restricted band of paid research-work-ers, but also for the man in the street, the day's ideal would be the wresting of another secret or another force from corpuscles, stars, or organised matter; a world in which, as happens already, one gives one's life to know, rather than to possess. That, on an estimate of the forces engaged, is what is being relentlessly prepared around us. (16)

Later we read: "In short, as soon as science outgrows the analytic investigations which constitute its lower and preliminary stages, and passes on to synthesis—synthesis which naturally culminates in the realisation of some superior state of humanity—it is at once led to foresee and place its stakes on the *future* and on the *all*. And with that it out-distances itself and emerges in terms of *option* and *adora-tion*" (17). And finally: "But there is another possibility. Obeying a law from which nothing in the past has ever been exempt, evil may go on growing alongside good, and it too may attain its paroxysm at the end in some specifically new form. 'There are no summits with-out abysses'" (18).

That is the message of Teilhard de Chardin as I see it. As for me, I care not whether the message is scientifically provable. I do not have to agree with the underlying theme that progress is built into the stuff of life, but I do agree that we should try to build it into our culture. I believe that Teilhard would accept the modern views of the origin and nature of life as spontaneous and operating in terms of the laws of chance, supervised and censored by natural selection.

I doubt that he would be classified as a vitalist, and I think that, like me, he would be a mechanist if he were aware of the fact that the only way a living organism can incorporate purpose into its mechanism is by the random development and ordered selection of feedback mechanisms, because these are the only ways the body machine can be made to work (Chapter 1).

It is my conviction that men's souls are products of their culture and that cultural evolution is in part analogous to biological evolution. The unit idea or concept in cultural evolution is analogous to the unit DNA molecule in biological evolution, and the emphasis of modern thought is that progress is based entirely on copy errors and hindsight, which is pretty unromantic compared with the ideas of Teilhard. But the essential message of Teilhard is this: "In short, as soon as science outgrows the analytic investigations which constitute its lower and preliminary stages, and passes on to synthesis—synthesis which naturally culminates in the realisation of some superior state of humanity—it is at once led to foresee and place its stakes on the *future* and on the *all.* And with that it out-distances itself and emerges in terms of *option* and *adoration*" (19). By option he means decision making and choice (the verb is *to opt*), and by adoration he means enthusiasm, which stems from the Greek *en theos,* or *in God.*

The Cybernetics of Human Values

In order to understand purpose as seen by Teilhard, I propose to describe man as an information-processing, decision-making, cybernetic machine whose value systems are built up by feedback processes from his environment. These feedback processes are built into the most primitive forms of life, and they form a continuous spectrum all the way back through prehistory and to times when no life existed. Throughout this whole development of man's history, coming up through biological evolution and extending into cultural evolution, the essential message is one in which disorder, or randomness, is used to generate novelty, and natural selection then generates order. Natural selection is the method by which survival information from the environment can be stored in the genome in the course of biological evolution and stored in the culture in the course of cultural evolution. Anthropologist Clifford Geertz has beautifully described how dependent we are on our culture in order to exist at all (20). According to Geertz, "culture is a set of control mechanisms for governing behavior and ... man is precisely the animal most desperately dependent on such extragenetic control mechanisms for ordering his behavior."

If we look at the human cybernetic machine more closely we can see that it is an information-processing device with a built-in normal tendency to make some copy errors (say, 0.01 percent to 1.0 percent) in the course of information processing, and this is the source of creativity, controlled in each individual case by the previously mentioned feedback from the environment at the moment or from memory storage of previous experiences coming from contacts with the environment. The normal tendency to generate novelty in the course of information processing varies from one individual to another and is based in the genome of the individual, although it may vary also in the same individual depending upon the environmental conditions in the individual's history, and, indeed, it can be cultivated and modulated. At the opposite pole, however, mental disease must be looked upon both in terms of hereditary capabilities and in terms of environmental history as uncontrolled modulation of reality.

The normal tendency to make copy errors is genetically based, but it is also strongly affected by the complexity of the information input as well as by the rate at which information is presented, in other words, the information load. The concept of information load (or overload or underload) has no meaning except the obligation of the individual to make decisions and carry out actions that involve choices based on the interactions between the incoming information and the previously stored information and beliefs. Peyton Rous, 1966 Nobel Prize winner, once said, "Beliefs are important because what men believe determines what men do." Every action is governed by feedback mechanisms in which the action is designed to close the gap between what the human cybernetic machine is doing and what it believes it should do. In other words, feedback mechanisms always involve a reading of an action and a comparison of the reading with a preset standard. This standard may be set by beliefs and tends to shift with time, but the man machine is always trying to close the gap between the actual performance and the standard.

The maximum rate of information processing coupled to action might be limited by the input, by the transduction and integration, or by the mechanical response; but experiments seem to show clearly that the rate-limiting step is not at the input or the output, but at the central nervous system, where the transduction and integration take place. And it has also been shown that there is a maximum rate for each individual, depending on the complexity of the problems, and that when this rate of input is exceeded, the individual becomes overloaded and begins to make errors or fails to respond completely. I am referring to studies by Dr. James G. Miller, recently of the Mental Health Research Institute, University of Michigan (21). Tests have shown that certain individuals classed as schizophrenic make errors at normal speeds in the way that normal people make errors at high speeds of input, that is, they make certain types of errors habitually. It appears that the capabilities involve inherent genetic properties as well as previous experience.

This concept of man as an information-processing, cybernetic machine bears an important relationship to cultural evolution, which is really what Teilhard was talking about. Because a culture can provide a person with a stereotyped decision to fit a particular situation and relieve him of the danger of information overload, cultures can be examined in terms of whether they decrease or increase the amount of information that individual members of the society have to process. And I would say that one of the dilemmas of our modern society is that people are confronted with more information and decisions in some areas than they can process. In other areas they have information underloads, as for example in a production-line job, where no choice except the right one is permitted, and this repetitively.

The Role of Knowledge, Ignorance, and Natural Selection in Further Evolution of Values

It seems that a reasonable way to build a value system would be to set up as a minimal requirement the survival of the human species under conditions that would permit further evolution and delay extinction. For if we admit with Teilhard that we do not now live in an ideal society and that we cannot change it overnight, we must agree that we have to have time to decide what kind of a society we want and what steps we must take to secure it.

However, if this is what we decide, we have already made a value judgment. There are many in the world who believe that we already have all the information that we need to build a perfect society and that for man to attempt to manipulate his destiny is contrary to some kind of natural law. Teilhard, on the other hand, felt that this *is* the natural law and that man must assume control of his destiny and must reach some kind of agreement on the ground rules for such an attempt. I agree with him. The choice between these polar views ("we know" versus "we don't know") probably cannot be resolved at once. But those who feel that man must take charge of his own destiny should identify themselves and clearly expound the basis of their views and the consequences of them; otherwise, there is little opportunity for those who hold opposite views to undergo the transformation that natural selection of ideas would bring about if all ideas were equally available.

If we agree that our environment is changing, and changing rapidly, then we must agree that we do not now possess all the information that we need to build a future society. We must ask what we can do to gain a better idea of how to predict the nature of the future problems that we will have to deal with.

Summation

The issue between Teilhard and all other evolutionists (including me) is that he believes that the growing tip of evolution, that is, man, can know where it is going and how to get there. He believes that by science plus inductive leaps based on Christian faith, the one true way can be found. He fails to specify clearly that he is really talking about cultural evolution and is not really supposing that biological evolution will achieve the desired end. Because he does not make this distinction, he sounds somewhat like a neo-Lamarckian, which is a view that we are all convinced is not tenable for biological evolution.

I believe, along with other contemporary evolutionists, that the ultimate destiny of the human race is unknown and cannot be predicted and that no path can be said to be assured of success. All we can hope to do is to keep the pathway open-ended and to permit several courses to be followed.

But we would agree with Teilhard that the problem of man's future is now a legitimate topic for discussion.

REFERENCES AND NOTES

1. Teilhard de Chardin, *The Phenomenon of Man* (New York: Harper and Row, Publishers, 1959), and *The Future of Man* (New York: Harper and Row, Publishers, 1964).

2. George Gaylord Simpson, "The World into Which Darwin Led Us." *Science* **131**:966–74, 1960.

3. Ernst Mayr, "Origin of the Human Races" (review of Carleton Coon's *The Origin of Races)*, *Science* **138**:420-22, 1962; "Cause and Effect in Biology," *Science*, **134**:1501–6, 1961 (see also the letters in response to this article, in *Science* , **135**:972–81, 1962); and "Accident or Design: The Paradox of Evolution in the Evolution of Living Things," from *The Evolution of Living Organisms*, a symposium of the Royal Society of Victoria, held in Melbourne, Australia, in December, 1959.

4. T. Dobzhansky, *Mankind Evolving* (New Haven: Yale University Press, 1962).

5. George Beadle, quoted in *Time*, June 29, 1962, pp. 53–54; cf. Kyle Haselden, "Science and Religion," *Christian Century*, June 20, 1962.

6. *The Phenomenon of Man*, p. 217.

7. *Ibid.*, p. 241.

8. *Ibid.*, p. 249.

9. See Chapter 4, this volume, pp. 55–68.

10. *The Phenomenon of Man*, p. 267.

11. *Ibid.*, p. 265.

12. *Ibid.*, p. 266.

13. *Ibid.*, p. 277.

14. *Ibid.*, p. 57.

15. *Ibid.*, p. 291.

16. *Ibid.*, p. 279.

17. *Ibid.*, p. 284.

18. *Ibid.*, p. 288.

19. *Ibid.*, p. 284.

20. cf. V. R. Potter, "Man and His Future" (book review), *Science*, **154:** 273–74, 1966, referring to Clifford Geertz, "The Impact of the Concept of Culture on the Concept of Man," in John R. Platt, ed., *New Views of the Nature of Man* (Chicago: University of Chicago Press, 1965).

21. James G. Miller, "Adjusting to Overloads of Information," in *Disorders of Communication* (Research Publications of the Association for Research in Nervous and Mental Disease, No. XLII, 1964), pp. 87–100; "Psychological Aspects of Communication Overloads," in R. W. Waggoner and D. J. Carek, eds., *International Psychiatric Clinics:*

Communication in Clinical Practice (Boston: Little, Brown and Company, 1964); "*The Individual as an Information Processing System,*" in W. S. Fields and W. Abbott, eds., *Information Storage and Neural Control* (Springfield, Ill.: Charles C. Thomas, Publisher, 1963).

CHAPTER THREE

Bridge to the Future: The Concept of Human Progress

Abstract The religious and the materialistic concepts of progress are contrasted with the scientific–philosophic concept in which wisdom is defined as the knowledge of how to use knowledge, and in which the destiny of mankind is placed in the hands of men, who must examine feedback mechanisms at biological and cultural levels.

The Idea of Progress

The idea of progress is deeply rooted in American tradition. We take it for granted. Not only we but also our forefathers assumed that progress is to be expected and that it is a legitimate goal. Indeed, the official seal of the state of Wisconsin, which was designed in 1851, exhibits a motto expressed in one simple, direct word: FORWARD.

Progress is in fact defined as motion toward a goal. The only problem that we have to resolve is, what is the goal? Which direction is *forward*?

I wish to develop the idea or concept of *progress* in relation to the development of the land-grant colleges and to contemporary developments on the American and world scene. Elsewhere I have reviewed the concept of progress in relation to our knowledge of Darwinian evolution (1), and I shall refer to Darwin again. The Morrill Act of 1862, which established the land grant colleges, came at a time of rapidly changing ideas. It was paralleled by one of the most earth-shaking ideas the scientific world has yet witnessed: the theory of the origin of species, which represented the culmination of years of study in the diverse phenomena of evolution. Darwin's theory was published in England in 1859, the year that the Morrill Act was introduced into the Congress of the United States.

Three Concepts of Progress

These, then, are my themes: progress, the land-grant colleges, and Darwinian evolution. I wish to begin by calling your attention to the fact that the world has not agreed on any single definition of the concept of progress. I submit that there are actually *three* separate and distinct ideas of progress and that these three separate concepts are in fact conflicting.

The three concepts of progress are (a) the religious concept, (b) the materialistic concept, and (c) the scientific–philosophic concept. No nation, almost no community, and few individuals can be cited as perfect examples of any one of these concepts of progress. All men and all societies are mixtures of the religious, the materialistic, and the scientific–philosophic concepts in various proportions.

It will be my contention that these three concepts of progress are chronologically related to one another and that individuals and societies tend to move from the religious to the materialistic (2) while the scientific–philosophic concept can, but not necessarily will, emerge only after a sufficient materialistic development has occurred. On the world scene the United States, Western Europe, and Russia are the materialistic giants while India is a country with essentially the religious attitude toward progress. In Russia the question of whether a country can develop a respectable scientific–philosophy without a religious foundation is being tested before our very eyes.

The Religious Concept of Progress

Let us now examine each of the three concepts of progress in turn. The religious concept of progress almost always includes speculations about the nature of death. How much of man's courage to face death or to cope with the vicissitudes of this life is fortified by a belief that by dying we can progress to a better world? Most primitive religions and in fact most Eastern cultures either simply do not believe in progress or survival on this earth as legitimate issues, or they believe that the only true progress is that which can be characterized as increased knowledge of the will of the gods. As for conflict between the religious and the materialistic concept of progress, I need only to quote Christ, who said: "It is easier for a camel to go through the eye of a needle than for a rich man to enter the kingdom of God." And in the same 19th chapter of Matthew: "If thou wilt be perfect, go and sell that thou hast, and give to the poor, and thou shalt have treasure in heaven."

The Materialistic Concept of Progress

If these views are examples of the religious concept of progress, what is the materialistic concept, and is it not a burden to religious progress? Here we come directly to an examination of the climate of the United States at the time the Morrill Act was passed. Was this a religious climate and have we moved toward or away from the preceding views? I would like to quote from E. D. Eddy's recent book on the land-grant idea in American Education entitled, *Colleges for Our Land and Time* (3).

The American of the early nineteenth century could be characterized as simple and agricultural. The population, 85 per cent of which was rural, lived on farms and in small towns along the Eastern seaboard. The center of knowledge was the church and the growing academy. The average person found little reason or desire to learn to read or write. Life was made secure by a strong religious faith. To the West lay vast miles of uninhabited territory. The conquering of this frontier became the stimulus to a gradual revolution out of which emerged the new form of American independence.

One of the phases of the revolution about to take place, and one of significance to education, was the break from the hold of orthodox religion on the minds of people. It took its most dramatic form in the emergence of a fixed belief in materialism as the credo of American life. The words *more* and *better* became guiding symbols of men who believed that anything was possible in the new nation. Man was considered both capable and close to perfect. He needed only the methods and the institutions by which to work out his ultimate perfection. Materialism gave vent to the concept of utilitarianism and to the final test of a process or an institution in its workability.

I shall return to a discussion of this concept of workability later when I draw a distinction between short-range pragmatism (which asks, is the thing working now?) and long-range pragmatism (which asks, how does the thing affect our society?). At this point I merely wish to bring out that the land grant colleges were spawned at a time in history when the juggernauts of *more* and *better* were just starting to roll; when Samuel Butler humorously stated the epitome of the new era: "All progress is based upon a universal desire on the part of every organism to live beyond its income." As this scene developed, it has been the voice of a minority that has continually pleaded for the long-range view, the view that I like to call the scientific–philosophic concept of progress. The conservationists have always stood in this corner, and it was Teddy Roosevelt who said: "The material progress and prosperity of a nation are desirable chiefly so far as they lead to the *moral* and material welfare of all *good* citizens" (italics mine). I speak of the scientific–philosophic concept of progress because I wish to distinguish it from the scientific–materialistic concept of progress. We are accustomed to hear people speak as if there were only two alternatives in defining progress, the religious or the materialistic; and the materialistic is always equated with science. Scientific materialism has been embraced by both capitalism and communism, and *neither* has made any real attempt to develop a scientific–philosophic concept of progress. However, we Americans have a much better chance for doing so than the Russians because we cherish the rights of individuals to express new ideas and to influence public opinion.

So far I have mentioned the religious concept of progress and the materialistic concept of progress and have indicated that these are not the only alternatives in our attempt to define progress.

Darwin and Spencer

At this point I should like to return to a discussion of Darwinian evolution because it is fundamental to an understanding of what I mean by a scientific–philosophic concept of progress. Darwin constantly referred to the *struggle for existence* and quickly adopted the phrase coined by Herbert Spencer—*the survival of the fittest*. He also coined the phrase *natural selection*, describing the principle by which each slight variation is preserved for inheritance if it is useful. Darwin believed in natural selection as a device with almost infinite possibilities, and at the end of his book he expressed the view that in man it would tend to cause *"progress towards perfection"* (italics mine). The same view was expressed by Spencer when he said: "Progress, therefore, is not an accident, but a necessity. ... It is a part of nature." The views of Darwin and Spencer, which provided for a mechanism that could be visualized as the operation of an infinite wisdom, permitted evolution to be taught as a part of a divine plan, thus avoiding any direct conflict with the clergy. The latter, however, were not all satisfied with this subtlety and many bitterly contested every inch of ground during a strategic retreat that has lasted a hundred years. If the idea of a fortuitously-operating system—in other words, an imperfect mechanism lacking infinite wisdom and thereby possibly not under a divine plan—should become widely accepted in scientific circles, the implications to theology could not escape unnoticed in nonscientific circles indefinitely (4).

The advent of Darwinism was not the only stimulating feature of the era between 1850 and 1900, the period during which the land grant colleges were founded. During this time the great German pathologist Virchow introduced the idea of the cell as the seat of all disease (1859). Pasteur seemingly disproved the spontaneous generation of life and showed the practical consequences of sterilization in preventing bacterial contamination. Edward Büchner discovered that fermentation could be accomplished by enzymes obtained from living cells. The beginnings of the sciences of biochemistry and genetics were in evidence. All of these developments were available to the more perceptive of the early scholars in the land grant colleges, who had a steady flow of fundamental discoveries from the European scientists. The opportunity and the incentive and the utilitarian trend of the times combined to make the American habit one of converting basic information from Europe into practical aids to production. The principles of natural selection were seized upon, and superior breeds of farm animals and farm crops were developed. The science of genetics explained how Darwinian evolution could occur and how it could be speeded up for agricultural purposes (5).

Spengler and Toynbee

However, as time passed the idea of inevitable progress began to be questioned by some, particularly after the occurrence of two World Wars. The first questionings did not come from the scientific field but from the historical. Spengler in *The Decline of the West* (6), Parkinson in *The Evolution of Political Thought* (7), and Toynbee in his many writings (8) have all rejected the Nineteenth Century historians' vision of history mounting on a single track to the heights on which we live. They have hinted at a uniform pattern of history in which civilizations rise and fall (9), a pattern from which they feel there may be no escape. That these writers have been influenced by Darwin is clearly shown by Parkinson when he says: "the belief that the present ... can represent finality is as old or older than Plato. It runs through many of the texts which the student is required to read. ... Is essentially pre-Darwinian as a mode of thought. No believer in evolution could expect to find that sort of finality." Thus Parkinson realizes that the Darwinian concept of survival of the fittest does not guarantee progression toward perfection; in fact, it almost guarantees progression toward extinction as far as any one group is concerned. Yet it was the concept of survival of the fittest that was seized upon with such satisfaction by the old *laissez faire* capitalists. It formed a bulwark of materialism, and as such it was a popular tenet of Karl Marx, who wished to dedicate his own book to Charles Darwin whose phrase "struggle for existence" undoubtedly inspired the "class struggle" of Marx. Interestingly enough, the autographed copy of *Das Kapital* with its pages uncut, remains to this day at Downe House (10).

Survival or Extinction?

Why does natural selection so often lead to extinction rather than to perfection? The reason is that natural selection stresses short-time gains on a generation-to-generation basis. It cannot anticipate changes in the environment, yet the environment is constantly changing. The survival of a species is determined by how well it is adapted to its environment, and progress is in part definable as change that permits survival in a changing environment. Following Thoday (11), we may propose a new definition of the survival of the fittest by saying that "the fit are those who fit their existing environments and whose descendants will fit future environments." What future environment will our descendants face? Will they be able to survive in the changing environment that we have set in motion? Are we "fit" if judged by this test? If we look at the record, we see that selection does not guarantee that a species will endure; most species of the past have become extinct without issue—not merely dinosaurs and dodos, but the vast majority of species. Dobzhansky (12) at Columbia University points out that no biological law can be relied upon to insure that our species, man, will continue to prosper or indeed that it will continue to exist. However man is the sole product of evolution who knows that he has evolved and who is capable of taking steps that might help to insure survival, which is the first requirement for progress. If the survival of man as a species is problematical, what then is the prognosis for nations or cultures, which must be even more transient?

More and Better?

The latter part of the Nineteenth Century in America was characterized, as Eddy said, by the words *more* and *better*, the foundations of a materialistic society. In this development the land grant colleges have played a key role in increasing agricultural production to the point that, whereas in 1862 one farmer was producing enough to feed himself and 3½ non-farmers, he now produces enough for himself and 27 non-farmers. What was once a pride in possession and achievement has given way to mixed feelings and confusion as to whether local surpluses here and general under-consumption elsewhere can be justified in a shrinking world whose overpopulated cities and underfed millions are crying the words *more* and *better* that we believed were the heritage of anyone who would do as we did. It is clear that the graduates of the land grant colleges have a role to play in the future of the world, but the message I would like to bring is that more and better are not enough. It is conceded that the materialistic concept of progress is the necessary stepping stone from primitive religions to the scientific–philosophic concept of progress, but the students at the land grant colleges need to combine productive and scientific know-how with an understanding of history and the humanities in order to take the step. This nation needs to control its materialistic instincts and to realize that some forms of production contribute more to national and world progress than other forms do. We need to compete with the Communists in the field of ideas and not merely in the production of corn, hogs, and missiles.

The Scientific–Philosophic
Concept of Progress

The scientific–philosophic concept of progress is based on the ideas

- that no knowledge is absolute
- that knowledge has no boundary other than ignorance (Virchow, 1858)
- that the limits of knowledge are infinite
- that no end of new knowledge is conceivable
- that no individual can begin to encompass even the knowledge that exists today
- that knowledge should be as widely disseminated as possible
- that the only solution to dangerous knowledge is more knowledge
- that wisdom is moral knowledge, the knowledge of how to use knowledge, and the most important knowledge of all.

Science is knowledge, but it is not wisdom. Wisdom is the knowledge of how to use science and how to balance it with other knowledge. Albert Schweitzer said: "Our age has discovered how to divorce knowledge from thought, with the result that we have, indeed, a science which is free, but hardly any science left which reflects"(13).

The scientific–philosophic concept of progress is a direct-line descendant of American traditions. It represents the Judaeo-Christian heritage, the Puritan heritage, and the Utilitarian heritage. It might be called the realistic concept of progress, because it cherishes no illusions. Its premises are all subject to test and modification. It places equal emphasis on the individual and society and regards the flowering of individuals as the supreme test of progress in a society. It follows Emerson in its philosophy of self-reliance and individual freedom, but it places less faith than did Emerson and Thoreau in the ability of individuals to operate independently of society in this modern world. It is completely foreign to communist ideology, and it is difficult to see how it could arise spontaneously in the communist system which places its emphasis on society and not on individuals. It is also opposed to the outworn political philosophies that regard individuals as taking supreme priority over society.

In advocating a scientific–philosophic concept of progress, we have tried to emphasize that we are not advocating social Darwinism, which was the sociological equivalent of the struggle for existence. In fact, we have gone out of our way to point up the limitations of the process of natural selection in any context. What we are advocating is the use of the scientific method in seeking wisdom; that is, we assume that wisdom can be found in the same way that other knowledge can be found. Can mankind find a way to pool individual knowledge in order to achieve a collective wisdom? Only if individual minds are free to organize overlapping pools of knowledge and to derive generalizations that will be widely understood and accepted. One of the persons who presumably believes in the scientific–philosophic concept of progress is David Lilienthal (14), former director of the Tennessee Valley Authority. He lists the scientific points of view that should be carried over into other areas of action as follows:

1. Imagination.
2. Appeal to reason rather than to authority.
3. Realism—face the facts.
4. Intellectual independence but listen to criticism and analysis by other competent experts.
5. Science is universal, not provincial.
6. Science is hopeful.

He asks: "Can the distinctive qualities and standards implicit in pursuing the scientific method so affect the minds and thinking of people who are not scientists as to lead to a change in their values, their horizons, in the things they hold fast to, and change the quality of their relations with their fellow men? In short, can Science be a helpful, perhaps even decisive influence in a kind of ethical revolution comparable in its importance to the physical revolution which science has wrought? My own answer is in the affirmative."

To Mr. Lilienthal's affirmation I must say that I heartily add my own, except that I believe this development will not come spontaneously. It will have to be evangelized, and *the chances that this will occur are desperately slim.*

Each scientist may have to be willing to stick his neck out and accept the risk of ridicule by attempting to relate his specialty to the long-range goals of society. I feel this urge with a peculiar sensitivity because my whole life has been spent in dealing with the control mechanisms of biological systems. Before the war I studied the relation between vitamins and enzymes and then took up the biochemistry of cancer. During the war I studied the breakdown in control that occurs in irreversible shock due to hemorrhage or wounds. After the war I studied physiological adaptation to high altitudes in the Andes of Peru, and from 1940 to the present I have maintained the cancer problem as my major concern. I have seen terminologies change from biochemical genetics to molecular biology, from cell regulation (15) to negative feedback and repression, but throughout this period I have seen the most rapid increase in knowledge of what makes living organisms tick that the world has ever seen. I believe that the discovery of chemical feedback in biological systems is the greatest event in the history of biological science since the development of the gene concept. No man can call himself educated who does not consider the knowledge of evolution. Mendelian heredity, mutation, and chemical feedback are as important as any of the laws of physics, the sonnets of Shakespeare, or the history of human conflict. It would be impossible to cram a semester course into the next few pages, but it really does not take very long to make some basic points. The hereditary genes are now known to determine the potential strength of any given ability in a person or organism, but they do not guarantee the expression of the ability. Secondly, we know that the expression of each gene is regulated by chemical feedback in such a way that if a talent or function is not used it diminishes in strength (16). The ability to increase the strength of any given function is the phenomenon of adaptability. But if an organism can adapt, by the same token it will de-adapt. When we carry a heavy load, our ability to carry loads increases, but the corollary is that when we have no loads to carry, our ability in this direction decreases. But the more our needs are supplied the more we are able to concentrate on other things. We are not only able to, but we in fact do, concentrate on other things, and I take this to have some kind of universal applicability.

The Judaeo-Christian admonition, "do unto thy neighbor as you would have him do unto you," should be interpreted in this light: help him in such a way that he gains the strength and desire to help himself *and* others. It has immense possibilities for good in our society if one farmer can feed 27 non-farmers, but if the 27 non-farmers are not contributing to the betterment of society, then nothing has been gained.

At this point in history we are committed to the idea of an

industrialized and urbanized society because we need the steel production, the industry, and the agricultural production that will support the research which provides the adaptability that makes survival possible in a changing world. But unless part of this research effort is devoted to the seeking of wisdom, it has served no useful purpose. There are many problems that are crying to be solved and which, if solved, would go far toward lessening world tension. I list a few:

1. Educational goals and methods
2. Race relations
3. Overpopulation
4. Overconsumption
5. Religious intolerance
6. Conservation of natural resources
7. Capture of solar energy
8. Desalinization of sea water
9. Liberation of creative talent
10. Reexamination of the role of advertising in our society

We hold that the scientific-philosophic concept of progress which places its emphasis on long-range wisdom is the only kind of progress that can lead to survival. It is a concept that places the destiny of mankind in the hands of men and charges them with the responsibility of examining the feedback mechanisms and short-sighted processes of natural selection at biological and cultural levels, and of deciding how to circumvent the natural processes that have led to the fall of every past civilization.

Let us not assume, as Spengler has, that we have already passed the point of no return; but in keeping with our best traditions, let us combine agriculture and industry, science, and the humanities to find a definition of progress that permits every man to develop to the maximum of his inherited talents not only in this country but everywhere in the world.

Let us pin our faith not on science alone, or on production alone, but on a search for wisdom, a wisdom that will recognize man's spiritual needs as well as his physical needs, a wisdom that will conquer by force of persuasion, a wisdom that will strengthen every individual member of society and make it possible for him to strengthen the society in which he lives. Let us use our tremendous capacity for production to produce the things that make us wiser, rather than the things that make us weaker. In this new challenge the Universities have the basic ingredients of *more* and *better*. The addition of curricula that will enable students to achieve a balance between the three concepts of progress that I have outlined and to translate them into action will, in my opinion, give the Universities a role of leadership in this complex world of today. Only by combining a knowledge of the sciences and of the humanities in the minds of individual men can we hope to build a "Bridge to the Future."

REFERENCES AND NOTES

1. V. R. Potter, *Nucleic Acid Outlines*, *Vol.II*, unpublished notes.

2. E. A. Burtt, *The Metaphysical Foundations of Modern Physical Science* (New York: Harcourt, Brace & World, Inc., 1925).

3. E. D. Eddy, *Colleges for Our Land and Time* (New York: Harper and Row, Publishers, 1957), p.1.

4. cf. *Teilhard de Chardin and The Concept of Purpose*, Chapter 2, this volume, pp. 30–41.

5. cf. S. A. Barnett, *A Century of Darwin* (London: William Heineman Ltd., 1958).

6. O. Spengler,*The Decline of the West*, *Vols. I and II*, translated by C. F. Atkinson (New York: Alfred A. Knopf, 1926).

7. C. N. Parkinson, *The Evolution of Political Thought* (Boston: Houghton Mifflin Company, 1958).

8. A. J. Toynbee, *Civilization on Trial* (New York: Oxford University Press, 1948).

9. cf. Stephen Raushenbush *Man's Past, Man's Future* (New York: Delacorte Press, 1969).

10. S. A. Barnett, *op cit.,* p. xv.

11. J. M. Thoday, in S. A. Barnett, *op. cit.*, pp. 313–333.

12. T. Dobzhansky, "Evolution at Work," *Science* **127**:1091–1098, 1958.

13. A. Schweitzer, *An Anthology* (Boston: Beacon Press, 1948). cf. Dobzhansky, *op. cit.*, p. 1098.

14. David Lilienthal, "Science and Man," *Chemical and Engineering News,* September 29, 1958, p. 115.

15. G. E. W. Wolstenholme and C. M. O'Connor, *Regulation of Cell Metabolism* (London: J. A. Churchill, Ltd., 1959).

16. Van R. Potter and Victor H. Auerbach, "Adaptive Enzymes and Feedback Mechanisms," *Laboratory Investigation* **8:**495–509, 1958.

CHAPTER FOUR

Society and Science

[Can science aid in the search for sophistication in dealing with order and disorder in human affairs?]

Abstract The most important contribution science can make to society is to increase the degree of sophistication with which mankind perceives "order" and "disorder" in individual lives and in the long range problems of society. Interdisciplinary scholars trained in molecular biology as well as in the nature of man should be organized into groups to arrive at new ways to improve the human condition.

Science and Disorder

How can science contribute to the betterment of the human condition? This is the dominant question that must be asked in any discussion of society and science. For years it has been assumed that the answer to this question is obvious and that it can be answered in terms of increased material well-being for mankind (1).

In addition science has been considered to be an organizing force in society. A large proportion of the human race is psychologically incapable of coping with large doses of disorganization and uncertainty. Mankind has an inborn desire to have some degree of organization in life, and this desire leads many to gravitate in the direction of religion or of science, both of which are identified as mechanisms for bringing order out of disorder.

The battle between organization and disorganization is a never-ending one and deserves to be examined with all the intelligence we can muster. We have to understand when to fight disorder and when to encourage it, when to stand fast for order and when to give ground. Science has contributed to society as an organizing force in the management of raw data and in the manipulation of nature, but it has produced "dangerous knowledge" and disorganization as well. It is important to look at some of the manifestations of order and disorder and to realize that disorder is the raw material from which order is conceived and selected. Attempts to establish societies based on order will always fail unless they incorporate some *disorder* (2). The most important contribution science can make to society is to increase the degree of sophistication with which mankind perceives "order" and "disorder."

The Quest for Order

Man has long been aware that his world has a tendency to fall apart. Tools wear out, fishing nets need repair, roofs leak, iron rusts, wood decays, loved ones sicken and die, relatives quarrel, and nations make war. One of the important functions of even the most primitive religions has been to establish order and meaning in mankind's way of life, to provide explanations for sickness and death, to rationalize suffering, to circumvent death and make it bearable (3). We instinctively resent the decay of orderly systems such as the living organism and work to restore such systems to their former or even a higher level of organization. As viewed in the context of order and disorder, both religion and science have been processes "of maximizing the quantity of organization in the matrix of perceived human experience," in the words of the anthropologist A. F. C. Wallace (3). Most religions offer some kind of "solution which assures the believer that life and organization will win, that death and disorganization will lose, in their struggle to become the characteristic condition of self and cosmos" (3). Science, meanwhile, attempted to provide ground rules for the organization of the universe and, more recently, of man himself. Knowledge led to power, and the power to alter the environment led to new dimensions of order and disorder.

Starting with essentially religious motivations, men like Copernicus, Galileo, Newton, Bacon, Descartes, Hobbes, Locke, Hume, and

Kant began to develop an understanding of science and to feel that all the facts of the universe could be sufficiently explained by the existence and nature of matter (4). It was felt that there were no problems too big for man to solve, and the concept of natural order in the world probably reached its highest point among philosophers. Many felt that the universe was a mighty clock that had been wound for all time and that each individual was born to suffer and die to serve a cosmic purpose (4).

By the middle of the Nineteenth Century we find Charles Darwin developing a comprehensive theory of evolution, based on the survival of the fittest. The phrase "nature red in fang and claw" was coined by Tennyson to dramatize the struggle for survival. Darwin felt that the struggle was difficult to rationalize except as a means to progress, which he believed was the inevitable result from the process of natural selection (5). The survival of the fittest was a brutal process for using the raw material or disorder to achieve order, but it served a noble purpose in selecting new and better species, which were widely understood to arise on a continuing basis. Until quite recently most educated people in both the sciences and the humanities accepted Darwin's idea of natural evolution as a mechanism for progress and found no discrepancy between Darwinism and the idea of a master plan or the concept of purpose in the natural world. But today a great uneasiness pervades the intellectual world, for a variety of reasons. In the field of biology a few individuals have begun to emphasize the view that natural evolution selects on the basis of relatively short-range decisions (5) and that most species become extinct. The process is unable to foretell the future, hence today the inevitability of progress and the existence of a master plan must be questioned.

Belief in the comprehensibility of all knowledge and implicit faith in human progress did not fade throughout the Nineteenth Century. In this period Rudolf Virchow, a German contemporary of Darwin, studied the ravages of disease, and he is known today as the father of pathology. An outspoken mechanist and an ardent believer in the power of the scientific method, he proclaimed that "knowledge has no boundary other than ignorance," and he plainly felt that this boundary could be pushed back indefinitely (6). In these times scientists were still considered the instruments of truth and order and were able to see the consequence of their work and call it good. The concept of human progress was a materialistic concept of more and better, and men like Louis Pasteur were proving that, in terms of taking the guesswork out of man's biological problems, science could pay for itself a thousandfold.

Rise of Unmanageable Knowledge

But as science grew more complicated and as the amount of relevant knowledge began to double in shorter and shorter time intervals, scientists began to specialize. As scientists began to know more and more about less and less, the individual scientist became less confident of his ability to organize his specialized knowledge in the larger context of science and society. He no longer was able to devote his time to cosmic issues or to worry about ultimate truth. He was convinced that the latter was not attainable and the former were neither important, useful, nor interesting. It was assumed that all new knowledge was basically good and that it contributed to order in a way that, if not immediately obvious, would become obvious in the fullness of time. If there were no individual scientists able or willing to cope with cosmic issues, neither were there philosophers of the Descartes variety who could hope to comprehend all available knowledge.

With the arrival of the Twentieth Century the divorce of science and letters was virtually complete, but the Louis Pasteur image was firmly planted in the public mind. Knowledge was power, and the key to knowledge was science. Science produced rayon, nylon, orlon, and dacron. Science produced vacuum tubes, transistors, and semiconductors. Science produced phosgene, mustard, and other deadly war gases.

I think that with the development of the war gases in World War I, the image of "dangerous knowledge" became a reality. When World War II came along, more war gases were developed, and this led to the concept of biological warfare. Crop-killing chemicals were invented, nerve gases were produced, and germ warfare was contemplated. The atom bomb was built and used. During and after the war, science produced crop killers, weed killers, and insecticides—2-4D, DDT, and others by the thousands (7).

By the end of World War II science, the source of material well-being; science, the law-giver; and science, the source of order and understanding could no longer be regarded as an unmixed blessing or an agent for inevitable improvement in the human condition.

In the field of biological science the counterrevolution reached a peak when a single writer, Rachel Carson, already established as the author of *The Sea Around Us*, wrote a best-seller called *Silent Spring* and outraged the chemical industry with her emphasis on the side effects of insecticides and weed killers [(8), see also (7)]. Then a single drug, thalidomide, sold as a sleeping pill and later proved to cause deformities in the babies of a large percentage of pregnant women who were critically exposed, caused the United States Senate to pass a drug control bill by unanimous vote. Except for the thalidomide tragedy, the bill might not have commanded a majority.

The new realization that science could produce chemical substances that had potentially dangerous consequences not intended by their designers, as in the case of thalidomide, led to other repercussions that may influence the established customs and traditions of society. An interesting example is the case of the young married couple who challenged the abortion laws because their unborn baby had been exposed to the effects of thalidomide. Although they were unable to get help in the United States, there were many who sympathized with their decision; and when they chose to go outside their own country for a legal abortion, the entire American public learned through the daily press that abortions are medically safe and legally and morally accepted in certain countries in the world. In this episode the message was clear that science can produce unforeseen complications in our lives and can challenge our traditional ways of thinking. By no means as widely understood is the fact that science has created tremendous problems in society by eliminating many causes of death and by greatly reducing the death rate without a proportionate lowering of the birth rate. A few individuals have come to believe that the only immediately effective solution to the population explosion is medically supervised abortion. (This is a solution officially sanctioned by the Japanese government.) Medically supervised abortions will undoubtedly become more widespread in the United States as the procedure becomes legalized, and will provide time for the development and adoption of more suitable methods of birth control.

Upsurge in Molecular Biology

While the fear inspired by the publication of *Silent Spring* and by the unforeseen thalidomide danger was severely shaking faith in the infallibility of science, that faith was being reinforced on another front. Biological science was proceeding in the Louis Pasteur tradition in a great humanitarian effort to increase the well-being of mankind. The era of greatly expanded medical research began with the March of Dimes, a fund set up to conquer poliomyelitis by means of research. The widespread support of this effort was followed by the American Cancer Society drive for funds, and this in turn was followed by United States Public Health Service support on a generous scale.

Just when the funds from the March of Dimes reached unprecedented heights, the Salk vaccine was developed, and dozens of laboratories that had been tooled up for attacking the poliomyelitis problem were free to think about other things. By this time the support for cancer research was at flood tide, and the hopes raised by the successful fight against poliomyelitis were encouraging both the virus approach and the molecular approach to the cancer problem.

This increased support for poliomyelitis and cancer research has permitted and encouraged the expansion of attacks at the fundamental level, which in biological science may be defined as research with no particular disease in mind or research that is directed toward understanding the nature of life processes in general. This support for the fundamental approach has increased because the cancer problem has proved to be more formidable than the poliomyelitis problem, and there is no agreement as to which road will provide the quickest answer. Whenever there are no easy answers, the fundamental approach is more easily justified. What has emerged is the new science of molecular biology, which is engaged in an attack on the problem of understanding the mechanism of life itself. This attack is a direct link-up between genetics and biochemistry; the techniques include physical methods, electron microscopes, ultracentrifuges, isotope tracers, and many elaborate semiautomatic electronic instruments, most of which were not available until recently.

Molecular biologists have a religion all their own in which Nobel Prize winner Francis Crick is the prophet and the DNA molecular model is the icon (9). Molecular biologists have a "trinity" of three kinds of molecules—DNA, RNA, and the protein molecules—which correspond to each other on a unit-for-unit informational basis. They have a "dogma" (and they call it a dogma) which says that "information"—that is, molecular pattern—passes from DNA to RNA to protein but does not pass in the reverse direction.

The DNA molecule is the chemical equivalent of the hereditary gene. It is the basis of evolution because of its five basic capabilities of (a) providing information, (b) replication, (c) mutation, (d) recombination, and (e) expression. These five capabilities of the DNA molecule epitomize the relation between order and disorder in the living world. Because the DNA molecules contain information and are capable of expression, protein molecules can be built according to exact specifications. Because the DNA molecules can be replicated in a highly ordered fashion, cellular reproduction along hereditary lines is possible. Because the replication is not completely ordered and copy errors called mutations inevitably creep in to form new DNA molecules containing new information that can be expressed in the form of new protein molecules, evolution through natural selection is possible. Finally, the properties of recombination and of sexual reproduction provide a further element of disorder by guaranteeing a reshuffling of the genetic information.

The ultimate expression of the DNA molecule or gene is the protein molecule, but between DNA and protein is a complicated protein-synthesizing mechanism that "transcribes" the DNA information into a "messenger RNA" and then "translates" the latter into a specific protein structure by reactions that seem logical and almost machine-like. The protein molecules then bring about the myriad chemical and structural changes that occur in living cells.

Perhaps this slight digression will give some idea of the basis for the modern view of man as a machine. But the view given so far is only the beginning. If the basic machine represented by the trinity DNA, RNA, and protein were to have no properties other than those already outlined, all forms of life would be too stereotyped in their response to their environment.

The Living Machine

The basic machine represented by the trinity DNA, RNA, and protein has another capability, in addition to evolution, that commands our attention. This is adaptation. The process of mutation explains evolution, but further clarification is needed to explain how evolution can lead to mechanisms for adaptation, one of the most exciting features of living cells.

Every living cell in every organism, from the lowest bacterium to man, has to come to terms with its environment. This coming to terms with the environment involves the regulation or control of the most intimate properties of life. The DNA, RNA, protein system does not grind out the gene products in endless succession; instead, the individual genes and protein-generating mechanisms are turned on or off according to a plan that is partly programmed internally and partly regulated by a process called "feedback." The feedback concept describes a process in which the formation of a product is speeded up or slowed down by the product itself. It is a purely mechanistic system that permits a machine or a cell or an organism to measure the gap between its performance and some standard of performance and to take action to close the gap between the standard and the actual performance. In this kind of machine, not only does the product of the activity regulate the activity, but if enough product arises from some extraneous source in the environment, the machine is frequently able to shut off its own production of the particular substance completely.

Thus, in individual bacterial cells we find that an organism that can make an essential metabolite for its own use, such as an amino acid for protein synthesis, will immediately shut off the synthesis of the essential metabolite the moment the compound is added to the nutrient medium (10). In addition, the synthesis of the enzymes needed to make the essential metabolite will be shut off. Thus, the bacterial cell seems to behave as if it had a kind of intelligence. It is as if the bacterium doesn't do anything it doesn't have to do—and neither do human beings, unless persuaded by education or tradition to follow a different course.

If man is a machine, what becomes of free will? If man is a machine, how can a machine develop a new idea? If a bacterium is a machine whose "intelligence" can be mechanistically explained, can we be sure that our intelligence is not generated in the same way?

I believe the dilemma is solved for man by a highly sophisticated combination of order and disorder. The problem of biological evolution is solved by a built-in "copy-error mechanism" for introducing novelty in DNA molecules in the form of mutations. My theory is that creativity in man is the result of a built-in "copy-error mechanism" in the reproduction of ideas. Our minds operate with a certain built-in amount of disorganization. Our minds are always reshuffling facts and racking them up in new combinations. If the new combinations come too slowly, we call a person stupid; and if they come too fast, we call him a schizophrenic. Most new ideas do not turn out as expected, but we can weigh them—sometimes subconsciously—in terms of our past experience, rejecting many of them without further test and predicting success for others. A person who does this skillfully is said to have common sense. The scientific method is simply a way of testing our common sense under a rigid set of rules that makes us reject the idea when the facts go against us. It is an acceptance of the fact that the correctness of an idea is not determined by how good the idea makes us feel at the moment of illumination.

If the theory is correct, inventive computers would be feasible (11). Instead of a fixed program, the machine would be built to let its mind wander a bit. If the theory is correct, the problem of free will is solved, because we can never be completely programmed like a computer with fixed responses. Because of the built-in disorder in our minds, we will always be able to come up with new combinations and put them to a test (11).

Chemical Control of Life Processes

While learning about the ways in which cells control their own activity, scientists are learning how to control life by adding chemical substances to the environment. In learning how to control life, however, we are forging a two-edged sword. The knowledge of how to kill cancer cells, poliomyelitis viruses, insects, lampreys, dandelions, crabgrass, and eventually, any form of life may be what the public is paying for, but such knowledge can lead to undesirable applications as well as to intended results. No matter what phase of life control is studied, there will be unintended by-products. Insecticides and weed killers will affect life other than the insects and weeds. Cancer killers will prove to be effective in producing abortions—in fact, they already have been. Compounds that prevent conception produce an increase in fertility when their use is discontinued. Even when insecticides or weed killers prove highly specific, the elimination of one form of life may have unanticipated consequences for other forms. Knowledge of how to control life is dangerous knowledge, since it is difficult to manage; and such knowledge is not just around the corner, it is here. Dangerous knowledge can never be put back into the laboratories from which it came. Dangerous knowledge is a major problem of society, and the only solution to dangerous knowledge is more knowledge. From the disorder of unevenly developed branches of knowledge, we must achieve some new kind of equilibrium.

The new knowledge of how to manipulate life processes involves not only the killing of various insects, weeds, pests, viruses, and cancer cells but also the development of chemicals that affect the emotional and psychological attitudes of human beings, and again we are dealing with dangerous knowledge. The new tranquilizers and energizers are certain to have unanticipated side effects and consequences that cannot be appraised by any means other than actual experience.

In describing knowledge of biological control as dangerous knowledge, I am really discussing science as a force in cultural evolution. While in the past science could be seen as a source of material well-being and as the organizer and source of new knowledge, it is now realized by many that science is in fact a source of considerable disorder and of knowledge that society is by no means prepared to manage (12).

Perhaps science should make a more conscious effort to determine the impact of new knowledge on society. One of the roles of science in society should be to clarify the meaning of *order* and *disorder* as they relate to both biological evolution and cultural evolution. I believe that the processes of natural selection and survival of ideas in cultural evolution are analogous to the natural selection and survival of DNA molecules in biological evolution, and that ideas are the key to understanding cultural evolution just as DNA molecules are the key to understanding biological evolution. Earlier I remarked on the five basic capabilities of DNA molecules. I noted that mutation and recombination represent elements of disorder without which the system could not evolve, while information, expression, and replication represent elements of order. I believe that ideas or concepts possess the same five capabilities, and that without the elements of disorder represented by mutations and recombinations of existing ideas, cultural evolution could not occur. At present it appears that science is to cultural evolution what a mutagenic mutation is to biological evolution. That is, science is a new idea that generates more new ideas at an ever-increasing pace. Many of the new ideas have had consequences that have not been foreseen.

Earlier I noted that biological evolution proceeds on the basis of short-range decisions arrived at by natural selection, with the result that many species become extinct. Is it possible that civilizations become extinct because they proceed on the basis of short-range decisions and are unable to estimate their future needs in relation to their future environments?

If we accept the ideas that science is flooding society with new and dangerous knowledge, that the knowledge of the consequences of biological control is incomplete and inadequate, and that more knowledge is needed, what long-range policies should be advocated?

Specific Suggestions

Specifically, I urge that more studies be made on the phenomenon of adaptability, which occurs in man as well as in lower forms. Knowledge of adaptability is important since, if an organism can adapt, by the same token it will "de-adapt." When we carry a heavy load, our ability to carry loads increases; but the corollary is that, when we have no loads to carry, our ability to carry loads decreases (cf. Chapter 3). Just how big a load should we be able to carry, and what kind of load-carrying program will be best for each individual? How can he be helped to find his way to a load that will make him a useful member of society? When I speak of load-carrying capacity, I am thinking of a load in the broadest sense. A load can be physical, or it can be intellectual or emotional. Many tasks call for a great expenditure of creative energy, and we know far too little about how to bring out the best in people, about how to determine when an individual reaches a point of no return in his educational or home environment. When I speak of helping an individual find the load that is best for him and that will make him a useful member of society, I speak from the conviction that the performance of useful function within the capacity of the individual is the only source of true happiness. In the present context of order and disorder, we assume that some kind of balance between routine and novelty is desirable and that tasks should stretch the capacity of the individual at some times and not at others.

While emphasizing the importance of a search for more knowledge on man's adaptability, I also urge that more studies on man's individuality be made, in line with the many interesting leads provided by Roger Williams et al. (13). If one man's meat is another man's poison, perhaps one man's stimulus may be another man's stress (14). In the studies of adaptability and individuality we should try to find methods for helping people discover themselves. We should encourage the development of individual differences and should look upon individual differences in terms of their contribution to society. Above all we should study the phenomenon of stress in all its aspects—physical, mental, and emotional—as well as the sensory channels through which stress is perceived. The concepts of audio stress and visual stress are particularly meaningful in this day and age. But we should not seek to eliminate all forms of stress; rather we should introduce the concept of "optimum stress" and seek to define its parameters and meanings in terms of individuals.

More generally, I urge the establishment of interdisciplinary groups that will study, on the one hand, cultural evolution and adaptation in the light of biological evolution and adaptation and, on the other, the accumulated knowledge and methods of the humanities and social sciences. In advocating such an organization I urge the study of contemporary and long-range problems that arise from the uneven application of scientific knowledge, but we should look for ways not only to avoid pitfalls but also to better the human condition. Science is not wisdom, but we can use the scientific method to seek wisdom. Wisdom is the knowledge of how to use knowledge to better the human condition, and it is the most important knowledge of all. Aristotle distinguishes between philosophic wisdom and practical wisdom. Practical wisdom, he says, concerns personal interests; philosophic wisdom combines scientific knowledge with intuitive reason about "things that are highest by nature" (15). If we may equate his philosophic wisdom with a proper balance between the highest good for present and future society, it is clear that the wisdom I refer to is close to Aristotle's philosophic wisdom.

In seeking wisdom by consensus of interdisciplinary groups we need to examine all the old ideas by means of the scientific method, and we need to establish a continuing exchange of new ideas between scientists and humanists. We need to develop a new breed of scholars: men who combine a knowledge of new science and old wisdom, men who have the courage of the men of the Renaissance who thought truth was absolute and attainable.

Although the dream of absolute truth has faded, there is today a large group of scholars who are familiar with the concept of the living machine and aware of the philosophic implications of the existence of truly random phenomena (16) and the terrible responsibilities these implications place upon individual scholars and groups of scholars. The time is past when individual intuitive reason or revelation can be relied upon to provide all the relevant scientific knowledge; instead there must be continuing group discussion, and conclusions must be continually subject to amendment.

Conclusion

I advocate further research on the concept of "optimum stress" and on the nature of adaptations in human performance and in the human environment. At the same time I advocate further inquiry into the role of random processes in biological evolution and cultural evolution—in other words, a search for a new sophistication concerning the meaning and roles of order and disorder in individual lives and in the long-range problems of society. To accomplish these ends we need a new breed of scholars, with rigorous training for understanding the fundamental nature of man. They should be organized into special groups, with the task of generating wisdom that represents a consensus of many minds. They should be rigorously trained in the humanities and social sciences, and, in particular, in molecular biology (which includes chemistry and physics). The new scholasticism should not be debating whether man is a machine, but rather it should ask, "What kind of machine is man?" The aim of the new studies will be to arrive at valid concepts of order in terms of morality, tradition, custom, and law, and to develop further understanding of the role of disorder in arriving at new positions on how to improve the human condition. The results of new studies should be incorporated into the educational system as rapidly as possible. The ultimate goal should be not only to enrich individual lives but to prolong the survival of the human species in an acceptable form of society.

REFERENCES AND NOTES

1. V. R. Potter, "Bridge to the Future: The Concept of Human Progress," *Land Economics* **38**:1, 1962. Chapter 3 of this volume, pp. 42–54.

2. See Plato's *Republic*, Book 8: "Democracy, which is a charming form of government full of variety and disorder ... "

3. A. F. C. Wallace, *Religious Revitalization: A Function of Religion in Human History and Evolution* (Boston: Institute on Religion in an Age of Science, 1962), p. 24. See also Chapter 7 of this volume, pp. 83–102.

4. T. V. Smith and M. Grene, *From Descartes to Kant* (Chicago: University of Chicago Press, 1940); see E. A. Burtt, *The Metaphysical Foundations of Modern Physical Science* (New York: Harcourt, Brace & World, Inc., 1925).

5. J. M. Thoday, in S. A. Barnett, *A Century of Darwin* (London: William Heinemann Ltd., 1958).

6. R. L. K. Virchow, *Disease of Life, and Man*, L. J. Rather, translation (Stanford: Stanford University Press, 1958).

7. R. L. Rudd, *Pesticides and the Living Landscape* (Madison: University of Wisconsin Press, 1964), p. 78. Rudd quotes a 1957 report by Lemmon in which it is stated that California had registered over 12,000 pesticidal products up to that time.

8. R. Carson, *Silent Spring* (Boston: Houghton Mifflin Company, 1962).

9. V. R. Potter, *DNA Model Kit* (Minneapolis, Minn.: Burgess Publishing Co., 1959).

10. R. A. Yates and A. B. Pardee, "Control of Pyrimidine Biosynthesis in Eschericia Coli by a Feed-Back Mechanism," *J. Biol. Chem.* **221**:757, 1956. This article refers to earlier studies by P. H. Abelson, E. T. Bolton, and E. Aldous, "Utilization of Carbon Dioxide in the Synthesis of Proteins by Eschericia Coli. II," *J. Biol. Chem.* **198**:173, 1952.

11. D. M. MacKay, "Mindlike Behavior in Artefacts," *Brit. J. for Phil. Sci.*2:105, 1951; "The Use of Behavioural Language to Refer to Mechanical Processes," *ibid.* **13**:89, 1962; "On the Logical Indeterminacy of a Free Choice," *Mind* **69**:31, 1960.

12. F. Lipmann, "Disproportions Created by the Exponential Growth of Knowledge," *Perspectives Biol. Med.* **5**:324, 1962.

13. R. J. Williams, R. B. Pelton, and F. L. Siegel, "Individuality as Exhibited in Inbred Animals; Its Implications for Human Behavior," *Proc. Nat. Acad. Sci. U. S.* **48**:1461, 1962.

14. N. A. Scotch, "Sociocultural Factors in the Epidemiology of Zulu Hypertension," *Am. J. Public Health* **53**:1205, 1963.

15. See R. McKeon, ed., *Introduction to Aristotle: Nicomachean Ethics* (New York: Random House, Inc. 1947), especially pp. 430 and 431.

16. I. Langmuir, "Science, Common Sense and Decency," *Science* **97**:1, 1943.

CHAPTER FIVE

Dangerous Knowledge: The Dilemma of Modern Science

[Some reflections on where we have been and some thoughts on where we may be going]

Abstract Knowledge can become dangerous in the hands of specialists who lack a sufficiently broad background to envisage all of the implications of their work. Educated leaders should be trained in both sciences and humanities. All the implications cannot be foreseen in any case, and all plans must provide for revision. Medical science provides many examples.

One of the dilemmas of modern society is the phenomenon of dangerous knowledge, and the task of educated men everywhere is to find ways to understand the significance of new knowledge and its potential misapplications. This is one of the facts of life now that was evident to only a few half a century ago.

It will be argued that knowledge can become dangerous in the hands of specialists who lack a sufficiently broad background to envisage all of the implications of their work and that educated leaders should be trained in both sciences and humanities.

At the same time it will be emphasized that no one can ever possess the omniscience to foresee all the implications of new knowledge, and the best we can hope for is increased multidisciplinary planning with a continual revision of ongoing plans based on actual experience, that is to say, on hindsight.

The idea of dangerous knowledge is not new, since it is mentioned in the Book of Genesis. Adam, we are told, was expelled from the Garden of Eden for eating from the tree of knowledge "lest he put forth his hands, and take also from the tree of life, and eat, and live forever."

The more modern view was expressed in the annual report from a leading private foundation in 1956 which said:

> The answer to dangerous knowledge continues to be more knowledge, broadly shared by an international community of science and scholarship, and reliance upon the determination of man to grow in wisdom and understanding.

In other words, once we have made the choice to open Pandora's Box of knowledge, we can never put back its contents, and mankind must continue to search forever for the wisdom that is needed to cope with the avalanche of new knowledge that is upon us.

When we speak of dangerous knowledge, we have to admit at once that knowledge in itself cannot be inherently good or bad. What has lent credence to the concept of dangerous knowledge is that knowledge is power, and once knowledge is available, it will be used for power whenever possible. Knowledge once gained can never be left to gather dust in a library or locked successfully in a vault. No one worries about knowledge that is not used. It is the uses to which knowledge is put that make it dangerous or helpful.

Dangerous knowledge is frequently not recognized as such at the time of its discovery. A chemical might be designed in an attempt to cure cancer, then found to be effective as a weed-killer, and finally be used as a herbicide to destroy the food supply of a whole nation. Similarly, the study of nuclear fusion was not carried out originally with the intent to develop an atomic bomb that would destroy a whole city or nation. When thalidomide was developed as a sleeping pill it was not foreseen that, if it were given to a pregnant woman at just the critical number of days after conception, the developing infant would probably be born without arms. Unfortunately, we seem to learn these things by hindsight, after the actual events have occurred.

One of the cries frequently heard is to stop all research or to stop certain kinds of research, but this is difficult for many reasons. In

1917 there were very few people who were professional scientists. Professors made their living by teaching and did research more as a hobby than a vocation. Students did research to earn an advanced degree and then went into industry or became teachers.

Today all this is changed. Research is carried out by many scientists on a fulltime vocational basis. They frequently demand and get complete freedom from other obligations.

Instead of solving the world's problems, it appears that science has created new ones. Discoveries that led to the control of malaria led to tremendous decreases in infant mortality, and the saved babies grew up to have families of their own and help create the population explosion. Everyone who has studied the problem is aware of the fact that new knowledge does not need to be in the hands of individual families to decrease the infant mortality that formerly held populations in check. The virtual eradication of smallpox, diphtheria, typhoid fever, typhus, yellow fever, and malaria from large segments of the world was the work of a handful of public health officers and sanitary engineers. The resulting population explosion was not the result of choices made by individual men and women, most of whom were not aware of having any choice in the matter of conception.

Today there are some who feel that we have already passed a point of no return with respect to the possibility of solving the population problem by humane methods. They predict that the widespread undernutrition in the world of 1967 will burgeon into massive famines in the 1970s. Others say that the famines can yet be prevented if maximum efforts to limit the birth rates and to increase food production are made. But the bitter truth is that present efforts are not adequate. If economic growth is charted together with population growth, Brazil, Costa Rica, and India all show a disastrous crossover between the period of 1955–60 and 1960–65. That is, the ratio of economic growth to population growth, which was 2.7, 1.1, and 2.3, respectively, in the first period, dropped to 0.2, 0.2, and 0.4, respectively, in the second period. When this index is 1.0, it means that a country is standing still or holding constant in the war against poverty. When the index drops below 1.0, it means that the population is increasing faster than the national economic production, and the war against poverty and famine is being lost. In the countries mentioned, the population increase in 1960–65 was 3.1, 3.7, and 2.5 per cent per year, respectively, compared with 1.4 per cent in the United States and Canada (1).

It is clear that the knowledge of how to prevent infant mortality was dangerous knowledge in the absence of how to organize and distribute the economic production that the increased populations would require, or of knowledge on how to effectively limit the birth rate, or a willingness to reorganize ancient taboos in the light of new knowledge. In all of the cases cited, one must conclude that it is not dangerous knowledge but dangerous ignorance that we have to fear.

Medical science, coupled with engineering, has contributed to the world's problems not only by decreasing infant mortality but also by decreasing mortality at the other end of the life span. Mankind not only wants to live, but wants to live forever. Many religions have the promise of immortality as a prime motivation for participation, and when this is coupled with a guarantee of paradise for those who die in battle, the result can be disastrous, especially when the beliefs are held by opposing armies.

But a belief in immortality does not make people enthusiastic about ending their life span on this planet. One of the strongest instincts in man is to stay alive as long as possible, and it is commonly believed that a desire to end one's life is proof of temporary mental derangement. But this idea is leading to problems that may prove to be as complicated as unwillingness to face realistically the need for birth control.

Not only do we avoid death ourselves but we do not permit people to choose death in a dignified manner, when this is what they sorely need. Must we insist that old people must have their lives prolonged for months of pain or vegetative life after they no longer have the means to end it all themselves? Do such people really give informed consent to the therapeutic trials to which they submit? Do they really have a choice in the matter?

Medical science has already reached the point of agonizing decisions, and every day some conscientious physician has to decide to withhold the support that would prolong life but not make it more bearable. Such a decision can readily be justified, but what about the situation in which an elderly cancer patient is condemned to painful death by the decision that medical intervention should not be attempted because it would not prevent death anyway, when in fact treatments are available that would greatly alleviate suffering? In either case, the patient at present has insufficient basis for choice in the matter.

With the increasing use of transistorized electronic aids, mechanical valves and pumps, artificial kidneys, organ transplantation, antibiotics, chemotherapy, and, more recently, the arrogant promises of gene rebuilding, the medical profession is in great need of a new set of principles (2) for sharing complex decisions with its patients and with society. Already the idea of an indefinite extension of life on this planet has become so reasonable to some that a group called the Life Extension Society has been formed to deep-freeze people at the point of death, with a promise to thaw them out at some future date as soon as their therapeutic problem has been solved by science.

Meanwhile the problems of preventive medicine, environmental decontamination, and positive health are relatively neglected, as René DuBos has pointed out (3).

What is needed is more vigorous life in childhood and the middle years and the possibility of ending it decently in old age in a brief but dignified episode such as frequently is the case with people who have lived past 70 in a vigorous state.

But what is to be the fate of the aging invalid? What is to be done while medical science tries to live up to the rising expectations of a society that breathes smoke-filled air frequently by choice, that consistently overeats and underexercises, and that places its faith in treatment rather than prevention? What is to be done with the aging invalid whose relatives expect and get all of the mechanical resources of medical science during the interval between now and the expected millenium? Surely many of the ill would prefer to end it all as quickly as possible, but they no longer have any freedom of action and frequently no basis for calculating the odds. Is it moral to prolong life when the chances for a return to sentient life are vanishingly small?

The moral problem arises because medical science has achieved partial success in maintaining the machinery without maintaining the man, and the individual physician can only do his best. The means to end life swiftly and painlessly are well known, but who is to make the decision? The knowledge of the means is dangerous knowledge, but in the long run it cannot be left in the hands of the physician alone or even in the hands of a committee. The decision cannot belong to anyone but the individual concerned; but as already indicated, when the decision is needed, it frequently cannot be implemented unless advance decisions have been made. As society moves into an era in which the individuals concerned accept the responsibility for conception, it will become increasingly apparent that the individual concerned should have a more informed choice at the end of life's span.

Meanwhile the future of medical science is being oversold by prophets who are not on the firing line at the present. For many years to come individual physicians will be unable to restore meaningful life to moribund patients despite the predictions about the future of medicine, and decisions involving the election to death will continue to be made by men.

Man will continue to be mortal, as indeed he should be; and choices will be made on the basis of insufficient, and therefore dangerous, knowledge.

REFERENCES AND NOTES

1. William D. McElroy, personal communication.

2. In September, 1968, I participated in a conference that brought scientists and theologians together to discuss these principles at the Ecumenical Institute, Chateau de Bossey, in Céligny, Switzerland, under the sponsorship of the World Council of Churches, from whom the final report may be obtained.

3. René DuBos, *Man Adapting* (New Haven: Yale University Press, 1965).

CHAPTER SIX

Council on the Future

[A Proposal to Cope With the Gulf Between Scientific Knowledge and Political Direction]

Abstract Dangerous knowledge was defined as knowledge that has accumulated faster than the wisdom to manage it. Present methods of coping with the gulf between scientific knowledge and political direction are inadequate. Existing mechanisms for arriving at complex decisions involving facts and values must be supplemented by a fourth arm of government instructed to consider the consequences of major research programs and to recommend legislation.

Moral philosophy may be able to pose some interesting questions about unlimited freedom of scientific inquiry but the debate is conditioned by absence of practicable alternatives. . . . The answer to dangerous knowledge continues to be more knowledge, broadly shared by an international community of science and scholarship, and reliance upon the determination of man to grow in wisdom and understanding. (The President's Review, The Rockefeller Foundation Annual Report, 1956.)

Dangerous Knowledge

As a scientist whose present and former students are engaged in the fight against cancer at a cost to the government of more than a million dollars a year, I am intensely concerned with the impact of science on society and the answer to the problem of "dangerous knowledge." As a professor at a major state university, I possess academic freedom in the highest degree, yet I feel accountable to society for the direction and consequences of my work. I cannot imagine a better world than the microcosm in which I live, but I am concerned about the future of the larger world that I will leave to my children and their generation.

The feeling grows that scientists are finding it increasingly difficult to predict the consequences of their work, that technology has become the sorcerer's apprentice of our age. The concept of dangerous knowledge appears in a variety of images—the mushroom cloud, the usurping robot, the armless child of thalidomide. Many scientists object violently to the idea of dangerous knowledge, taking the position that all increases in knowledge are inherently good. This attitude is undoubtedly interwoven with our religious heritage, which assumes that the world exists for the benefit of man and that human suffering and evil serve part of a greater purpose. I believe that the concept of dangerous knowledge is valid, if for no other reason than that it calls attention to one of the dilemmas of our society. Dangerous knowledge has been defined as knowledge that has accumulated faster than has the wisdom to manage it; in other words, knowledge that has produced a temporary imbalance by outpacing other branches of knowledge.

Knowers and Doers

Basically, the problem arises from the gulf that is driven between the knowers or scientists and the doers or technologists. The expanding scientific enterprise appealed to its own practitioners, the knowers, on abstract grounds, as a mode of progressively uncovering the truth —a good in itself. But it also drew the support of a widening circle by its demonstrable utility in improving the ways of doing. The knowers hesitate because knowledge is never final, and the number of possible combinations of hazards is always greater than the number of individual hazards. Pragmatism, however, has always been the test of success in our culture, and our technology has proceeded almost on the basis of a single motto: "If it can be done, and sold at a profit, let's do it." This viewpoint may seem in harmony with the world of the conservatives, but in fact it has been most responsible for changing that world.

The consequences of new knowledge have always been unpredictable—hence Michael Faraday's classic remark in 1831 when asked what good is electricity: "Sir, what good is a new-born baby?" The present world differs from that of Faraday, particularly in the speed with which technology seizes upon new knowledge and converts it to action that will combine with other actions in ways that are unpredictable. In a world so rapidly absorptive, all new knowledge is potentially dangerous, but the word "unpredictable" needs qualification. The danger of new knowledge lies only in its application, and the unpredictability prevails to a very great extent because no specific effort is made to foresee the consequences and the interactions that may result from that application. Such effort should be organized as quickly as possible, because our political system—using the labels Democratic or Republican or the subtitles liberal or conservative—has not up to now been able to grapple with this dominant political issue of our time. Yet no other form of political organization is inherently as suitable for such a development. Our basic devotion to the dignity of the individual, to nonviolent change, to the right of the minority to be heard, are minimal guarantees that must be maintained in any attempt to foresee the consequences implicit in the application of new knowledge *and to take more vigorous political action to control technology*, while at the same time preserving its magnificent potentialities.

A Council on the Future

We need to supplement the existing mechanisms for arriving at complex decisions that involve both facts and values. In this area present communications between scientists in different fields, or between scientists and humanists, are not adequate. Occasional symposia such as "Science and Culture," reported in the Winter 1965 *Daedalus*, are exceedingly valuable; but they are not sufficiently specific, and they involve only a tiny fraction of the nation's intellectual resources.

I propose the formation of an institution that would be charged with predicting the consequences and interactions that might result from the application of new knowledge, an institution above politics and not responsible for political action. Such a "Council on the Future" would be interdisciplinary in the broadest sense and would necessarily be composed of "insiders" representing various associations from the sciences and the humanities. This professional group could be balanced by a democratic forum that will be mentioned later. The proposed Council on the Future would be a fourth arm of the government, instructed to consider the consequences of major research programs and to recommend support according to national needs. The council should represent not only the natural sciences but the social sciences and the humanities as well. It would have no legislative power but should be able to recommend legislation in published reports to be considered by the Congress. Such a council could be formed by existing professional organizations. However, to be effective, it would need financial support and recognition from the Congress. It seems to me that the proposed fourth arm of government is needed to do a job that cannot now be carried out by the existing political party system.

This country and the entire world suffers from political systems that penalize the group in power if it initiates a program that will not come to fruition until the other group is in power, especially if the program involves a sacrifice at its inception. Thus, long-range goals are sacrificed to short-range expedients. What greater barrier to progress could be imagined? In general, it appears that conservatives make all decisions on the basis of the profit system, while liberals feel that if someone is making a profit there is probably something wrong with the project. The conservatives are pragmatists with the present in mind. The liberals are pragmatists with the future in mind and the present never quite in hand. The conservatives correspond to the classicists whose beliefs were defined by T. E. Hulme in 1926: "Man is an extraordinarily fixed and limited animal whose nature is absolutely constant. It is only by tradition and organization that anything decent can be got out of him." The liberals correspond to Hulme's romanticists: "Man, the individual, is an infinite reservoir of possibilities; and if you can rearrange society by the destruction of oppressive order, then these possibilities will have a chance and you will get Progress."

The Tree of Knowledge

Perhaps what is needed is not conservatism or liberalism but realism —realism about the nature of man and realism about the nature of the world we live in. We are now talking about what every educated person ought to know and does not. There is not presently available within a single cover any reliable authoritative summary of what one would hope a college graduate, or even a high school graduate, might be expected to know about man and his world and the relationship between order and randomness in each. Knowing involves knowing what we do not know as well as what we do know, and there is little doubt that if a group of the best minds from seven continents were mobilized, they could come up with surprisingly large areas of agreement on knowledge and ignorance.

It is altogether likely that a documentation of the worldwide intellectual view of the nature of man and his environment would confirm the worst fears of those who are convinced that our stockpile of dangerous knowledge is already too large. As a matter of fact, the concept of dangerous knowledge has always been with us, and the public mind has always had an instinctive ambivalence toward science. Ever since Adam and Eve were expelled from Paradise for eating from the tree of knowledge, the popular image of science has been less than holy.

As the old religious taboos on the search for knowledge have been progressively weakened by the onslaughts of Darwinism and neo-Darwinism, and while all the Christians except the fundamentalists have managed to incorporate evolution as "the technique of Creation" into their beliefs, the modern biologists have gone far beyond the simple man-from-monkey image that was debated in the Scopes trial. They now take the position that "if you believe in a little evolution, you have to believe in all of it." Evolution now embraces cosmology, and calculations seem to converge back to a reference point about 4.77 billion years ago, when it appears that inorganic elements first began to form from subatomic particles. Such calculations seem incredibly academic examples of "knowing," but they are part of the web of knowledge that led to atom splitting and atom fusion and to "doing" that changed the future of the world.

Similarly momentous are the theoretical extrapolations of evolution back to the point at which organic molecules began to form in the absence of life, back to the origin of the first nucleic acids and proteins, and back to the spontaneous origin of the single cells that were the ancestors of man and all other forms of life on this planet. Momentous because, in the words of Oscar Handlin (*Daedalus*, Winter 1965, pp. 156–170) " . . . science grew ever less inclined to replace old with new certitudes; it ceased to deal with deterministic laws and yielded instead tentative statements of probability. At the same time, it probed the most important aspects of human existence and did so with increasing confidence. Since Darwin's day it had been busily destroying the fixed universe of tradition; now it made clear that it offered no consolatory alternative of its own." No consolatory alternative because most modern biologists look upon evolution, from nucleic acid molecules to man, as a long series of nondirected mutations in which truly random events play an enormous role. Thus Ernst Mayr recently emphasized that even the regularities appearing in certain evolutionary lines are caused by natural selection rather than by any teleological, finalistic principles. The basic mechanism of evolution continually generates novelty and then asks of the product, will it work? will it do a job? will it survive? will it reproduce? If this is design, it is a design that is not concerned with the destiny of man.

Value Systems in Peril

In *The National Purpose*, published in 1960, a group of distinguished Americans appeared to conclude that the United States as a society is "uncertain of itself, confused as to the values it should be pursuing and the direction in which it should be tending." Almost simultaneously, a group of educators released a joint statement in the *Saturday Review* on the occasion of the Dewey Centennial calling for an educational policy that would "nurture minds intolerant of such immoral responses as cynicism, apathy, complacency, hysteria and despair." They pointed out that our society is precarious and not automatically self-perpetuating. Its future is guaranteed only to the extent that men are equipped with the intellectual skills and loyalties that the future may require.

It is now clear that the accelerated rate of development of science and technology will continue, and that our national and international politics must deal with both the possibilities and the dangers of the revolution that has occurred in the ways of knowing and of doing. Society must pay more attention to the long-range consequences of our day-to-day governmental decisions. I believe that most scientists would regard the peaceful preservation of our earthly environment, and the balance between the population and the environment, as high-priority goals for the future. I believe they would agree with John Dewey that progress consists of movement toward a society of free individuals in which all, through their own work, contribute to the liberation and enrichment of society as a whole. I believe that a revitalization of our value system is both necessary and possible.

A Journal for Mankind

The problem we face is how to harness science and technology to the above goals, how to arrive at specific value judgments that would serve them. Earlier I proposed the formation of a Council on the Future, composed of "insiders." In addition, we need a new international publication that might be called the *Journal for Mankind*, in which dozens of symposia in print would operate on a continuing basis and be open to the "outsiders." All contributions would be brief and documented with adequate bibliographies, and the majority would be in the form of extended letters to the editor confirming or challenging previous statements in the journal. The contributions would be classified according to the problems under discussion and might deal with a variety of topics that could be identified and segregated. Essays could be invited on the definition of human progress, the definition of a great society, the elimination of poverty, the question of goals and their priorities, educational goals and methods, race relations, religious revitalization, political revitalization, overpopulation, overconsumption, conservation of natural resources, help to underdeveloped countries, liberation of creative talent, the role of advertising, and redesign of urban communities. Each contribution would be subject to continuing criticism and rebuttal, and each author would render an opinion and try to support it on the basis of his particular knowledge or background. Much has been said about the "two cultures," but only the phenomenon has been discussed. The time has come to provide a forum in which views from all sides of the academic community may be heard for what they are worth in specific situations and in defining new problems.

The proposed journal would provide a source of expert testimony that could supplement the Council on the Future. It could help inform legislators and administrators and could provide source material for journalists and writers. It would permit busy scientists and other scholars to maintain their primary professional competence while at the same time bringing their knowledge to bear on the building of a better world. The proposed journal should be partly subsidized in order to achieve wide distribution and low subscription rates.

It may be thought that the volume of contributions might be either overwhelming or negligible or that none of the right people would contribute; but when a leading physiologist wrote an article on race problems for a recent issue of *Science*, numerous readers were moved to comment at length. At the symposium mentioned earlier, Margaret Mead made a series of proposals on "The Future as the Basis for Establishing a Shared Culture" which would serve admirably as a type of article that would invite comment and continuing discussion.

Conclusion

It is clear that world opinion is reaching a shared body of assumptions that, for better or worse, place the destiny of man in the hands of science and technology. If we are to preserve the dignity of the individual, and if the human species is to survive and prosper, we need to cultivate the world of ideas and perfect the techniques for arriving at value judgments in areas where facts alone are not enough. I have suggested specific kinds of organized, printed, and circulated, continuing, open-ended discussion in which we maintain the right of the minority in the House of Intellect to be heard. Some effort at humanistic cooperation along these lines is the least that science can do to advance the human condition, and to help improve the balance between the knowers and the doers, between values and technology. Unless the present imbalance is corrected soon, our world will be lost whether or not there is a nuclear war.

CHAPTER SEVEN

The Role of Disorder in Human Activity and Thought

Abstract The instinct to combat disorder is a basic drive which leads to the formation of organized religions and scientific disciplines. But disorder is built into both inanimate and living systems, and without it life and culture would be impossible. Understanding the nature and function of disorder can help us to be rational about irrational events. Primitive religions may need to be revised and revitalized in the light of increasing knowledge about disorder.

The Essence of the Religious Process

One of the modern scholars who has had a profound effect upon my own thinking is the anthropologist, Professor A. F. C. Wallace, of the University of Pennsylvania. I first encountered his analysis of the relation of science and religion in a printed report of a paper that he presented in 1961 at the Eighth Institute on Religion in an Age of Science (1), and his remarks seemed to make more sense than anything I had previously encountered in this area. When I later looked up his other scholastic endeavors, my respect for him was increased; and when I participated in a symposium on science and religion, I learned to further appreciate the sincerity and high motivation of his work, which includes an analysis of the psychology of people who have been overwhelmed by a natural disaster such as a hurricane. The tendency to think in simplistic terms seems to have uneasy parallels with the tendencies of people who are beginning to think of the present and future as an inevitable natural disaster. Briefer quotations from his work have appeared elsewhere in this volume, but in this chapter I would like to present an unabridged section from his paper which was presented under the heading I have employed above. His statement was as follows:

In view of the near-universality of religion among men, its antiquity, and the multiple functions which it seems to serve, it would seem that we may speak of "the religious process" as a type of event which occurs among human beings under very widely varying conditions. The essential theme of the religious event is, nevertheless, definable: it is the dialectic of disorganization and organization. On the one hand men universally observe the increase of entropy (disorganization) in familiar systems: metals rust and corrode, woods and fabrics rot, people sicken and die, personalities disintegrate, social groups splinter and disband. And on the other hand, men universally experience the contrary process of organization: much energy is spent preventing rust, corrosion, decay, rot, sickness, death, and dissolution, and indeed, at least locally, there may be an absolute gain of organization, a real growth or revitalization. This dialectic, the "struggle" (to use an easy metaphor) between entropy and organization, is what religion is all about. The most diverse creeds unite in the attempt to solve the sphinx-riddle of the relationship between life and death, between organization and disorganization; the ideas of the soul, of gods, of world cycles, of Nirvana, of spiritual salvation and rebirth, of progress—all are formal solutions to this problem, which is indeed felt intimately by all men.

But religion does not offer just any solution: it characteristically offers a solution which assures the believer that life and organization will win, that death and disorganization will lose, in their struggle to become the characteristic condition of self and cosmos. And religion further attempts to elucidate and describe the organization of self and cosmos. Religion then may be said to be a process of maximizing the quantity of organization in the matrix of perceived human experience. Religion maximizes it, perhaps, beyond what rational use of the data of this experience would justify, but it thereby satisfies a primary drive. We must, I think, postulate an organization "instinct": an "instinct" to increase the organization of cognitive perception. Religion and science, from this point of view, would seem to be the more direct expressions of this organizational instinct.

Categories of Religious Viewpoints

In my opinion there are two main types of religion, and all the others are mixtures of these two. First, there is the primitive type of religion, incorporating ignorance, superstition, and magic in the attempt to provide answers to the relationship between life and death and to the meaning of the struggle between organization and disorganization so graphically described by Professor Wallace. Second, there is the humanistic type of religion, including scientific humanism, which seeks to maximize human values and to arrive at rational understandings of the world we live in. It is recognized that both the extreme types and many intermediate groupings are still among us in this nation and in the world.

When I refer to primitive religions, I include those that believe in revelation, prophecy, and an afterlife that is more important than the life that is lived on this earth. I refer to any and all religions that take it as given that there is a master plan being carried out for the benefit of mankind here on this earth and that there are a privileged few who have been chosen to read it. Teilhard de Chardin (see Chapter 2, pp. 30–41) was aware of the frightful dilemma presented by the existence of a hierarchical, rigid superstructure of man's need for certitude on the one hand, and adaptation and this-worldly hope on the other. In this present era when the survival of mankind may depend upon erasing the religious and cultural ideas that help to maintain the population explosion among other anachronisms, we can no longer afford to continue to be obscure in discussing what aspects of religion are worthy of mankind and what aspects are in danger of hastening our destruction. The discussion to follow may be obscure and irrelevant at times, but it is only a small glimpse of the potential material that needs to be collated and integrated in an effort to understand the nature and meaning of disorder.

Disorder, Chaos, Randomicity and Chance

Disorder is the absence of order. It can be examined in terms of causation or the lack of causation. In general I shall be concerned with the existence of disorder as an uncaused or spontaneous phenomenon. I will insist that there is such a thing as spontaneous disorder and that the many examples of this do not merely have obscure causes (3). There are many semantic discussions of the meaning of disorder, but I am inclined to dismiss most of them as literary exercises.

The disorder that is deliberately generated, or the disorder that is stepped up to a higher level by discernible causes, would be subjects for separate discussion. What we are concerned with here is disorder that is related to natural chaos (as in cosmogenesis), to randomicity, and to chance. Examples of randomicity and chance are to be found in flipping (tossing) a coin, rolling dice, drawing a card from a shuffled deck, or in an honest roulette wheel or a game of "Russian roulette" (one cartridge in a six-chambered revolver). In these cases one can discuss the role of "causes" that are merely obscure but which produce "random" distributions. In the case of many atomic phenomena there appears to be an inherent random behavior that is sufficiently insensitive to external causes that the decay rate of various radioactive isotopes can be used as clocks to date archaeological, fossil, or mineral specimens over periods of time ranging up to millions and even billions of years (4). It is probably merely a matter of the degree of sensitivity or insensitivity to external forces that differentiates the flipping of a coin from the atomic clock, and even though the result of one toss of a coin may be subject to unseen external determining factors, the process is so insensitive to these factors that it can be used to reliably generate a statistical model of randomicity. Thus, it can be said with confidence that there is an equal 1:1 or 50-50 chance that the next toss of a coin will be heads or tails and that this prediction is not affected by any previous number of successive heads or tails. We have to keep telling ourselves that this is a fact because our common sense operates in precisely the opposite way. If we know there are two possibilities, we tend to think a series of "heads" will increase the probability of the next toss being different. But if something happens in a particular way every time we do a certain maneuver and we are unaware of the other possibilities, we assume that it will behave that way on the next occasion. Thus, in an extreme example we assume that the sun will come up tomorrow morning because we understand that it came up yesterday morning and on every yesterday that we know of. In brief, we go through life passing judgment on ordered events that can be depended upon and disordered events that cannot be depended upon. If they are sufficiently disordered to generate a truly chance phenomenon, we have a kind of "ordered disorder" that is sufficiently disordered to enable us to make exact predictions about the outcome of a sufficient number of trials, that is, the "probability" of an individual toss of a coin or the number of automobile deaths that will occur on Labor Day weekend in the United States.

The idea of *chance* is a basic part of Darwinian evolution. Random or chance mutations occur spontaneously during the operation of an almost perfect gene-copying system, and the probability of mutation is increased by cosmic rays, X-rays, ultraviolet rays, viruses, and certain chemicals from the natural and the industrial environment. These mutations can be carried along if they are beneficial or even if they are not beneficial, if they are not harmful (5). Natural selection will eliminate those that are harmful (Chapter 1).

Teilhard de Chardin and Disorder

Teilhard de Chardin believed in Darwinian evolution, and, unlike many present-day primitive religionists, he was fully aware of the role of chance and natural selection in it. Moreover, Teilhard made a strong effort to evangelize the Darwinian idea (Chapter 2, pp. 30–41) while at the same time trying to evoke the master plan idea and to keep within the boundaries of his religion. He was aware of the role of reckless procreation as nature's method, coupled with random mutations and natural selection.

> But it is not the individual unit that seems to count for most in the phenomenon. What we find within the struggle to live is something deeper than a series of duels; it is a conflict of chances. By reckless self-reproduction life takes its precautions against mishap. It increases its chances of survival and at the same time multiplies its chances of progress.
>
> Once more, this time on the plane of animate particles, we find the fundamental technique of *groping*, the specific and invincible weapon of all expanding multitudes. This groping strangely combines the blind fantasy of large numbers with the precise orientation of a specific target. It would be a mistake to see it as mere chance. Groping is *directed chance*. It means pervading everything so as to try everything, and trying everything so as to find everything. Surely in the last resort it is precisely to develop this procedure (always increasing in size and cost in proportion as it spreads) that nature has had recourse to profusion. [(2), pp. 109–110]

It is interesting to note how Teilhard differentiates between *mere chance* and *directed chance*, and this differentiation of course leaves between the lines the question *directed by whom or by what*? Modern molecular biology would offer suggestions not available to Teilhard, but undoubtedly he would have understood their message.

Directed chance is built into every living organism from the most primitive to the most complex in terms of *feedback* in the general sense to cover all aspects of the process by which the organism or the species judges how well it is doing (Chapters 1 and 12).

Teilhard was troubled by the dilemma of feedback-directed systems and the problem of free will, or as he put it "To connect the two energies of the body and the soul, in a coherent manner: science has provisionally decided to ignore the question, and it would be convenient for us to do the same. ... It is impossible to avoid the dark: we must advance" [(2), p. 62].

Teilhard solved the problem by setting up two categories that he referred to again and again: the *within* and the *without*. "The *within, consciousness* and then *spontaneity*—three expressions for the same thing. ... Determinate *without*, and 'free' *within*—would the two aspects of things be irreducible and incommensurable? If so, what is your solution?" [(2), p. 57].

Teilhard equated feedback mechanisms (Chapter 1) with determinism:

> At an early stage of their discoveries biologists were surprised and fascinated by the fact that living beings, however perfect their spontaneity, were always decomposable into an endless chain of closed mechanisms. From this they thought they could deduce a principle of universal materialism. But they overlooked the essential difference between a natural whole and the elements into which it is analysed. ... [The fact] that what is 'free,' even in man, can be broken down into determinisms, is no proof that the world is not based on freedom—as indeed I maintain that it is. [(2), pp. 110–111]

I wish to emphasize that throughout living systems there are built-in indeterminacies, built-in disorder, and that the life mechanisms are not as determinate as Teilhard assumed. My solution to the dilemma posed by Teilhard is that the freedom he strove to preserve, as opposed to determinism, may be keyed into the disorder that I assume is built-in and actually preserved by natural selection. Some of these issues have been discussed by Irving Langmuir (3), George Wald (6), and John Platt (7), each with an interpretation that differs from the others and from my own.

Beyond Teilhard: The Next Step

It is my opinion that those who lean toward the humanistic type of religion are still greatly troubled by the fact that science appears to destroy the groundwork of our ancient value systems without providing an adequate foundation for our present and future cultural evolution. Thus we seem to be living at a time when, in Wallace's words, "the process of maximizing the quantity of organization in the matrix of perceived human experience" is no longer possible by religious revelation, but neither has science provided any beacons that the man in the street can follow to satisfy his instincts for classifying information into signals that read red or green.

My contribution to this situation is not one that will satisfy those instincts. My role will appear to be nihilistic to some and merely destructive to others, but if we can begin a dialogue, I hope to show that the mysteries of disorder are not entirely irrelevant and inimical to man's nature. If we will but examine the realities of the situation we may be able to accept the mystery of it.

Let me begin by quoting from Arthur Koestler's *The Ghost in the Machine* (1968) in which he attacks biological science in general and modern psychology in particular (8).

> The citadel of orthodoxy which the sciences of life have built in the first half of our century rests on a number of impressive pillars, some of which are beginning to show cracks and to reveal themselves as monumental superstitions. The four principal ones, summarised in a simplified form, are the doctrines
>
> (a)   that biological evolution is the result of random mutations preserved by natural selection;
>
> (b)   that mental evolution is the result of random tries preserved by 'reinforcements' (rewards);
>
> (c)   that all organisms, including man, are essentially passive automata controlled by the environment, whose sole purpose in life is the reduction of tensions by adaptive responses;
>
> (d)   that the only scientific method worth that name is quantitative measurement; and, consequently, that complex phenomena must be reduced to simple elements accessible to such treatment, without undue worry whether the specific characteristics of a complex phenomenon, for instance man, may be lost in the process. [(8), p. 3]

In making my own position as a life scientist and a humanist quite clear, I will say that with respect to (a), I would affirm the orthodox scientific view as stated with some recent additional insights referred to earlier (5). With respect to (b), I would affirm that random tries preserved by reinforcements are an important *part* of mental evolution *and* mental development. With respect to (c), I will say that science is divided on this point and that it is precisely in the area of free will versus determinism that I feel some clarification is possible. With respect to (d), Mr. Koestler is setting up a thesis that no scientist would regard as patent, that is, that quantitative measurements cannot be applied to complex phenomena but only to their simpler elements. The modern emphasis is quite opposite to Koestler's view that science abhors complexity and, indeed, is increasingly based on systems analysis. The name of the game is biocybernetics, the science of feedback control in biological systems whether subcellular, cellular, in the whole animal, or in populations (Chapter 12). It is the existence of feedback that makes it possible to say that *disorder is the raw material from which order is conceived and selected* (Chapter 4).

Disorder in Human Affairs

Now I will turn to the documentation of disorder in human affairs. As a scientist engaged in cancer research for some 30 years, I have been led to examine the phenomenon of cancer not only from a scientific point of view but also from a religious and philosophic point of view. I have read and reread the Old Testament Book of Job many times, and I have read the critical review of the Book of Job as a literary example of Greek tragedy (9). It is a magnificent piece of literature and represents the mythical answer to the question of why must good people suffer? God's answer to Job was that you cannot expect to be virtuous and escape suffering; that is, you cannot make demands of the system. In modern terms we would have to say that the system operates as it can, not as we would have it. But the Book of Job shows that the ancient Hebrews were keenly aware that disorder was a real element that intervened in their relationship with their God. Job had to learn to accept suffering and not be swerved from loyalty to his faith.

The Greeks and Disorder

We find the role of disorder in Greek affairs discussed at length by E. R. Dodds in a charming book entitled *The Greeks and the Irrational*, first published in 1951 and reissued in 1964 (10). He says on page 10 and following pages:

But the most characteristic feature of the *Odyssey* is the way in which its personages ascribe all sorts of mental (as well as physical) events to the intervention of a nameless and indeterminate daemon or "god" or "gods." These vaguely conceived beings can inspire courage at a crisis or take away a man's understanding, just as gods do in the *Iliad*. But they are also credited with a wide range of what may be called loosely "monitions." Whenever someone has a particularly brilliant or a particularly foolish idea; when he suddenly recognizes another identity or sees in a flash the meaning of an omen, when he remembers what he might well have forgotten or forgets what he should have remembered, he or someone else will see in it, if we are to take the words literally, a psychic intervention by one of these anonymous supernatural beings. Doubtless they do not always expect to be taken literally: Odysseus, for example, is hardly serious in ascribing to the machinations of a daemon the fact that he went out without his cloak on a cold night. But we are not dealing simply with an "epic convention." For it is the poet's characters who talk like this, and not the poet: his own convention is quite clear—he operates, like the author of the *Iliad*, with clear-cut anthropomorphic gods such as Athena and Poseidon, not with anonymous daemons. If he has made his characters employ a different convention, he has presumably done so because that is how people did in fact talk: he is being "realistic."

And indeed that is how we should expect people to talk who believed (or whose ancestors had believed) in daily and hourly monitions. The recognition, the insight, the memory, the brilliant or perverse idea, have this in common, that they come suddenly, as we say "into a man's head." Often he is conscious of no observation of reasoning which had led up to them. But in that case, how can he call them "his"? A moment ago they were not in his mind; now they are there. Something has put them there, and that something is other than himself. More than this he does not know. So he speaks of it noncommittally as "the gods" or "some god," or more often (especially when its prompting has turned out to be bad) as a daemon. And by analogy he applies the same explanation to the ideas and actions of other people when he finds them difficult to understand or out of character. A good example is Antinous' speech in *Odyssey* 2, where, after praising Penelope's exceptional intelligence and propriety, he goes on to say that her idea of refusing to remarry is not at all proper, and concludes that "the gods are putting it into her chest." Similarly, when Telemachus for the first time speaks out boldly against the suitors, Antinous infers, not without irony, that "the gods are teaching him to talk big."

Professor Dodds sums up this section as follows:

We have now surveyed, in such a cursory manner as time permits, the commonest types of psychic intervention in Homer. We may sum up the result by saying that all departures from normal human behaviour whose causes are not immediately perceived, whether by the subjects' own consciousness or by the observation of others, are ascribed to a supernatural agency, just as is any departure from the normal behaviour of the weather or the normal behaviour of a bowstring. This finding will not surprise the nonclassical anthropologist: he will at once produce copious parallels from Borneo or Central Africa. But it is surely odd to find this belief, this sense of constant daily dependence on the supernatural, firmly embedded in poems supposedly so "irreligious" as the *Iliad* and the *Odyssey*. And we may also ask ourselves why a people so civilized, clearheaded, and rational as the Ionians did not eliminate from their national epics these links with Borneo and the primitive past, just as they eliminated fear of the dead, fear of pollution, and other terrors which must originally have played a part in the saga. I doubt if the early literature of any other European people—even my own superstitious countrymen, the Irish—postulates supernatural interference in human behaviour with such frequency or over so wide a field.

Nilsson is, I think, the first scholar who has seriously tried to find an explanation of all this in terms of psychology. In a paper published in 1924, which has now become classical, he contended that Homeric heroes are peculiarly subject to rapid and violent changes of mood: they suffer, he says, from mental instability (*psychische Labilität*). And he goes on to point out that even today a person of this temperament is apt, when his mood changes, to look back with horror on what he has just done, and exclaim, "I didn't really mean to do that!"—from which it is a short step to saying, "It wasn't really I who did it." "His own behaviour," says Nilsson, "has become alien to him. He cannot understand it. It is for him no part of his Ego." This is a perfectly true observation, and its relevance to some of the phenomena we have been considering cannot, I think, be doubted. Nilsson is also, I believe, right in holding that experiences of this sort played a part—along with other elements, such as the Minoan tradition of protecting goddesses—in building up that machinery of *physical* intervention to which Homer resorts so constantly and, to our thinking, often so superfluously. We find it superfluous because the divine machinery seems to us in many cases to do no more than duplicate a natural psychological causation. But ought we not perhaps to say rather that the divine machinery "duplicates" a psychic intervention—that is, presents it in a concrete pictorial form? (Pp. 10–14 in reference 10.)

Confusion Theory

Coming now to modern times, we find an interesting discussion of two theories of history in an anonymous review (11) of Arthur Schlesinger's book *A Thousand Days* (12).

> Schlesinger believes in the "confusion theory" of history as opposed to the "conspiracy theory." According to Political Scientist James Mac-Gregor Burns, the conspiracy theory holds that "if something happened, somebody planned it." Schlesinger, on the other hand, believes in "the role of chance and contingency, the sheer intricacy of situations, the murk of battle." Schlesinger is also scornful of the "prophetic" historians—Marx, Spengler, Toynbee—who use "one big hypothesis to explain a variety of small things." Says he: "They have reduced the chaos of history to a single order of explanation, which can infallibly penetrate the mysteries of the past and predict the developments of the future. . . . "
>
> His White House tour only reinforced his confusion theory. "Nothing in my recent experience has been more chastening," he wrote, "than the attempt to penetrate into the process of decision. I shudder a little when I think how confidently I have analyzed decisions in the ages of Jackson and Roosevelt, traced influence, assigned motives, evaluated roles, allocated responsibilities and, in short, transformed a disheveled and murky evolution into a tidy and ordered transaction."

I hope that there can be more thought given to the confusion theory of history in relation to the present theme of "disorder in human thought and activity." As a scientist I am keenly aware of the role of the accidental happening that turns out to be a great discovery (as in the case of penicillin) recognizing, of course, the validity of Pasteur's aphorism that "Chance favors the prepared mind." But not all great victories in battle can be ascribed solely to brilliant generalship.

Time does not permit me to describe all the facts that have led me to the conclusion that the "confusion" theory of history epitomizes many aspects of our innermost nature and of the external world. I believe that a certain minimal amount of disorder is required for biological evolution by mutation and natural selection, and I believe that a certain minimal amount of disorder has to be built into our brain function in order to permit us to be more than the "passive automata controlled by the environment" that Koestler claims is the standard model postulated by the life scientists.

Protean Behavior

That an *ordered disorder* is built into brain function is a difficult proposition to prove, but since I have been looking for proof for about ten years, I can now report that I believe that something approaching proof is at hand. If we could show that disorder in the form of nonsystematic behavior was built into lower forms that would ordinarily be considered as "passive automata controlled by the environment," we would have a strong base for tracing the phenomenon up through higher forms to man. This can now be done, entirely apart from each man's personal observations and experiences. The phenomenon has been described and reviewed by Humphries and Driver of the Mental Health Research Institute at the University of Michigan.

They have reviewed the subject of *protean* behavior (13) and briefly reported on it in *Science* in 1967 (14). The word, meaning erratic or unpredictable, was coined by Chance and Russell (see 14). It is derived from the mythological Greek character Proteus, who constantly changed form in a highly erratic manner. I quote Humphries and Driver:

> We define protean behavior as behavior that is sufficiently unsystematic to prevent a reactor from predicting in detail the position or actions (or both) of the actor. It includes many reactions that are released only when the animal is in immediate and obvious danger. For example, if small insects resting on tree bark are disturbed, they usually take to the wing in a characteristically erratic spinning and looping action; there is no known aerodynamic or physiological reason for such flight. The flight path is much more direct and simple when the insect leaves its resting place of its own accord. Similarly, noctuid and geometrid moths show a bewildering variety of unoriented maneuvers when exposed to the ultrasonics of hunting bats; their behavior has been shown to have a selective advantage of about 40 percent. . . .
>
> In many species of birds, including waders, gulls, ducks, and starlings, the erratic pattern is shown by flocks and may then be termed a united erratic display; it acts as a deterrent against the attacks of aerial predators like the peregrine falcon. On appearance of the predator the birds draw together into a tight group, which zigzags unpredictably in swift flight, sometimes splitting into subgroups, with the individuals continually shuffling their relative positions. . . .
>
> We propose that the essential feature of all protean displays is that they are likely to arouse mutually incompatible tendencies in the reactor. These tendencies may be of simple orienting components or of

fundamental behavioral categories like escape or defense. [(14), p. 1767]

In their extensive review, Driver and Humphries (13) discussed the behavior of moths:

> The most instructive data have been supplied in relation to moths by Roeder (1962). The noctuid moth is enabled to react to predatory bats by virtue of possessing a pair of tympanic organs. Roeder and Treat (1961) show that when the bat is less than 10 to 20 feet away, its cries produce a maximum neurophysiological response in both tympanic organs. Since the moth requires a differential response from the two organs in order to assess direction, it clearly lacks directing cues when the bat is at close quarters. Roeder (1962) shows that when at some great distance from the ultrasonic source, the moths give directed movements away, with few erratic manoeuvres. The typical full protean single erratic display occurs only when the moths are close enough to saturate both tympanic organs. Thus here we have clear evidence that the single erratic display can occur due to the activation of an escape tendency in the absence of adequate directing stimuli. . . .
>
> Roeder and Treat observed 402 field encounters between moths and feeding bats, recording the behavior of the moths and whether they were captured by the bats. They say (Roeder and Treat, [1961]) "the changes in flight path were dramatic in their abruptness and bewildering in their variety." Further, "bats soon learn to plot an interception course with food propelled through the air in a simple ballistic trajectory. The random behavior . . . seems to be a natural answer to this predictive ability in bats." They compared the percentage of survivors in moths which gave such manoeuvres, to the percentage surviving when there was no reaction. This showed that for every 100 reacting moths which survived there were only 60 surviving non-reactors, a selective advantage of 40%. Roeder and Treat suggest that this figure is "more than adequate to account for the evolution of the moth's ear through natural selection." We suggest that the same may be said for the evolution of the protean nature of the flight paths.

Driver and Humphries summarized their discussion as follows:

> In conclusion we wish to stress that all the variability seen in protean displays, the changes in appearance and alternations of role, are not random in the sense of lacking causal relations. The very effectiveness of their protean nature arises from the fact that the causal and systematic relations are *hidden* from the predator. Indeed, it is because these relations have been effectively hidden that biologists have largely overlooked the fact that unpredictability is so widely and sys-

tematically employed in the animal kingdom. *For it is the tendency of most scientists, even biologists, to concentrate their attention on the description of systematic features and to reduce, balance out, or even ignore variability. Thus Markgren (1960), in his monograph on fugitive reactions in avian behaviour, regards variation in behaviour as a source of error. Our present paper shows that, on the contrary, the variability of behaviour has distinct survival value. . . .*

We have surveyed the great store of evidence, already contained in the literature, for the occurrence of protean properties in nature. We have demonstrated on theoretical grounds that such displays arouse conflict and interfere with information processing capacities of the predator, so reducing the effectiveness of the predator mechanisms. Further, the quantitative evidence of actual encounters between predators and prey supports these theoretical conclusions and indicates that the capacity to behave in a protean manner confers a selective advantage. Many diverse forms of behaviour, most of which have been poorly understood in the past, have thus been united within a single theoretical framework and placed in their ecological and evolutionary perspective. Viewed in this perspective, new ethological problems have appeared. We have attempted to define, describe, and outline the possibilities of this new field of inquiry—the specific aspects of which now await more detailed analysis. [(13), italics mine.]

Variable Behavior

The term *protean* was used by Humphries and Driver to describe erratic behavior on the part of species under attack by a predator. Meanwhile a most interesting study by Kavanau (15) has been reported in which wild mice were placed in complicated laboratory environments in the form of highly instrumented running wheels or complex maze systems. One of the latter contained 427 meters of linear runways with a 96-meter path from access to exit. There were 1205 90-degree turns, 48 meters of vertical passageways, and 445 blind alleys occupying 53 percent of the total space. White-footed mice captured in the wild and placed in this environment learned to traverse it in as few as 2 or 3 days *without extrinsic reward or deprivation.* Once they had learned them, the mice negotiated the mazes with remarkable speed and agility. Kavanau commented that because the patterns of spontaneous movement are established and followed without extrinsic reward, the activities appear to be the extension of inherited tendencies to explore and to develop wide-ranging locomotor activities. One of the most interesting aspects of

Kavanau's work is discussed under the heading of "Incorrect" Responses. Referring to a particular captive mouse, he noted that it did not always press the reward levers correctly despite long practice. On a typical night it obtained 50 food pellets using the correct lever-pressing sequence but failed 23 times using incorrect sequences. Kavanau commented that behavior which deviates fairly frequently from stereotyped "correct" responses, coupled with a high degree of spontaneous activity, underlies the remarkable facility with which white-footed mice can be taught to cope with complex contingencies. The wealth of detail and ingenuity in Kavanau's experiments cannot be repeated here, but they are highly relevant to objections to the conclusions drawn from experiments with conditioned responses as exemplified by the work of Skinner and discussed at length by Koestler (8). But Koestler seems to neglect the idea of *ordered disorder,* although he is aware that many "great inspirations" are incorrect and that they can be evaluated only in the light of hindsight. In the case of the white-footed mouse in the wild, the animal cannot afford to assume that a correct response will invariably pay off. By incorporating "incorrect" responses in his behavior, he, in effect, hedges his investments and, by accepting some failures, gains some rewards. Thus, to quote Kavanau:

> The tendency of trained [captive white-footed mice, *Peromyscus maniculatus, P. crimitus*] to give some so-called "incorrect" responses even after long experience can be interpreted most reasonably in terms of the adaptive value of a certain degree of variability of behavior in the wild. . . . The basis of these responses is that the animal has a certain degree of variability built into many of its behavior patterns. This variability is adaptive to conditions in the wild, where there are many relationships that are not rigidly prescribed. [(15), pp. 1628, 1639]

Kavanau uses the conservative term "variability" for what Humphries and Driver might call "protean behavior" (13), what Koestler calls "pathological" (8), and what I am inclined to call "ordered disorder," that is, disorder that is ordered by natural selection.

Here I may point out that no extrapolations to the human situation were attempted by Humphries and Driver or by Kavanau (other than "consistent with anthropomorphic interpretations"), but I suggest that the occurrence of random events or perhaps protean "ordered disorder" in the human brain should be examined much more extensively by behavioral psychologists. Unfortunately, as Humphries and Driver suggest, scientists tend to regard disorder as unmanageable and unscientific. Thus, W. Ross Ashby of the University of Illinois in a 1967 article, "The Place of the Brain in the Natural World" in *Currents in Modern Biology,* was apparently unaware of the concept of protean behavior, for he referred to the "behaving organism" as follows:

> The second point of view *considers its creative aspect,* as when a man invents a new system of musical harmony or produces Joyce-like prose. *I shall say nothing of this matter, for I have no objective criterion by which I can distinguish such productions from the squeakings of a gate, or from a sequence of words generated by a dictionary and a table of random numbers.* When "anything goes," science has little to say. [(19), italics mine.]

The Human Brain

In contrast to this point of view, and of great interest vis-à-vis the articles on protean behavior is a book recording the BBC Reith Lectures given by Professor J. Z. Young of Oxford in 1950. The book is entitled *Doubt and Certainty in Science: A Biologist's Reflections on the Brain.*

If we examine his views in relation to those of Koestler and the articles by Humphries and Driver, we can begin to see what is bothering Koestler and why he is perhaps attacking an incorrect image. In his fourth lecture Young commented as follows:

> The doctrine that learning is all of a conditioned reflex type has had an immense vogue in Russia and is said to be a basic part of the theory of Soviet education. Like all systematizations it has some advantages over no systematization at all. But somehow we feel that Pavlov's analysis leaves out some essential feature of learning as it occurs in man, or at least man as we know him. Because of the limitation of his method, Pavlov actually took elaborate precautions to rule out the very phenomenon he should have studied. He did not include the *random trial-and-error behaviour* by which an animal or man searches for actions that shall produce satisfactory solutions for its needs. The Russian Government built him a wonderful laboratory with every room sound-proof and complicated arrangements to ensure that the dogs should stand quite still and be educated. With his outlook this seemed the right thing to do. It was the right thing to do to get that sort of result, but study by this method alone will not include the most useful forms of human behavior.

If the attempt to show how patterns of action grow up in the brain has been successful, you may now, perhaps, begin to see how this is going to help us in the search for the nature of scientific inquiry. I hope to be able to show in later lectures that in this system of brain action lie clues for understanding the development of *man as a communicating, family, social, religious, and scientific animal. At all stages we find first random behaviour,* as we call it experiment or doubting. Then through observations of connections between features that occur repeatedly, there is the recognition of similarities and recurrences, the establishment of laws, of certainty.

But we must notice that this process of replacing *randomness* by law may be a one-way, non-reversible process. The cortex of the new-born baby has perhaps few innate traits, it is in the main a blank sheet of possibilities. But the very fact that it becomes organized minute by minute, day by day, throughout the years, reduces progressively the number of possible alternative ways of action. Learning the laws of behaving in certain ways makes it increasingly difficult to learn others. We know surprisingly little about what determines the stability of the systems that we get built up in our brains. They can certainly be to some extent reversed by new circumstances. We may forget, or learn new ways of speaking about the world. Some people manage to go on learning new ways much longer than others. Probably a part of their secret is that they constantly seek new circumstances. The temptation to go on relying only upon the rules already used year in year out is very strong. A really useful and interesting brain is always starting off on new ways. But it is a common experience that this gets more difficult as we grow older. [(17), pp. 69–70, italics mine.]

In his eighth and final lecture of the series, Young concluded,

Perhaps instead of focusing on beginning as the act of creation we should do exactly the opposite and centre our speech on continuity. The sense in which we do see creation is in the building of organization that goes on in the life of each individual, especially in the case of man, in our brains. Each individual thus forms his own way of life, his own order and rules, and these are valuable to the race because each is unique. Certainly our rules are largely acquired, but it is because individuals are not all alike that our kind is so adaptable and maintains its dominance. *Each individual uses the store of randomness with which he is born to build, during his life, rules that are useful and can be passed on.*

Similarly we can detect in the progress of evolution a decrease in randomness of all living things. The higher animals are in a sense more different from their surrounding than are the lower. *We might therefore take as our general picture of the universe a system of continuity in which there are two elements—randomness and organization —disorder and order if you like, alternating with each other in such a fashion as to maintain continuity.* [(17), p. 160, italics mine.]

Rationalizing the Irrational

The time is not yet ripe for a thorough integration of the foregoing material with my own views, with the reports by Kavanau (15), by Humphries and Driver (13, 14), by Dodds (10), and by Koestler (8), and with history, philosophy, and religion (9, 11, 12). Such an integration can only come about by a continuing multidisciplinary discussion between people who are experts in their chosen discipline but who, in addition, have some degree of competence in fields other than their own. It is my belief that protean behavior occurs in human beings, that there is a kind of ordered disorder in the human brain, and that this is necessary for cultural evolution, religion, art, science, invention, and creativity as well as much that is evil. As I said, I feel that the time is not ripe for firm conclusions, but I feel that the time for opening a dialogue on the occurrence and implications of protean behavior in the human is long overdue. If we could move beyond the primitive religionists' view of random events, we might advance to a rational view of the irrational in ourselves and in our friends and neighbors and in the world. If history really is explained to a significant degree by "confusion" rather than by "conspiracy" alone, could we not decrease the confusion by improving insight into the nature of man and his world and by communicating with others who might hold similar views or be converted to them? [cf. additional readings, (18–23).]

REFERENCES AND NOTES

1. A. F. C. Wallace, "Religious Revitalization: A Function of Religion in Human History and Evolution," paper presented at the 8th Institute on Religion in an Age of Science at Star Island, Portsmouth, N. H., July 26, 1961. Subsequently included in his book *Religion: An Anthropological View* (New York: Random House, Inc., 1966), pp. 38–39.

2. Teilhard de Chardin, *The Phenomenon of Man* (New York: Harper and Row, Publishers, 1961).

3. I. Langmuir, "Science, Common Sense and Decency," *Science* **97**:1–7, 1943.

4. P. T. Furst, "Radiocarbon Dates from a Tomb in Mexico," *Science* **147**:612–13, 1965.

5. J. L. King and T. H. Jukes, "Non-Darwinian Evolution," *Science* **164**: 788–98, 1969.

6. George Wald, "Determinacy, Individuality, and the Problem of Free Will," in John Platt, ed., *New Views of the Nature of Man* (Chicago: The University of Chicago Press, 1965), pp. 16–46.

7. John R. Platt, *The Step to Man* (New York: John Wiley and Sons, Inc., 1966). (See especially pp. 141–55, "Man and the Indeterminacies.")

8. Arthur Koestler, *The Ghost in the Machine* (New York: The Macmillan Company, 1968). See also his excellent book *The Act of Creation* (New York: The Macmillan Company, 1964).

9. Horace M. Kallen, *The Book of Job as a Greek Tragedy* (New York: Hill and Wang, 1959).

10. E. R. Dodds, *The Greeks and the Irrational* (Berkeley: The University of California Press, 1969), pp. 10–14.

11. *Time*, pp. 54–60, Dec. 17, 1965.

12. Arthur M. Schlesinger, Jr., *A Thousand Days* (Boston: Houghton Mifflin Company, 1965).

13. P. M. Driver and D. A. Humphries, *Protean Behavior* (Preprint No. 197, Mental Health Research Institute, University of Michigan, Ann Arbor, 1966, to be published in book form).

14. D. A. Humphries and P. M. Driver, "Erratic Display as a Device Against Predators," *Science* **156**:1767–68, 1967.

15. J. L. Kavanau, "Behavior of Captive White-Footed Mice," *Science* **155**: 1623–39, 1967.

16. W. Ross Ashby, "The Place of the Brain in the Natural World," *Currents in Modern Biol.* **1**:95–104, 1967.

17. J. Z. Young, *Doubt and Certainty in Science: A Biologist's Reflections on the Brain* (Oxford: The Clarendon Press, 1951).

Additonal Readings Not Cited

18. L. Gilkey, "Evolutionary Science and the Dilemma of Freedom and Determinism," *The Christian Century,* March 15, 1967, pp. 339–43.

19. D. E. Berlyne, "Curiosity and Exploration," *Science* **153**:25–33, 1967.

20. R. Bellman, "Dynamic Programming," *Science* **153**:34–37, 1967.

21. A. Iberall and W. S. McCulloch, "1967 Behavioral Model of Man, His Chains Revealed," *Currents in Modern Biol.* **1**:337–52, 1968.

22. Michael A. Arbib and Roy M. Kahn, "A Developmental Model of Information Processing in the Child," *Perspectives in Biol. and Med.* **12**:397–416, 1969.

23. Burns B. Delisle, *The Uncertain Nervous System* (London: Edward Arnold [Publishers] Ltd., 1968).

CHAPTER EIGHT

The Role of the Individual in Modern Society

Abstract The possible analogies between biological and cultural evolution are discussed using the DNA molecule and the idea or concept as the least common denominators in the respective systems. Seven principles of optimum environment are elaborated with emphasis on adaptive functions. Individuals generate biased ideas which may be improved by multidisciplinary evaluation in groups composed of individuals that are competent in one or more disciplines.

The Individual and His Environment

How can we in the university system help to develop a society in which individuals are able to live happy and productive lives? This question can also be examined from the standpoint of the individual member of society. What can the individual member of society do to insure himself a happy and productive life? At this point we may as well state the underlying assumption that this recurring phrase "happy and productive" will be used repetitiously and without further defense. We will not assume the burden of trying to prove that a human life can be happy and *unproductive*, and we would be willing to concede that a life can be productive without being happy all of the time. We will assume that there is some kind of a linkage between the concepts of happy and productive and leave the documentation to the psychiatrists.

My recent work has involved oscillating biochemical systems in experimental animals, and I am inclined to believe that life in whatever form is never in a completely steady state. Perpetual happiness is psychologically impossible; what we should aim for is a kind of happiness in which we oscillate between states of satisfaction and states of dissatisfaction in what might be called a "continual revision of our on-going intentions." A happy and productive life is certainly one in which physiological and mental health is as near optimum as possible, but I would like to express the opinion that medical science has thus far not penetrated very deeply into the question of what constitutes an optimum environment for the human species. It will be one of the themes of this chapter that an optimum environment is *not* one which presents a fixed temperature, a constant food supply, and freedom from manual labor. Rather, it is an environment which requires the utilization of the adaptive powers of the individual members of the species, both at the physiological and the psychological level.

Elsewhere, I have attempted to define an optimum environment as one which "induces each individual to develop continually from birth to death as a result of systematic challenges by physical and mental tasks which elicit normal adaptive responses within his rapidly increasing and eventually declining capabilities"(1). In the present context I would say that this aspect of an optimum environment would help achieve the goal of a happy and productive life, but we have to qualify the word "productive." I should say that no life is productive unless it contributes to the welfare of others, in the family, in a group, in the community, or in the context of the nation or of mankind. A productive life is one that involves a sense of commitment which may be fulfilled in many ways, including commitment to a search for principles that may not be utilized until some distant future.

In Table 1, I have listed seven different categories that I consider important in the human environment. These are advanced as goals that organized society should strive to provide for every individual member of society and as principles that should be taught to individuals during their development.

TABLE 1. How to Define an Optimum Environment

1. *Basic needs* that can be satisfied by effort

2. *Freedom* from *toxic chemicals,* unnecessary *trauma,* and preventable *disease*

3. A respect for sound *ecological principles* with a long-range point of view

4. *Adaptive responses* in each individual, continually from birth to death, as a result of systematic challenges by physical and mental tasks which come at appropriate times and are within individual capabilities, which increase rapidly at certain periods and decline later

5. Individual *happiness* that involves oscillation between satisfaction and dissatisfaction, with a sustained sense of *identity* despite a continual revision of on-going intentions.

6. Productivity that directly or indirectly involves *commitment* to other members of society

7. A continual search for *beauty* and *order* that does not deny the role of *individuality* and *disorder*

I have serious doubts as to whether or not the individual *can* do very much to insure himself a happy and productive life after a certain age has been reached (2). I mean that by the time an individual is able to ask the question it may be too late for him to change his attitudes and value systems. I suspect that the individual is not equipped by instinct to choose either an optimum environment or a course of action that will lead to a happy and productive life in this modern world. The question we are all concerned with assumes that the individual can be *taught* how to cope constructively with the vicissitudes of modern life, if the teaching comes early enough in life and if the vicissitudes are not overwhelming. We are all somewhat appalled by the thought that there may be severe limitations on the teaching process as the child approaches adolescence and in the post-adolescent years, yet the whole anti-poverty program and the goals of the "Great Society" were approached as if no one ever reached an age at which he was incapable of learning to change basic attitudes.

Thus, we have the *practical* problem of dealing with individuals who may have become fixed in their outlook and have difficulty in learning new attitudes, and the *theoretical* problem of what might be done under ideal conditions if the teaching process could be started at birth. In either case, I believe that the dialogue between the various biological specialities and the humanities has been inadequate and that our discourse on the questions of the role of the individual in modern Society can only be superficial until we have had much more opportunity to hear diverse viewpoints on certain fundamentals.

I shall approach the subject mainly as a scientist attempting to encompass the reductionist approaches of the molecular biologist and the holistic approaches of the organismic physiologist. This professional role is a natural outgrowth of my academic obligation, which has been to pursue cancer research according to my own best judgment for over 25 years. This preoccupation with the cancer problem undoubtedly accounts for the gradual enlargement of my horizons to the philosophical problems of the meaning of human suffering and the role of science in society.

On an earlier occasion I raised the question, "How can science contribute to the betterment of the human condition?" I proposed that, "The most important contribution science can make to society is to increase the degree of sophistication [insight] with which mankind perceives 'order' and 'disorder' " (3). I shall persist in defending that viewpoint, taking the position that until modern society as a whole and the individual members of society can achieve a better understanding of the nature of man and the nature of the world, we shall be almost hopelessly handicapped in attempting to write prescriptions for happy and productive lives. Yet we in the cancer field have not abandoned "courage" as the priceless ingredient to substitute for knowledge when ignorance is still overwhelming; there is no reason why educators should not follow the same rule.

The Nature of Man and His Ideas

If we are to talk about productive living for the individual, it may be worthwhile for me as a scientist to take the extreme view that man is a purely physical–chemical mechanism in which purposeful behavior is brought about by the natural selection of feedback mechanisms that in the past have proved effective in the relationship between the human species and its external environment. The fact that man now exists as a member of society and that his environment is largely determined by the cultural context in which he lives

(4) does not alter the fact that man is basically a cybernetic machine with molecular mechanisms for continuously reading the environment and responding with behavior that is partly instinctive and partly learned, and partly disordered in both of these categories.

I think that most people rebel at the idea of man as a machine because they at once form a mental image of an automaton in which the responses are fixed. But I am convinced that the phenomenon of man can only be understood in terms of a multifeedback mechanism in which there is a certain amount of built-in disorder—an idea which may be as repugnant as that of an automaton. I think, however, that it is the possibility of partly random response that gives man his freedom and at the same time makes cultural evolution possible.

Just as an understanding of the relationship of disorder to order is essential to the understanding of biological evolution, I maintain that cultural evolution comes about because of the built-in disorder in our mental processes (Fig. 8.1) (5).

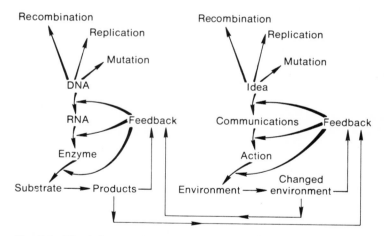

Fig. 8.1 The informational analogy between the basic unit of biological evolution (DNA, shown on the left) and the basic unit of cultural evolution (Idea, shown on the right) (5).

If the DNA molecules that constitute our genetic makeup were replicated with no error and passed from generation to generation without reshuffling the contributions from the respective parents, there could be no biological evolution. *Ideas* are to cultural evolution what *DNA molecules* are to biological evolution. They are the basic unit of information and, as such, are subject to mutation, recombination, replication, and expression. Tools and other material things are ideas in physical form. If every student or every child or every citizen were to store every idea and play it back exactly as it was given to him, there would be no cultural evolution. Because every concept, every image, every abstraction that enters our minds is subject to both conscious and unconscious modifications in which random copy errors play a part, there is a continual production of new raw material to be subjected to the process of natural selection by which cultural evolution takes place. Ideas never arise *de novo*. Each new idea is always a modification, a recombination, an analogy, a new combination of parts, or some other synthesis from previously available images that have been recorded in the brain presumably by processes involving intermolecular recognition (6). Great ideas are not chronologically predictable. They may be inevitable, but they cannot be called forth on demand. I maintain that ideas, whether they occur in the mind of a scientist, poet, or politician, involve not only the raw material and the motivation but also the phenomenon of the built-in margin of copy error or random reshuffling that is constantly a feature of mental activity (7). According to Livingston (8), the central nervous system contains some 10 billion neurons; there are only 1.7 million afferent neurons, about two-thirds of which are accounted for by the optic nerves alone. There are only about 250,000 neurons which leave the central nervous system to command all of our visceral and bodily performances. Thus, there are roughly 5000 *internal* neurons for *each* neuron that enters or leaves the central nervous system, and each of them has some degree of spontaneous activity (7). These elementary facts imply that information entering the system comes under the direct or indirect influence of a very large population of spontaneously active central neurons. "Evidently, then, no stimulus can enter upon a *tabula rasa*" (7). These considerations seem to lend support to my suggestion that new ideas involve processes containing a certain amount of built-in indeterminacy or change (cf. 8, 9).

The most amazing feature of the spontaneous idea is the feeling of euphoria that accompanies the moment of illumination (10). Archimedes was undoubtedly not the first to say, "Eureka, I have found it!", although he is certainly the most quoted. But the merit of an idea is not measured by how good it makes one feel. We can be just as happy with an incorrect idea as with a correct one, if we have no way to tell the difference. As scientists, we learn that a new idea must be tested and rejected or shelved if the experiments go against it. Few indeed are the scientists who can say as Einstein did, "Tell them to repeat their experiments," when the data do not agree with the idea.

When we leave the realm of science and come to that of the poets and politicians, the test of an idea is its acceptability. This test, as Galbraith (11) has pointed out, is always based on the conventional wisdom of the time and place, and the march of events is continually modifying conventional wisdom. There is a process of natural selection of ideas in cultural evolution just as there is a natural selection of DNA molecules in biological evolution. Many will wonder whether this analogy can be used to argue that good ideas and good DNA molecules are assured of survival. The answer is no. This can be an interesting topic for extended discussion, but I believe it can be understood more readily if we realize that natural selection in either case is based upon short-term considerations rather than on long-term considerations. There is a fatal flaw in the vital machinery of evolution, and it arises from the fact that the process makes its value judgments as to what is good on the basis of only two parameters: (a) survival to the point of reproductive success and (b) survival in terms of the present environment. Thus, in terms of the first point, fatal diseases that occur only after the period of reproductive activity are not easily eliminated by natural selection unless they affect the survival of the tribe. In the second instance, natural selection is incapable of seeing into the future, and as each species becomes genetically adapted to a special environment, it becomes increasingly vulnerable to a change in environment. Thus, extinction without issue has been the fate of most species.

In the case of cultural evolution, an idea is usually judged in terms of the present and not in terms of the future. Only the combined intellects from many disciplines will be able to assess the ideas that will best chart the course of mankind through an environment that is undergoing unparalleled cultural and physical changes. Only *man* has the capacity to think about the future, and only *man* has the power to take steps to prevent his own extinction. At the moment, however, no one can say whether or not these powers can be mobilized soon enough. The best recommendation that can be made at present is for open-ended solutions that avoid the dead-end pathways of overspecialization.

Application

If our interpretation of man as a cybernetic machine with instinctive and acquired feedback responses—plus a certain degree of random or unpredictable response—has any validity, it must have a profound meaning for our image of ourselves and of our neighbors and of the relationship between individuals and society.

As individual men, we can feel that we are not automatons with no escape from a predetermined fate. On the other hand, the free will that we possess is subject to considerable constraint. We can get new ideas but they will be conditioned by the raw material that goes into the process, and the ideas we get will not necessarily be correct. We must test our ideas and submit them to the tests imposed by others. We can take satisfaction, however, from knowing that we are biologically and culturally unique and that we can make unique contributions in two ways: (a) we can specialize to the point of carrying out experiments that no other creature in the world has ever done and (b) we can develop knowledge that can be tested within a specified operational framework and confirmed by others. Or we can widen our horizons and interact at the interdisciplinary level and attempt to develop a philosophy that is applicable to modern society. I believe that it is possible and desirable to combine science and philosophy, but I admit that the top-level specialists cannot devote much time to matters outside their specialty. Moreover, it seems difficult to obtain fruitful interdisciplinary discussions unless the various disciplines are represented by people who have mastered their discipline. In either case we as individuals, whether as specialists or as educated citizens in a decision-making process, must develop the humility to realize that when we deal with ideas involving action and other people, we must be able to listen as well as to advocate. We must look upon all ideas as tentative and subject to test. We must realize that there is a difference between ideas that apply to ourselves alone and ideas that we feel should be applied to others.

For our neighbors we should be able to develop a tolerance for occasional irrational behavior. We should understand the momentary enthusiasm for a new idea and should not discourage its exposition. Questions that lead to new ideas should be propounded.

For society the problem is one of recognizing and utilizing the resources represented by the interdisciplinary group and of encouraging individual participation in interdisciplinary groups at all levels of action. The problems of society have often been turned over to small panels of technical experts who are all indoctrinated with the same point of view and who have all been trained in the same discipline. Many of the current problems of urban society and of widespread pollution may be due to the failure of our society to give sufficient impetus to the development of wisdom that could encompass the consequences of our expanding technology. How can society develop the wisdom needed to deal with its problems? I believe that a wider participation in the discussion process by representatives of various disciplines is needed, while at the same time more individuals need to be trained in the specific skills that each discipline represents. Fortunately, the formation of broad interdisciplinary panels is accelerating. One example is seen in the report of the Environmental Pollution Panel of The President's Science Advisory Committee ("Restoring the Quality of the Environment," November 1965).

For a discussion of the role of the individual and his participation in interdisciplinary groups, I have prepared a chart on "Decision Making in a Free Society" (Fig. 8.2), which includes my ideas on the role of disorder in both the external and internal worlds. I have

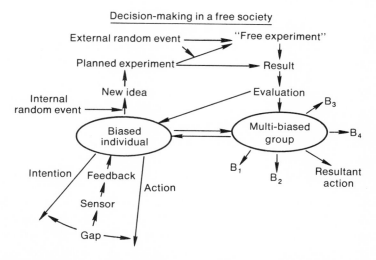

Fig. 8.2 The concept of random events as components of cultural evolution.

used the concept of the "free experiment" to indicate an unplanned circumstance that leads to a result that can be evaluated.

Certain historians have referred to the existence of two theories of history: the "confusion" theory and the "conspiracy" theory. My concept of the "free experiment" is a further development of the "confusion" theory. That is, certain things just happen without plan (in contrast to the conspiracy theory), but, having happened, the events are just as available for evaluation as if they were planned. The figure also shows the individual as a biased feedback mechanism that is trying to close the gap between its actions and its intentions. Finally, group decisions as the resultant of individual vectors are indicated.

It is my contention that the "free experiment" is the escape hatch from any predetermined fate and that the result of a "free experiment" can break through the bias of the individual in two ways: (a) it can be so overwhelming that it overcomes all bias or (b) it can be incapable of overcoming certain individual biases but capable of overcoming others. Thus, in any evaluation by a diversified group, there will be a greater chance of overcoming the bias factor.

Adaptation

Up to this point we have said very little about the basic problem of productive living for the individual, although I indicated at the outset that the *adaptive* powers of the individual should be called upon. By adaptation I do not mean conformity. Conformity is that state of affairs in which the individual has adapted to the status quo. After that no further mental effort is required. Society has traditionally exerted pressure on its members, forcing conformity to certain norms that require adaptation on the part of individuals. This adaptation has considerable advantage if it can result in the release of energy for the exploration of new modes of thought and action. However, very little has been done to consider ideal goals which modern society might set up (other than materialistic goals) or the methods by which society might influence individuals to exercise their adaptive powers while at the same time encouraging creative ability and a free society.

A basic problem requiring further study is this: the individual appears ill-equipped by instinct to select an optimum environment for himself. Each of us has to be indoctrinated by society to get more exercise than we choose voluntarily, to eat less than our appetites demand, to learn new skills, to carry extra loads, and to develop interests outside of ourselves.

As long ago as 1890, William James said, "Keep the faculty of effort alive in you by a little gratuitous exercise every day. That is, be systematically ascetic or heroic in little unnecessary points, do every day or two something for no other reason than that you would rather not do it, so that when the hour of dire need draws nigh, it may find you not unnerved and untrained to stand the test." A similar thought was expressed by Thomas Henry Huxley in 1877 when he said, "Perhaps the most valuable result of all education is the ability to make yourself do the thing you have to do, when it ought to be done, whether you like it or not; it is the first lesson that ought to be learned; and however early a man's training begins, it is probably the last lesson that he learns thoroughly."

These ideas are now believed to be old-fashioned, but I believe that with newer developments in molecular biology and physiology, we will come to appreciate their meaning and relevance to the subject of productive living with which we are concerned in this chapter.

Somehow we have to learn why the rat or human will eat more and exercise less than is good for him and probably think less if given the opportunity. The answer lies in the understanding of man and rat as feedback-controlled machines that were designed to adapt to an economics of scarcity. The difference between simple cause and effect and a feedback-controlled machine is that the latter is constantly measuring its output and regulating its production according to the amount of product. If we introduce the product from the surrounding environment, the organism will shut down the production machinery; while if we decrease the amount of product, the organism will adapt by increasing its production machinery. That is, if an organism can adapt to a given situation, by the same process it can *de-adapt* if the need is met through an outside source. So what happpens if all the immediate needs of an organism are met from the outside? It appears to me that there will be a rapid weakening of the organism's physiological capacities.

Recently we set up experiments with rats to determine whether or not we could develop animals that were superior to the ordinary laboratory rat, the epitome of the organism with all its needs provided. We reasoned that the process of natural selection has developed rats that desire food every night, but it has also developed rats that will survive if they *do not* find food every night. That is, they can go hungry one of every two nights and still survive. We provided food for 12 hours on every other night and provided voluntary exercise wheels. On the nights that no food was available, the rats traveled an average of 15 kilometers. The combination of exercise and restricted feeding time resulted in rats that weighed 225 grams, in comparison with 325 grams for the rats that had food available at all times. Biochemical studies showed that the rats that fasted periodically were undergoing marked swings in enzyme activity corresponding to the alterations in fasting and feeding (12). Studies elsewhere showed that rats of similar weight on low calorie diets lived longer and had much lower incidence of cancer than control rats [cited in (12)].

Of the rats which were allowed access to food for only 8 hours out of each 48, nearly all died within a week when they had exercise cages available, while none died if housed in their usual cages. That is, when the animals were given an opportunity to react instinctively, the drive to search for food resulted in an expenditure of energy in excess of what could be stored in the period available. Thus, in two examples the animals' instinctive reactions misled them. In the one case they overeat; in the other case they overexercise. These interpretations are, of course, going beyond the bare facts of the experiments and are subject to further discussion. Nevertheless, I would like to see what might be done with human volunteers who might wish to control obesity with a combination of exercise and periodic fasting.

The concept of optimum stressor level as a necessary component of an optimum environment apparently has not been extensively studied from a biochemical standpoint, and I am not familiar with the psychological literature. Students in the field of Environmental Design should be encouraged to develop new proposals on the subject of optimal stressor levels alternating with periods that are not stressful.

The concept of an optimum environment as one that includes a demand for physiological and psychological adaptation and a respect for biological rhythms also interacts with programs in education, recreation, and leisure time. I wish to raise the question of how to develop programs to test the proposition that happy and productive lives will be more likely if adaptive functions are called upon at levels appropriate to the individual. Much has been left unsaid about goals and values, but it is implicit that my concept of "happy and productive" includes the idea of contribution to the welfare of others in the family, the community, and to society as a whole, depending on the capacity of the individual.

Human Welfare

There is a curious relationship between the concept of an optimum environment in which the individual is exercising his full capacity and the concept of brotherly love which calls for support of the weak. The relationship is resolved by stating that all efforts to promote human welfare should bear in mind that too much support will make the recipient weaker instead of stronger. Every support program should be designed to restore function and to build up adaptive capacity. Such programs may be more expensive in the beginning, but in the long run they will prove superior.

Conclusion

In this chapter I have emphasized the concept of a happy and productive life as one which utilizes the physiological and psychological adaptive powers of each individual and which contributes to the welfare of other members of society.

The individual human has been characterized as a special kind of machine whose activities are based on multichannel feedback relationships with the environment and whose responses include a certain built-in irrationality. Thus, individual behavior, though inherently based on feedback loops, was suggested to be partly instinctive, partly learned, and partly disordered (random, unpredictable, or irrational).

The inclusion of the built-in factor of unpredictability was related to the "confusion" theory of history and was regarded as the basis of the unplanned or "free-experiment" which, in turn, provided for further cultural evolution despite the limitations of the biased individual. Group consideration by individuals having divergent biases was suggested as an essential device for overcoming individual bias.

Welfare programs based on the concept of brotherly love were considered good if they developed strength in the recipients and bad if they resulted in further deterioration. Modern knowledge of physiological and psychological adaptive functions should be expanded and applied to problems in environmental design.

REFERENCES AND NOTES

1. Van R. Potter, "How Is an Optimum Environment Defined?" Delivered in a *Symposium on Physiological Characterization of Health Hazards in Man's Environment,* Sec. IV: "The Future" (Bretton Woods, N. H., Aug. 22–25, 1966). *Environmental Research,* **2:**476–87, 1969. (See Chapter 10, this volume, pp. 133–48.)

2. S. Levine and R. F. Mullins, Jr., "Hormonal Influences on Brain Organization in Infant Rats," *Science* **152:**1585–92, 1966.

3. Van R. Potter, "Society and Science," *Science* **146:**1018–22, 1964. (See Chapter 3, this volume, pp. 42–54.)

4. Clifford Geertz, "The Impact of the Concept of Culture on the Concept of Man," in John R. Platt, ed., *New Views of the Nature of Man* (Chicago: University of Chicago Press, 1965), pp. 93–118.

5. Van R. Potter, "Models as Aids to Communication," in *Metabolic Control Mechanisms,* National Cancer Institution Monograph No. 13 (Bethesda, Md., 1964), pp. 111–16.

6. F. O. Schmitt, "The Physical Basis of Life and Learning," *Science* **149:** 931–36, 1965.

7. Similar ideas have been independently expressed by Dr. Robert B. Livingston, a neurophysiologist and psychologist at the National Institutes of Health, Bethesda, Maryland. In a lecture in honor of Stanley Cobb at the Harvard Medical School on October 14, 1960, entitled "Possible Biological Foundations for Creativity," Dr. Livingston spoke as follows: "Perhaps information-gaining systems characteristically depend upon the incoming information ultimately getting down to a real level of *indeterminacy—within a system that exercises some systematic control over input and output....* Turning to our own fields, where specialized information-gaining instruments are available to examine—our attention is drawn first to those circuits of the brain where a diffusion of heterogenous impulses takes place, the neuropil. Ordered input becomes exposed to time-space intervals of presumed indeterminacy, of 'noise,' before it is reconstituted again along channels arranged for orderly output.

"It may be that a descent to a noise level, to a level of indeterminacy, would be meaningless *unless,* and this is important, such 'noise' takes *place within a system that is controlling its own input and output.*"

8. R. B. Livingston, "How Man Looks at His Own Brain: An Adventure Shared by Psychology and Neurophysiology," in S. Koch, ed., *Psychology: A Study of Science* (New York: McGraw-Hill Book Company, 1959), volume I, pp. 52–59.

9. Jacques Hadamard, *The Psychology of Invention in the Mathematical Field* (Princeton, N.J.: Princeton University Press, 1945).

10. W. I. B. Beveridge, *The Art of Scientific Investigation* (New York: W. W. Norton and Co., Inc., 1951), pp. 72ff.

11. John K. Galbraith, *The Affluent Society* (Boston: Houghton Mifflin Company, 1958), pp. 7–20.

12. Van R. Potter, R. A. Gebert, and H. C. Pitot, "Enzyme Levels in Rats Adapted to 36-Hour Fasting," *Advances in Enzyme Regulation* **4:**247–65, 1966.

CHAPTER NINE

Intracellular Responses to Environmental Change: The Quest for Optimum Environment

Abstract Walter Cannon's book on the wisdom of the body drew from French and German physiologists of the late Nineteenth Century and was written in 1932 without any knowledge of cellular metabolism or the wisdom of the cell as manifested by changes in enzyme concentration. Adaptation is the key to biology and may be evolutionary, physiological, or cultural. An optimum environment would not be constant but would provide an optimum range and frequency of change in the environment.

The Wisdom of the Body

One of the great milestones in biology occurred in 1932, when Walter Cannon published a book called *The Wisdom of the Body* (1), which was an extension of his earlier article, "Organization for Physiological Homeostasis," which appeared in *Physiological Reviews* in 1929 (2). Shortly before the review article, Cannon had coined the phrase *homeostasis* on presenting his paper at a jubilee celebration in honor of Charles Richet, but this earlier paper was buried in the *Transaction of the Congress of American Physicians and Surgeons* and is not widely available, in contrast to his more extensive later publications.

In his review article Cannon listed six general postulates of *homeostasis*. These are reproduced in Table 1 because so few among our modern molecular biologists have considered it appropriate to refer to these early examples of feedback dogma.

TABLE 1. WALTER B. CANNON'S SIX POSTULATES
REGARDING HOMEOSTATIC REGULATION (REF. 2)

1. In an open system such as our bodies represent, compounded of unstable material and subjected continually to disturbing conditions, constancy is in itself evidence that agencies are acting, or ready to act, to maintain this constancy.

2. If a state remains steady it does so because any tendency towards change is automatically met by increased effectiveness of the factor or factors which resist the change.

3. Any factor which operates to maintain a steady state by action in one direction does not also act at the same point in the opposite direction.

4. Homeostatic agents, antagonistic in one region of the body, may be cooperative in another region.

5. The regulatory system which determines a homeostatic state may comprise a number of cooperating factors brought into action at the same time or successively.

6. When a factor is known which can shift a homeostatic state in one direction it is reasonable to look for automatic control of that factor or for a factor or factors having an opposing effect.

What makes Cannon so interesting to us today is that his laws pertaining to "the wisdom of the body" could be applied with almost no change in wording to a new set of phenomena under the rubric of "the wisdom of the cell," a title which, so far as I am aware, is still looking for an author (begging I suppose, because of the inevitable comparison with Cannon's book that would follow).

But if Cannon's six postulates of homeostasis could be applied to "the wisdom of the cell," it would not be on the basis of knowledge available to Cannon when he wrote the book. As far as I have been able to discover, Cannon had no concept whatsoever of enzymes in the modern sense and did not even mention the word enzyme in the book or the review. To him, "cellular activity" embodied all that we now dissect into metabolic schemes and pathways, induction, adaptation, repression, allosteric activation, and so on. Since he was in no position to think of individual enzymes as such, it is not surprising that he was unable to anticipate adaptive changes that come about through changes in enzyme amount, as we have come to expect in many cases.

Cannon, however, was not unaware of his debt to his scientific predecessors. His chief benefactor was the great French physiologist Claude Bernard who in 1878 coupled his famous dictum on the constancy of the *milieu intérieur* (which certainly made *homeostasis* an unoriginal concept) with the words" . . . all the vital mechanisms, however varied they may be, have only one object, that of preserving constant the conditions of life in the internal environment." Moreover, in 1877 the great German physiologist Pflüger, probably independently of Bernard, said, "The cause of every need of a living being is also the cause of the satisfaction of the need." In 1885 Fredericq and in 1900 Charles Richet expressed similar ideas. Fredericq commented, "The living being is an agency of such sort that each disturbing influence induces by itself the calling forth of compensatory activity to neutralize or repair the disturbance. The higher in the scale of living beings, the more numerous, the more perfect and the more complicated do these regulatory agencies become. They tend to free the organism completely [sic] from the unfavorable influences and changes occurring in the environment." Richet said of the living being, "In a sense it is stable because it is modifiable—the slight instability is the necessary condition for the true stability of the organism." All of these men were well-known, reviewed, and quoted by Cannon (2), but all were physiologists. The time of the biochemists had not yet come.

Changes in Enzyme Amount

In 1939 a new era began. A brilliant young German investigator proposed the metabolic cycles for which he was later to receive a Nobel prize and to become known as Sir Hans Adolf Krebs of Oxford. The urea cycle was under attack as a test tube phenomenon, and two American investigators sought supporting evidence by asking whether or not the concentration of arginase, one of the enzymes in the Krebs urea cycle, was increased in the liver of rats on a high protein diet. Lightbody and Kleinman (3) showed that the enzyme was increased, thus providing collateral support for the urea cycle and initiating a new era in the enzymatic aspects of adaptation. They were aware of the distinction between enzyme amount and enzyme activity. They remarked, "In general, changes in enzyme systems caused by changes in type or quantity of food ingested may be expected to result in two types of adaptations, those that may be considered emergency measures, and those requiring slow changes in physiological processes. Those of the first group may consist of changes of velocity and duration of enzyme action, rate of delivering of the substrate to, and removal of the end products from the site of action, and activation or inactivation of a reserve enzyme supply. Those of the second group may be considered *adaptations in the quantities of the enzyme required* to accomplish a given purpose" (italics mine). It appears that the idea of quantitative change of enzyme concentration was not among the mechanisms considered by Cannon, who was more concerned with the switching of organ functions from standby to active duty and vice versa. The early studies by Lightbody and Kleinman have more recently been greatly amplified by the elegant studies on arginase carried out by Schimke and his associates (4) who have established that both synthesis and degradation are independently controlled.

About this same time the Potter–Elevehjem homogenate technique for enzyme quantitation (5) was gaining a wide acceptance, and I published (5) one of the earliest feedback diagrams linking physiology and molecular biology. This was in 1944 and the words *feedback* and *molecular biology* had not yet appeared in biochemical literature. At that time, however, I wrote as follows:

These specialized tissues differ in at least three important respects from primitive, growing, nonspecialized tissues. First, the tissue must be equipped to hold energy reservoirs intact until the functional demand occurs, at which time the reservoirs must be mobilized rapidly to provide energy for the function. Second, the remainder of the organism must be regulated so as not to interfere with the needs of the functioning part. Third, there must be a mechanism by which the specialized organ can grow and develop to meet functional demands which may temporarily tax its capacity. The first point has been investigated in terms of enzymes and intermediate metabolism. The second point represents the contribution of physiologists, endocrinologists, and pharmacologists. The third point is perhaps of greatest interest in connection with the cancer problem, in which growth appears to occur in the absence of a continuing stimulus. These three steps in the response of a specialized tissue to a stimulus are in reality control mechanisms, and must be finally correlated with each other and with the original stimulus through common denominators. It is here proposed that the adenosine triphosphate system may be just such a common denominator, which will serve to integrate the above control mechanisms. . . . "

Reviewing that publication, the late Jesse Greenstein commented (6), "The central position of ATP in muscle metabolism has long been recognized. Whether it is possible to generalize from muscle physiology to other kinds of tissues is an open question." (Subsequent events appear to justify the generalization.) The 1944 feedback diagram was published in a modified form in a study of the shock problem in collaboration with McShan et al. in 1945 (7) and is reproduced here (Fig. 9.1) as a kind of bridge between Cannon's writings (1, 2) and the present-day studies on enzyme adaptation at the cellular level.

The first real milestone to gain recognition for enzyme adaptation in mammals was the epic review in 1956 by Knox, Auerbach, and Lin (8), "Enzymatic and Metabolic Adaptations in Animals." Like the masterful review by Cannon, it was published in *Physiological Reviews*. Although strong in citations (there were 752), it was weak in historical perspective, and it failed to even mention the name of Walter B. Cannon or the word *homeostasis* in connection with the role of enzyme adaptations as measures designed to maintain constancy in the internal environment. Instead of citing *The Wisdom of the Body,* it took as its precedents the many publications by bacteriologists, who had shown many times over that the amount of an individual enzyme can vary independently of the total protein in the bacterial cell. This review was mainly a heroic compilation of references intended to document the fact of enzyme adaptation in animals with little concern for the historical connections to physiology or for the theoretical mechanisms, which were not quite ready for discussion. The latter were discussed in terms of molecular biology by Potter and Auerbach (9) in 1959, at the very threshold of the explosive developments in this area of gene expression as modified by environment.

Three Kinds of Adaptation

As we come to the present day, I would like to emphasize that *adaptation* is what biology is all about. If I had but one lecture to give in the field of biology to undergraduates who had no other

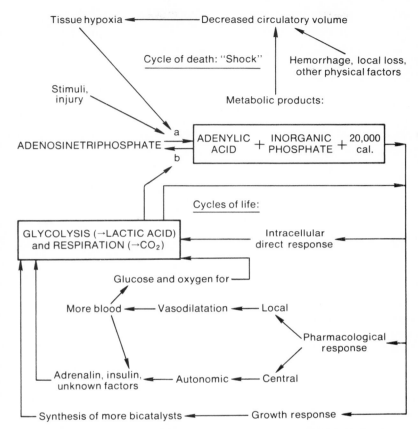

Fig. 9.1. A 1945 proposal regarding adenosine triphosphate (ATP) as a possible common denominator of cell physiology and organismic physiology in relation to enzyme adaptation. (Reproduced from reference 7.)

contact with the subject—and this is in fact what I do once a year —I would lecture on *adaptation*.

We live in a changing environment from the day we are born until the day we die. We live because we adapt, and we live only if we adapt. Each year is different from the preceding year, and the things we learn to do one year may help us the next. But if we can learn what is involved in learning, perhaps we can learn again, and again, and again. Adaptation is a kind of learning, and we need to learn what is involved in adapting. If we learn that adaptation is a way of life, perhaps we can begin to think about what kind of a world we would live in if we had a choice, and we could begin to ask "what would be an optimum environment for mankind?" as I shall attempt to do later.

The first thing we have to learn about adaptation is that the word is ambiguous at this time. It carries too big a load and the load can only be lightened by sharing it with qualifiers. The word becomes meaningful only if we use it in conjunction with the words *evolutionary, physiological,* or *cultural.*

Evolutionary adaptation involves populations over a period of many generations. It is the process by which natural selection acts on a population of nonidentical individuals and selects those whose heredity is best suited to reproduce in the given environment. This kind of adaptation cannot foresee future environments and often leads to extinction but need not do so.

We need to understand *physiological adaptation* in great depth, because it is the process that each of us as individuals are capable of over time periods that range from minutes to weeks to years. In the mind of Walter Cannon, physiological adaptation was the orchestration of a symphony of individual organs and it still is. But within those organs we can now see the wisdom of the cells; that is to say, adaptation at the cellular level, wherein enzyme activities and enzyme amounts wax and wane in response to need. When we go to high altitudes, we increase certain aspects of our cellular machinery; when we go to busy street intersections and breathe toxic gases, we may develop another set of enzymes, as I shall describe.

Finally, *cultural adaptation* is the psychological counterpart of physiological adaptation in the individual, but cultural adaptation can also be analogous to evolutionary adaptation when populations are involved. Here we can say that a desirable cultural adaptation would be an increase in dissemination of knowledge of all the kinds of adaptation as well as a decent respect for the depths of our ignorance in the significance of long-range aspects of adaptation. Moreover, we would have to consider the analogies between cultural shock and physiological shock as failures in the respective adaptations.

Systematic Oscillations in Animals on
Controlled Feeding Schedules

Recently in my laboratory various enzymes were studied in the livers of white rats, because we were concerned with nature of the conversion of normal cells to cancer cells. We asked the question, "are the enzymes of the cancer cells responding to the same signals that the normal cells respond to?" In the course of this work we became aware of the fact that homeostasis of certain bodily functions such as pH, alkali reserve, body temperature, and blood constituents must be achieved in the presence of marked changes in the external environment by rather marked shifts in certain enzyme concentrations, some of which increased and some of which decreased. We began to develop an experimental protocol in which rats were routinely divided into three different groups that received diets containing, respectively, 12, 30, or 60 percent protein, with compensating changes in the carbohydrate content at 79, 61, or 31 percent. The other 9 percent was made up with 5 percent corn oil plus minerals and vitamins (10). We carefully regulated the light to give 12 hours light and 12 hours darkness, and the animals had food available only during the first 8 hours of the dark cycle. This regimen was designated the "8 + 16" cycle because it consisted of 8 hours with food and 16 hours without food. Partly to exaggerate the enzyme changes and partly to test our belief that healthier rats might result, we arranged for other groups to be on an "8 + 40" cycle, in which food was available only 8 hours in 2 days and was then withheld for 40 hours. Such rats were shown to weigh about 100 grams less than rats on the "8 + 16" regimen or on *ad libitum* feeding in experiments lasting about a month, when males weighed 225 to 250 grams in comparison with 325–350 grams in the case of the rats on the "8 + 16" or *ad libitum* regimen. Recently we have completed experiments lasting over a year with rats on the "8 + 40" regimen and, in addition, inoculated with a slow-growing tumor. The rats remained within the 250-gram weight range for the entire period, and we believe that a significant slowing of tumor growth occurred. The data has been published (*Cancer Research* **29:**1691–98, 1969) and is mentioned to indicate that the "8 + 40" regimen can be sustained for long periods. We observed that the rats on the

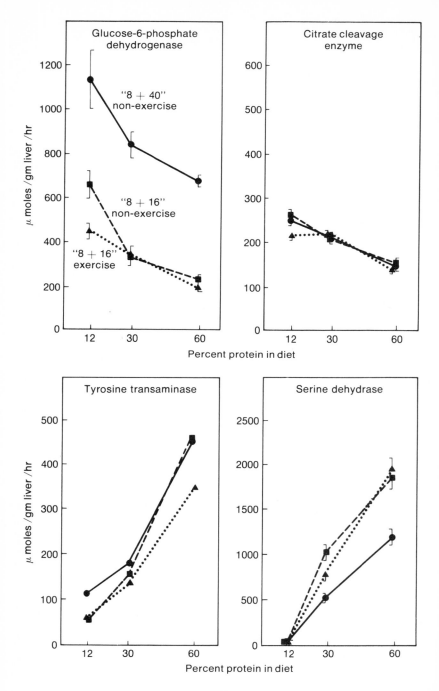

126

"8 + 40" regimen were hyperactive, and we arranged exercise cages with mileage recorders to measure this aspect of behavior.

Many experiments in the literature have measured only one enzyme at a time or only one variable at a time, but with the advent of partially automated equipment it is possible to increase the number of kinds of measurements. This was possible in the present instance through the efforts of Professor H. C. Pitot to develop such equipment. We thus present data on four different enzymes measured in rats who received three different diets under three different feeding regimens as indicated in Fig. 9.2, reproduced from a recent report by Potter, Watanabe, and Pitot (10). It will be seen first that tyrosine transaminase and serine dehydratase increase in proportion to the protein in the diet but that serine dehydratase synthesis is not "switched on" until the protein level exceeds 12 percent. Second, the glucose-6-phosphate dehydrogenase and citrate cleavage enzymes increase in proportion to the carbohydrate in the diet; that is, they increase in inverse proportion to the protein percentage. Third, the level of glucose-6-phosphate dehydrogenase is affected not only by the diet composition but also by the spacing of the feeding periods.

During the development of these protocols we systematically killed rats at different times of the day and discovered that several enzymes showed oscillations in activity during the daily cycle. Most outstanding was tyrosine transaminase, which showed an increase every night in the animals on the "8 + 16" regimen (10); but in the animals on the "8 + 40" regimen the enzyme activity increased at night during feeding and then showed a secondary rise during the daytime preceding the night that food was not offered [Fig. 9.3 (reproduced from reference 10)]. The oscillations in tyrosine transaminase activity also occur in animals that are not on controlled feeding schedules, but in the latter circumstances the amplitude of the oscillating mean values is less pronounced (11). In line with this

Fig. 9.2 Enzyme patterns of tyrosine transaminase, serine dehydratase, glucose-6-phosphate dehydrogenase, and citrate cleavage enzyme in the liver of rats as a function of protein content in the diet. Each closed circle connected with a solid line represents a mean value in rats adapted to "8 + 40" regimen under the nonexercise condition; each closed square connected with a dashed line represents "8 + 16" regimen under the nonexercise condition; each closed triangle connected with a dotted line represents "8 + 16" regimen under the exercise condition. Standard errors are indicated by brackets. (Reproduced from reference 10.)

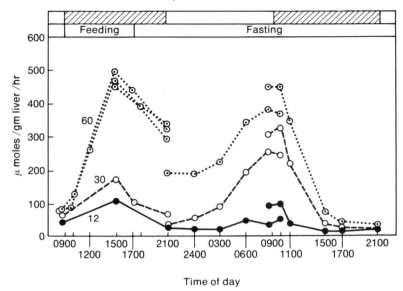

Fig. 9.3 Tyrosine transaminase in the liver of Holtzman rats adapted to "8 + 40" regimen with 12, 30, and 60% protein diets. Darkness during alternate 12 hours is indicated by cross-hatched bars. Each closed circle connected with a solid line represents a mean value of 2 to 4 rats fed 12% protein diets; open circles connected with a dashed line represent rats fed 30% protein diets; a point within an open circle connected with a dotted line represents rats fed 60% protein diets. Separate experiments are shown by groups of points connected by a single curve. (Reproduced from reference 10.)

observation is the fact that when the ability of the liver to concentrate an amino acid analogue was studied, oscillations could be demonstrated in the animals on controlled feeding schedules, but the data from animals on *ad libitum* feeding gave data that could not be resolved into any systematic fluctuation. These various relationships were recently summarized in a "Symposium on Nutrition and Metabolic Regulation" (11) and need not be detailed here. At that time, however, we listed five categories of objectives that might be served by the substitution of controlled feeding schedules for *ad libitum* feeding in experimental work designed to be relevant to human welfare. One of these categories was the search for a definition of an optimum regimen of nutrition in terms of various criteria of health such as longevity, fertility, and performance. After the symposium someone pointed out to me that those three criteria did not take into account the issue of "compatibility with others," and I agree that an optimum nutritional regimen does have to consider more than the factors I originally listed.

The Quest for Optimum Environment

As I have pointed out elsewhere (11), we originally developed the "8 + 40" regimen on the assumption that it would provide animals that were calorie-restricted and that the nonrestricted or *ad libitum*-fed animals were less healthy than they could be. There is an abundant literature, some of which has been cited (11), showing that animals on a reduced caloric intake develop less spontaneous cancer and live longer for a variety of reasons than animals that eat their fill. It seemed to us that a laboratory rat, confined to a small cage with an abundance of food under its nose and nothing else to do but eat, is in a highly unnatural situation and, indeed, a situation for which its natural instincts had not been prepared. I think there is some analogy with the human situation, but I do not wish to overstate the case. In the case of the rat we reasoned (11) "that natural selection must have operated to produce rats that desire food every night, but also to produce rats that will survive if they don't get food every night." Hence we set up the "8 + 40" regimen and, as I mentioned earlier, we now have data on rats that have been on this regimen for over 13 months. This regimen is truly a feast or famine procedure, and we really have no idea whether we can demonstrate any virtue in it. It should be said that there is a school of thought that advocates many small increments of food intake ("nibbling") as an optimum feeding regimen, and there is a substantial literature on the subject, especially by Cohn and associates (12, 13). Most previous studies have not been carried out using our technique of "8 + 40" feeding, and it is clear that if this regimen or a modification of it has any virtue, the proof remains to be demonstrated. We are continuing experiments with this regimen and its effect on fat metabolism in rats. The initial results have been published (*Federation Proceedings,* 29:1553–59, 1970).

In terms of an optimum environment we are inclined to refer back to all of the expressions that were cited in the introduction and to anticipate that a constant external environment, one that exercises the adaptive capacities the least, is absolutely undesirable for the health of an animal. Not only can an animal adapt to change but it somehow expects to adapt to change (but not *any* degree of change). If we adopt this philosophy, we can rephrase the problem of optimum environment so that, instead of asking what is the optimum *constant* environment, we ask what is the optimum frequency and amplitude of change in the environment; not what is the optimum temperature, but what is the optimum temperature *range* and frequency of change; not what is the optimum diet that is constantly available, but what is the optimum quantity and frequency of feeding.

In extrapolating rat experiments to the human there is no doubt that compatibility with others is an important issue to be considered as a product of environmental manipulation. But compatibility with others is not an end in itself. We have to take a more long-range view of the problem than merely the one of how to keep complaints out of the "Suggestion Box." We have to eventually ask what kind of an environment will be most helpful in sustaining and improving the civilized world.

In this connection society has not been doing too well recently in terms of controlling overall pollution, and some of the vagaries of civilization have led to the accidental discovery that certain insecticides lead to a marked increase in liver enzymes that destroy the toxic compounds. This is now a classic example of enzyme adaptation to the environment, and there are many examples of compounds that induce a variety of so-called detoxifying enzymes, not only in liver but also in lung and intestine. Among the inducers are a number of the tranquilizing compounds (14). So, if we can produce enzymes to destroy the toxic compounds in our environment, why worry? Isn't our adaptive power being exercised, and won't we be able to just go on smoking cigarettes, breathing engine exhaust, and eating tranquilizers? Unfortunately it is not that simple. We know far too little about all the different products of drug metabolism; and, in fact, some compounds that are not carcinogenic can be metabolized to compounds that do produce cancer (15). Moreover, any kind of adaptation is weighed in an overall balance that includes all the rest of the organism. At this moment we simply do not know whether there is any kind of overall advantage or disadvantage to the adaptive formation of a hundredfold increase in a particular drug-metabolizing enzyme.

Conclusion

First, I would emphasize that the hereditary genes are now known to determine the potential strength of any given ability in the organism, but they do not guarantee the expression of the ability. Second, we know that the expression of each gene is regulated by chemical feedback from the environment and from the products of the other genes to produce the phenomenon of adaptability (16).

We have much to learn in asking what criteria to consider in seeking an optimum environment, and surely there is no single environment that can be considered optimal. But surely in seeking a pluralistic answer to the question of optimal environments, we need to consider the role of evolutionary adaptation, physiological adaptation, and cultural adaptation. Finally, we need to recall an earlier admonition when, in reference to our industrial and agricultural capabilities, I said, "Let us use our tremendous capacity for production to produce the things that make us wiser, rather than the things that make us weaker" (17). This is the message that I hope emerges from a discussion of adaptation.

REFERENCES AND NOTES

1. Walter B. Cannon, *The Wisdom of the Body* (New York: W. W. Norton and Company, Inc., 1963).

2. Walter B. Cannon, "Organization for Physiological Homeostasis," *Physiol. Reviews* **9:**399–431, 1929.

3. H. D. Lightbody, and A. Kleinman, "Variations Produced by Food Differences in the Concentration of Arginase in the Livers of White Rats," *J. Biol. Chem.* **129:**71–78, 1939.

4. R. T. Schimke, "The Importance of Both Synthesis and Degradation in the Control of Arginase Levels in Rat Liver," *J. Biol. Chem.* **239:** 3808–3817, 1964.

5. V. R. Potter, "Biological Energy Transformation and the Cancer Problem," *Advances in Enzymology* **4:**201–256, 1944.

6. J. G. Greenstein, book review, *Cancer Research* **5:**62, 1945.

7. W. H. McShan, V. R. Potter, A. Goldman, E. G. Shipley, and R. K.

Meyer, "Biological Energy Transformations During Shock as Shown by Blood Chemistry," *Am. J. Physiol.* **145**:93–106, 1945.

8. W. E. Knox, V. H. Auerbach, and E. C. C. Lin, "Enzymatic and Metabolic Adaptations in Animals," *Physiol. Review* **36**:164–254, 1956. (Contains 752 references.)

9. V. R. Potter, and V. H. Auerbach, "Adaptive Enzymes and Feedback Mechanisms," *Lab. Invest.* **8**:495–509, 1959.

10. M. Watanabe, V. R. Potter, and H. C. Pitot, "Systematic Oscillations in Tyrosine Transaminase and Other Metabolic Functions in Liver of Normal and Adrenalectomized Rats on Controlled Feeding Schedules," *J. Nutr.* **95**:207–227, 1968.

11. Van R. Potter, E. F. Baril, M. Watanabe, and E. D. Whittle, "Systematic Oscillations in Metabolic Functions in Liver from Rats Adapted to Controlled Feeding Schedules," *Fed. Proc.* **27**:1238–45, 1968.

12. C. Cohn, "Feeding Patterns and Some Aspects of Cholesterol Metabolism," *Fed. Proc.* **23**:76–81, 1964.

13. C. Cohn, and D. Joseph, "Feeding Frequency and Lipogenesis in Undernutrition," *Can J. Physiol. Pharmacol.* **45**:609–612, 1967.

14. L. W. Wattenberg, and J. L. Leong, "Effects of Phenothiazones on Protective Systems Against Polycyclic Hydrocarbons," *Cancer Research* **25**:365–370, 1965.

15. E. C. Miller, and J. A. Miller, "Mechanisms of Chemical Carcinogenesis: Nature of Proximate Carcinogens and Interactions with Macromolecules," *Pharmacol. Reviews* **18**:805–838, 1966. (Contains 223 references.)

16. V. R. Potter, "Society and Science," *Science* **146**:1018–1022, 1964. (Chapter 4, this volume, pp. 55–68.)

17. V. R. Potter, "Bridge to the Future: The Concept of Human Progress," *Land Economics* **38**:1–8, 1962. (Chapter 3, this volume, pp. 42–54.)

CHAPTER TEN

How Is an Optimum Environment Defined?

Abstract Physiologists, molecular biologists, and geneticists must combine with humanists to build a society that can help each individual steer a course between too much leisure and information overload. Genetic capabilities can be fully expressed only in the presence of an optimum stressor level applied discontinuously. Environmental physiology should emphasize the genetic basis of individuality and the physiological basis of adaptation by individuals.

Optimum Stress

Any discussion of the future in the context of the physiological hazards in man's environment will inevitably have to be broad enough to consider leisure as a possible health hazard and, at the other extreme, information overload (15) or future shock (25) as hazards which society will have to consider. A full-page advertisement that appeared in 1958 illustrates what I mean by the hazards of leisure. It is entitled "Power companies build for your future electric living," and subtitled, "Electricity may do your yard work." I think it was this ad that first aroused my interest in the physiological hazards of leisure.

133

An optimum environment is one that delivers what I would like to call an "optimum stress," but I have come to realize that the word "stress" produces stress in many physiologists. Therefore I will not again refer to "optimum stress." Instead, I will follow the definitive "Perspectives of Adaptation" presented by Prosser and Adolph in Section 4 of the *Handbook of Physiology*, "Adaptation to the Environment" (7). Prosser defines a "stressor" as an environmental circumstance that induces adaptations, and what I shall be talking about is the concept of deliberately promoting an optimum stressor level (Fig. 10.1). Indeed, I wish to promote the idea of a merger between physiology, genetics, and molecular biology on the one hand, with anthropology, psychology, and philosophy on the other. Our goal for the future should be to adapt our evolving culture to the fact that adaptation is a normal feature of life and that we need to know much more about the process than we do now. But it is not enough to consider adaptation as an esoteric topic dealt with by physiologists. It is a topic that is fundamental to all the specialties mentioned above. Moreover, it is a topic that needs to be incorporated into our educational system and into our cultural milieu.

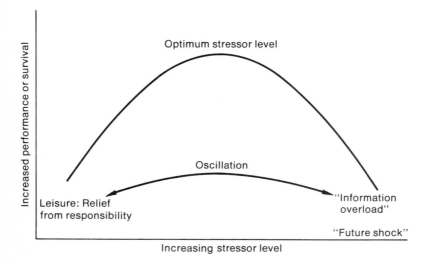

Fig. 10.1 Definition of the optimum environment in terms of the stressor level.

Culture as Environment

Professor Clifford Geertz (10) of the Anthropology Department of the University of Chicago has contributed an excellent chapter to *New Views on the Nature of Man,* edited by John R. Platt. Entitled "The Impact of the Concept of Culture on the Concept of Man," its thesis is that (a) culture is a set of control mechanisms for controlling or programming human behavior and (b) man is precisely the animal most desperately dependent upon such extragenetic, outside-the-skin control mechanisms for ordering his behavior. He says, "One of the most significant facts about us may finally be that we all begin with the natural equipment to lead a thousand kinds of life but end in the end having lived only one."

The question is whether we, as physiologists, molecular biologists, and geneticists, are prepared to tell society how to move toward a cultural tradition that can help each individual find an optimum stressor level and steer successfully between the Charybdis of too much leisure and the Scylla of information overload.

The question I am raising is whether our Twentieth-Century culture is providing the proper kind of "extragenetic, outside-the-skin control mechanisms" that the human animal is so "desperately dependent upon." Do prospective parents know that every individual is genetically different from every other individual, that only those genetic capabilities that are possessed can ever be expressed, and that every genetic capability can be fully expressed only in the presence of an optimum stressor level applied at the right time—and then not continuously? Do we, as scientists and humanists, have any idea what to tell these hypothetical prospective parents if they ask us for practical answers to these questions?

There are historical precedents for these questions. In 1890, we find William James saying, "Keep the faculty of effort alive in you by a little gratuitous exercise every day. That is, be systematically ascetic or heroic in little unnecessary points, do every day or two something for no other reason than that you would rather not do it, so that when the hour of dire need draws nigh, it may find you not unnerved and untrained to stand the test" (2). And in 1919 we hear Twentieth-Century cynicism replying, in the words of Somerset Maugham, "I forget who it was that recommended men for their soul's good to do each day two things they disliked . . . it is a precept that I have followed scrupulously; for every day I have got up and I have gone to bed." In the same vein, I believe it was Robert

Maynard Hutchins who spoke for academicians in general, when he said, "Whenever I feel the urge to exercise coming on, I lie down until the feeling goes away."

Physiologic Adaptation

What Maugham and Hutchins do not seem to realize is that adaptation is not just a physiologic response to some abnormal or novel situation, some hypoxic condition at a mountain top where average people never go. The living animal is adapting during every moment of life. Adaptation is not merely a mechanism "for the adjustment of organisms to the action of unfavorable [sic] factors in the environment" (Barbashova in reference 7, p. 49). Adaptations are part of the everyday life mechanism, and they are noted as adaptations by the physiologist only when they differ from "ordinary responses" sufficiently to be "increments or decrements in the ordinary response" that "require time to develop" (Adolph in reference 7, p. 34). The word "adaptation" is frequently misunderstood because it has come to have two meanings. Some people think of evolutionary adaptation, which involves natural selection of mutants that fit a particular environment. This kind of adaptation occurs in populations over a large number of generations. The other kind of adaptation is physiological adaptation, which applies to the individual members of a population.

In the present discussion I am concerned only with physiologic adaptation and follow Prosser (in reference 7, p. 11) who defines it as "any property of an organism which favors survival in a specific environment," although Prosser adds the words that narrow the meaning when he says, "particularly a stressful one." Prosser states that "an adaptation permits maintenance of physiological activity and survival when the environment alters with respect to one or more parameters."

As a biochemist and molecular biologist, I have the thesis that, if we examine the organism at the molecular level, the environment is changing on a minute-to-minute basis and the "ordinary responses" at the enzyme or nucleic acid level are constantly undergoing adaptive increments or decrements in enzyme activity or amount in a complex feedback system that is designed to maintain certain features of the internal milieu within limits that will promote survival. We can either cultivate this adaptive capacity or we can let it atrophy. The idea that an effort should be made to define "health" as more than the absence of disease was emphasized by René Dubos in *Man Adapting* (8), when he said (p. 391), "A medical philosophy which assumes a priori that the ideal is to make human life absolutely safe and effortless may paradoxically create a state of affairs in which mankind will progressively lose the ability to meet the real experience of life and to overcome the stress and risks that this experience inevitably entails." I think that Dubos would be willing to include individual men as well as mankind in the above statement.

Elsewhere, Dubos comments (pp. 362-363) that " . . . in the United States, the emphasis is on controlling disease rather than on living more wisely. . . . The public health services themselves, despite their misleading name, are concerned less with health than with the control of the specific diseases considered important in the communities they serve. They do little to define, recognize, or measure the healthy state, let alone the hypothetical condition designated 'positive health'."

I suspect that most of us feel that the name of the public health service is not so misleading and that the evolution of concepts will naturally move toward the concept of positive health as infectious diseases and malnutrition are conquered and degenerative diseases continue to increase. In this event we must not only eliminate dangerous chemicals from our environment as much as possible, but also learn how to live more wisely.

Enzyme Adaptation to Toxic Hazards

Physiologic adaptation at the enzyme level is a subject that is fundamental to any discussion of the health hazards in man's environment. Should we aim for an environment that is completely free from toxic hazards? We can answer that question very quickly by recognizing that such an achievement is not only improbable, it is impossible! Then what is the effect of a low dose of a toxic substance, a dose that does not produce death or obvious pathology in a time that is short enough to suggest an obvious cause-and-effect relationship? The answer is that for many toxic substances at dosages that produce no rapid overt symptoms in the intact animal, there is a rapid increase in activity of a variety of enzymes within 24 hours which appears to be a result of the synthesis of increased amounts of enzyme proteins, first indicated by the experiments of Conney, Miller, and Miller (6). Numerous examples are now available(9).

The next question is whether the animal is any worse off or any better off for having an increased level of certain enzymes in liver (6, 9) or intestine (26). In the study of Wattenberg and Leong (26), it was shown that 6 mg of phenothiazine increased the activity of benzpyrene hydroxylase in rat liver from 14 to 311 units/mg, and in intestinal mucosa from 16 to 55 units/mg. Chlorpromazine, a phenothiazine derivative that is a well-known tranquilizer, had almost identical results for liver and increased the value in intestine to 114 units. At a dose of only 1 mg per rat given 48 hours prior to exposure to 30 mg of dimethylbenzathracene, phenothiazine protected nine of ten rats against adrenal necrosis. This study has as its overall objective the determination of "optimum methods for achieving protection from the effects of chemical carcinogens in experimental animals and, possibly, eventually in man." Further studies on the protective effects of smaller daily doses, such as are used over long periods of time as tranquilizers, will be of interest.

Meanwhile, a clinical application of the induction of enzyme activity in a human has come to our attention. Yaffe, Levy, and Matsuzawa (27) have reported the use of phenobarbital (15 mg daily) to enhance glucuronide conjugation capacity in a congenitally hyperbilirubinemic infant. The authors claim that theirs is the first demonstration of the apparent induction of the glucuronide conjugating system by phenobarbital in man and the first therapeutic application of enzyme induction. There is no reason to doubt that phenobarbital did cause increased synthesis of the enzyme, since enzyme induction by phenobarbital is well known (9).

At the present time, it appears impossible to answer the question as to whether amounts of toxic substances that will induce certain enzymes are intrinsically helpful or harmful. Of course, we have been made aware that even noninducing doses of some compounds may be capable of producing irreversible damage to DNA and hence capable of acting as carcinogens. Recently, Siperstein (23) has reported deletion of the negative feedback system for cholesterol biosynthesis in liver by aflatoxin at a level of 10 parts per billion in the diet of trout and in the liver of rats after only 2 days of a diet containing aflatoxin at a level of 10 ppm. In this case, it is not yet established whether the change is irreversible or reversible, but it is clear that the phenomenon could give the appearance of enzyme activation or induction. It should be noted that trout receiving aflatoxin at 10 parts per billion from birth develop hepatomas to the extent of 80–100 percent. Thus, we are in the position of having to make considerable efforts to find any virtue in the ingestion of any foreign compound if it can be avoided, unless there is clear indication that the benefits outweigh the possible or known risk. Further discussions on animals in toxic environments are available in the handbook (7) referred to earlier. No beneficial effects seem to be mentioned in the section on polluted air (by E. B. Morrow, on pp. 795–808 in reference 7) or in the section on man and industrial chemicals (by H. W. Gerarde, on pp. 829–34 in reference 7), although in both chapters there are suggestions of adaptation in various instances. Tables showing levels to which workers can be exposed day after day without adverse effect do not appear to have been based on criteria other than the ability to work efficiently and the absence of claims of pathology. Thus, we can suggest that although there is evidence that humans can adapt to some extent to a variety of toxic chemicals, there is still no basis for assuming that there are no disadvantages to the adapting individual and no basis for complacency about the increasing levels of ambient toxicity. Meanwhile, let us investigate the type of adaptive changes that might be considered in examining the life of a completely healthy man or animal.

Enzyme Adaptation to Daily Regimens

Changes in enzyme amount resulting from changing rates of synthesis and degradation of enzyme protein occur not only in physiological adaptation to toxic hazards in the environment. Such changes can also be observed in the course of each 24-hour cycle, as a result of feeding habits and as a result of changes in dietary composition. In 1961 Ono and I (21) reported enzyme changes in liver of rats fed *ad libitum* under controlled lighting conditions, in which food was eaten in the dark hours. The liver glycogen decreased in the light hours and increased in the dark hours, and glucose-6-phosphate dehydrogenase showed mild oscillations in opposite phase. More recently, we studied a number of enzymes in livers and hepatomas of rats fed diets containing 0 percent, 12 percent, 30 percent, 60 percent, and 90 percent protein during 12 hours of darkness with no food during 12 hours of light in each 24-hour period (20). We noted oscillations in liver glycogen with both peak and minimum levels that were inversely related to protein and directly proportional to carbohydrate in the diet. In this study there was a marked oscillation in tyrosine transaminase in rat liver, with maximum values proportional to protein intake at midnight, six hours after the onset of feeding, with declines to resting levels thereafter even while the glycogen values were still rising. Recently, this phenomenon has been studied in more detail by Dr. Minro Watanabe in our laboratory, and the detailed data confirm the discontinuity between liver glycogen and liver tyrosine transaminase. In addition they show that the plasma corticosterone decreases while the rise in tyrosine transaminase occurs. The induction of this enzyme by injections of adrenal steroids was well known, but the rapid increases during food ingestion had not been previously reported, possibly because in the rat the peak is at midnight and tends to reach daytime levels by 6 A.M. (28–31).

These examples show that metabolic transitions occur throughout the daily routine of sleeping and waking, eating and not eating, and that these transitions are accompanied by marked changes in several enzyme activities.

Enzyme Adaptation to Fasting

In the 1961 study (21) we also carried out the procedure of fasting rats for three days and then refeeding various diets, as has been carried out by Tepperman and Tepperman (24). In this situation owing to a changed feedback relationship, the glucose-6-phosphate dehydrogenase activity in the liver responds by rising to unusually high levels compared with the daily cycle and greatly overshoots the normal range. The enzyme level rises to about 20 times the usual level during about 72 hours, and then slowly returns to normal levels over a period of about 10 days. It is clear that the optimum stressor level for the synthesis of this enzyme is not attained in the *ad libitum* feeding regimen.

In a recent symposium on feeding patterns and their consequences, Mayer (14) emphasized that the pattern of metabolism may be influenced by the distribution of the food intake in one, two, three, or a number of meals. Tepperman and Tepperman (24) and others have carried out many experiments on rats that have been fasted for 21 or 22 hours in each 24, and correspondingly fed for only two or three hours per day. Such animals showed a striking increase in fat production from both acetate and glucose, and they stored liver glycogen to higher levels than animals fed *ad libitum*. Moreover, the fat pads showed an increased level of fat deposition. From these studies, there has been a tendency to conclude that frequent snacks are better than one meal a day for the human, as well as the rat or mouse; and there is a widespread belief that frequent small meals represent a regimen that can be recommended as one feature of an optimum environment. It is my purpose here to question this point of view and in fact to take the opposite position. Incidentally, it is reported that the custom of three full meals a day had been established only since 1890; that in Anglo-Saxon tradition there were only two meals a day, breakfast and dinner; and in the 16th century dinner was eaten at 11 A.M. (4).

We start from the assumption that the animal or human is not equipped by instinct to do what is best for him in circumstances other than those under which his species evolved to its present state. Particularly for rats in small cages or men in small rooms, with no exercise imposed by circumstances, the provision of food on an *ad libitum* basis has no instinctive support to provide information on "living more wisely," a goal emphasized by Dubos (8), as mentioned earlier. True, our society has come to value the slim figure achieved by a low-calorie diet; but this has been coupled with the idea of frequent snacks and never, to my knowledge, with the idea of one good meal once a day.

Secondly, we start from the assumption that fasting is normal, beneficial, and not unnatural. This view is probably contrary to popular and medical opinion, both of which are probably influenced by the knowledge that stomach ulcers are given palliative treatment by frequent small meals of milk. My assumption is that physiological functions are meant to be used, and that atrophy of disuse is not limited to skeletal muscle. It is also assumed that brain function, both intellectual and characterwise, is influenced by bodily function. Animals possess metabolic machinery for storing fuel far in excess of what can be stored in the form of liver glycogen. According to Cahill (5), the liver glycogen in man is able to maintain blood glucose for only about 12 hours, and, of course, muscle glycogen is not directly available as a source of glucose. Thus, in the absence of food intake the human must initiate the process of gluconeogensis from protein within 12 hours, and the evidence suggests that in rodents the situation is not greatly different. Cahill shows the relative sizes of the various glucose reserves in comparison with the total potential reserves, and the total glucose pool is only about 290 moles, or a little less than 1 percent of the total of about 30,000 moles, based on the fact that men can survive a total fast of 60–90 days.

It has commonly been assumed from studies on laboratory rats that fasting leads to a rather prompt adrenal cortical stimulation, which in turn leads to increased gluconeogensis from protein (1, 22). However, in a recent study by Kollar et al.(13), two men were fasted four days and three men six days with no evidence of adrenal activation in any of them. However, an as yet unidentified "stress responsive indole substance," normally absent from the urine, was maintained at high levels in all six subjects after the second day of starvation. What lends interest to this observation is the finding by Rosen and Nichol (22) that two tryptophan metabolites, 5-OH-tryptophan and serotonin, are effective inducers of tyrosine transaminase in rat liver. It appears that the stress of fasting may lead to adaptive changes mediated both by indole-containing substances and by cortisone and that the two classes of inducers are merely separate stages in a sequence of adaptive changes, which vary in different species.

The interest in my laboratory has not been in the effect of fasting per se, but rather in the effect of prolonging the intervals between food intake as an approach to an optimum stressor level. The typical laboratory rat lives at a constant temperature, with food constantly available, and with little opportunity or incentive to exercise. In rats that have been trained to eat their daily allotment of food in two or three hours, the result is obesity (12, 24). Under natural selection, rats have been selected to desire food every night and to sleep in the daylight hours, but they have also been selected for the ability to survive if they do not obtain food every night. We decided to explore the consequences of training rats to undergo cycles of feeding and fasting with durations of 48 hours, rather than 24 hours.

From the experience with *ad libitum* feeding regimens, with food limited to 12 hours in each 24 (20), and with food *ad libitum* after a three day fast (21), we went on to develop regimens that have attempted to attain the hypothetical optimum stressor levels corresponding to an environment that might be optimum for the greatest number of parameters. Starting with rats that were fed 12 hours in each 24, which is not much different from *ad libitum* feeding, we adopted the simple expedient of feeding every other night instead of every night. Thus, these animals were fed 12 hours in every 48, and were fasting for 36 hours. We refer to them as "36-hour fasting-adapted rats" (19). There have been some experiments with a 48-hour cycle in which food is available for only 8 hours in 48, and these are called "40-hour fasting-adapted rats" [(28)–(32)].

It was soon noticed that the fasting-adapted rats were hyperactive. We therefore installed activity cages and recorded mileage for each animal. It can be reported that 40-hour fasting-adapted rats will survive in small cages of the usual type, but if allowed access to activity cages, they will all run themselves to death in 5–10 days, illustrating the breakdown of instinctive "wisdom." In contrast, the 36-hour fasting-adapted rats are able to survive and adapt to the regimen with or without exercise.

The 36-hour fasting-adapted animals ran an average of 15 km during the 12-hours of darkness when no food was available (19), and on the following day, still hungry, they slept much of the time and ran much less. The *ad libitum* control-rats exercised and ate at night and slept most of the day, with almost no day activity recorded.

We have studied a number of enzymes and have also studied nucleic acid metabolism, but data for only one enzyme will be mentioned here. Glucose-6-phosphate dehydrogenase shows great fluctuations and averages much higher values than the *ad libitum* controls (19). We feel that these data adequately demonstrate the fact that adaptive enzyme changes are part of normal physiology and that these changes can be exaggerated by increasing the time between meals.

The animals on this regimen have not been studied for longevity; but it is clear that obesity does not result during 30 days, and the growth curve during this period does not develop a steeper slope than the control curve, as in the case of rats fed two hours per day (12). The growth rate is quite similar to that of male rats studied by Berg (3) at the levels of 33 percent and 46 percent restriction of food intake and falls midway between the rates for his groups. Berg's studies demonstrated increased longevity and general health without evidence of immaturity. In the 36-hour fasted rats, it is as yet unknown whether the food intake would increase to the level of the *ad libitum* feeding in time, or whether in the long run, restricted feeding on a once-per-day basis would be preferable. It can be suggested, however, that the usual restricted food intake always results in fasting periods of 22–23 hours and that fasting may be partly responsible for the beneficial effect of the caloric restriction.

At this time, we can only speculate that the fasting-adapted animals derive benefit from the active use of their abilities to produce large shifts in intracellular enzyme patterns and leave it to the future to determine whether mental powers, motivations, and character would be helped or hindered in humans on similar regimens.

Definition of Optimum Environment

Turning now to the actual task of defining an optimum environment, I have tried to make the point that the culture in which we live is an important part of our environment. What we recommend as physiologists may become a part of our culture or it may be ignored, depending on the force of our logic and the force of counterpressures. A cogent example is the relationship between cigarettes and lung cancer, where the experts are pretty much agreed but the counterforces still prevail.

In the case of defining an optimum environment, I think it is essential to go beyond a mere consideration of toxic hazards and to recommend positive steps that could raise men above mere absence of disease to the concept of "positive health" mentioned by Dubos (8). My basic concern is that physiologists should be in the forefront of describing and analyzing the mechanisms of physiologic adaptation, not only in physiologic terms, but in behavioristic and molecular terms—not only in the academic sense, but also with the aim of guiding mankind during the next 20 or 30 years of rapid change to we know not what. If affluence is not conducive to an optimum environment, then what can we say to those who seek it? What are the minimum requirements for a world that physiologists could recommend and work toward?

I have made a list of seven points, not as a physiologist but as a scientist and a humanist. I present them as the whole package recognizing that, as I am a physiologist, my main concern is the fourth point, which has to do with physiological adaptation. However, I might emphasize that, until we know more about the nature of adaptation and the molecular targets of toxic hazards, we can say very little about the problems of threshold and potentiation, which are the crux of the pollution problem.

My seven points are as follows:

1. I would begin with basic needs that can be satisfied by effort. These include food, shelter, clothing, space, privacy, leisure, and education, both moral and intellectual. [Regarding the ethical basis of science, see Glass (11).]

2. I would insist on freedom from toxic chemicals, unnecessary trauma (primarily war and traffic injuries), and preventable disease.

3. I would demand a culture that had a respect for sound ecologic principles with a long-range point of view. The aim must be to live with nature as in a balanced aquarium, with no assumptions about the ability of future science to rescue a sick planet.

4. The point that is the most personal with me, as it is based on my research experience over many years, is that the culture should prepare us for and expect of each individual adaptive responses continually from birth to death, as a result of systematic challenges by physical and mental tasks which come at appropriate times and are within individual capabilities, which are known to increase rapidly at certain periods in life and decline later. This proposition is based on molecular genetics, which shows that our genetic capacity does not automatically express itself, and that each capability is called forth maximally only in response to an optimum stressor level.

5. The next point calls for individual happiness that involves oscillation between satisfaction and dissatisfaction, with a sustained sense of identity, despite a continual revision of ongoing intentions as the new messages from a rapidly changing world show up in our private information centers.

6. The next point calls for productivity that involves commitment to other members of society; directly to our family, our church, our community, or indirectly to mankind.

7. Finally, each of us can contribute to the further evolution of our culture, to our present society, and to our own satisfaction by a continual search for beauty and order that does not deny the role of individuality and disorder (16, 17).

In connection with the subject of adaptive responses, which is my main concern under my assigned topic of defining an optimum environment, I feel it is within the scope of environmental physiology (a) to postulate that individual organisms show a wide variation in their tendency to seek out such challenges unaided and that most individuals in fact are equipped by instinct and natural selection to satisfy only their basic physiological needs by the easiest possible route and no more; (b) to inquire what counsel to give to a society that is basically uninformed as to the nature of man as well as to the goals, attitudes, and personal values which should be inculcated into pre-school and in-school individuals in order to build a free society worthy of mankind; and (c) to inquire whether individuals are in general unwilling to challenge systematically their own adaptive capabilities and whether society should attempt to influence the attitude of the young in favor of systematic exercise, periodic fasting, and continual development of new mental and motor skills, and, if so, how these adaptive challenges can be initiated by society but maintained by free individuals, perhaps reinforced by some kind of voluntary grouping.

The first step in any program that might hopefully assist in the evolution of our culture toward better concepts of positive health is to secure more knowledge. I advocate that the study of the individualistic aspects, as well as the principles, of physiological adaptation is an especially important sector of environmental physiology and that much more research which combines both organismic and molecular biology should be our first objective.

REFERENCES AND NOTES

1. J. Ashmore, S. R. Wagle, and T. Uete, "Studies on Gluconeogenesis," *Advan. Enzyme Reg.* **2**:101–114, 1964.

2. William James, *The Principles of Psychology* (New York: Holt, Rinehart and Winston, Inc., 1892).

3. B. N. Berg, "Nutrition and Longevity in the Rat. I: Food Intake in Relation to Size, Health, and Fertility," *J. Nutr.* **71**:242–254, 1960.

4. R. Brasch, *How Did It Begin?* (New York: David McKay Co., Inc., 1966).

5. G. F. Cahill Jr. "Some Observations on Hypoglycemia in Man," *Advan. Enzyme Reg.* **2**:137–148, 1964.

6. A. H. Conney, E. C. Miller, and J. A. Miller, "The Metabolism of Methylated Aminoazo Dyes V: Evidence for Induction of Enzyme Synthesis in the Rat by 3-Methylcholanthrene," *Cancer Res.* **16**:450–459, 1956.

7. D. B. Dill, "Handbook of Physiology," *Am. Physiol. Soc.* (Baltimore: The Williams and Wilkins Co.,1964), Section 4.

8. René Dubos, *Man Adapting* (New Haven: Yale University Press, 1965).

9. L. Ernster, and S. Orrenius, "Substrate-Induced Sythesis of the Hydroxylating Enzyme System of Rat Liver Microsomes," *Fed.Proc.* **24:** 1190–1199, 1965.

10. C. Geertz, "The Impact of the Concept of Culture on the Concept of Man," in John R. Platt, ed., *New Views on the Nature of Man* (Chicago: University of Chicago Press, 1965).

11. B. Glass, "The Ethics of Science," *Science* **150:**1254–1261, 1965.

12. G., Hollifield, and W. Parson, "Metabolic Adaptations to a "Stuff and Starve" Feeding Program II: Obesity and the Persistence of Adaptive Changes in Adipose Tissue and Liver Occurring in Rats Limited to a Short Daily Feeding Period; *J. Clin. Invest.* **41:**250–253, 1962.

13. E. J. Kollar, G. R. Slater, J. O. Palmer, R. F. Docter, and A. J. Mandel, "Measurement of Stress in Fasting Man," *Archiv. Gen. Psychiat.* **11:**113–125, 1964.

14. J. Mayer, "Introductory Remarks, Symposium on Feeding Patterns and their Biochemical Consequences," *Fed. Proc.* **23:**59, 1966.

15. J. G. Miller, "Psychological Aspects of Communication Overloads," in R. W. Waggoner and D. J. Carek, eds., *International Psychiatric Clinics: Communication in Clinical Practice* (Boston: Little, Brown and Company, (1964), pp. 201–204. Other reports by Miller include: "Adjusting to Overloads of Information," in *Disorders of Communication* (Volume XLII: Research Publications, Association for Research in Nervous and Mental Disease, 1964), pp. 87–100; and "The Individual as an Information Processing System," in W. S. Fields and W. Abbott, eds., *Information Storage and Neural Control* (Springfield, Illinois: Charles C. Thomas, Publisher, 1963), pp. 1–28.

16. R. S. Neutra, *Survival Through Design* (New York: Oxford University Press, 1954).

17. V. R. Potter, "Society and Science," *Science* **146:**1018–1022, 1964. (See Chapter 4, this volume, pp. 55–68.)

18. V. R. Potter, and V. H. Auerbach, "Adaptive Enzymes and Feedback Mechanisms," *Lab. Invest.* **8:**495–509, 1959.

19. V. R. Potter, R. A. Gebert, and H. C. Pitot, "Enzyme Levels in Rats Adapted to 36-hour Fasting," *Advan. Enzyme Reg.* **4:**247–265, 1966.

20. V. R. Potter, R. A. Gebert, H. C. Pitot, C. Peraino, C. Lamar, Jr., S. Lesher, and H. P. Morris, "Systematic Oscillations in Metabolic Activity in Rat Liver and in Hepatomas I: Morris Hepatoma 7793," *Cancer Res.* **26:**1547–1560, 1966.

21. V. R. Potter, and T. Ono, "Enzyme Patterns in Rat Liver and Morris Hepatoma 5123 During Metabolic Transitions," *Cold Spring Harbor Symp. Quant. Biol.* **26:**335–362, 1961.

22. F. Rosen, and C. A. Nichol, "Studies on the Nature and Specificity of the Induction of Several Adaptive Enzymes Responsive to Cortisol," *Advan. Enzyme Reg.* **2:**115–135, 1964.

23. M. D. Siperstein, "Deletion of the Cholesterol Negative Feedback System in Precancerous Liver," *Abst. J. Clin. Invest.* **45:**1073, 1966.

24. H. M. Tepperman, and J. Tepperman, "Adaptive Hyperlipogenesis," *Fed. Proc.* **23**:73–75, 1964.

25. A. Toffler, "The Future as a Way of Life," *Horizon* **7**:No. 3, 108–115, 1965.

26. L. W. Wattenberg, and J. L. Leong, "Effects of Phenothiazines on Protective Systems Against Polycyclic Hydrocarbons," *Cancer Res.* **25**:365–370, 1965.

27. S. J. Yaffe, G. Levy, T. Matsuzawa, and T. Balliah, "Enhancement of Glucuronide-conjugating Capacity in a Hyperbilinemic Infant due to Apparent Enzyme Induction by Phenobarbital. *New Eng. J. Med.* **275**: 1461–1466, 1966.

28. E. F. Baril, and V. R. Potter, "Systematic Oscillations of Amino Acid Transport in Liver from Rats Adapted to Controlled Feeding Schedules," *J. Nutr.* **95**:228–237, 1968.

29. V. R. Potter, E. F. Baril, M. Watanabe, and E. D. Whittle, "Systematic Oscillations in Liver from Rats Adapted to Controlled Feeding Schedules," *Fed. Proc.* **27**:1238–1245, 1968.

30. M. Watanabe, V. R. Potter, and H. C. Pitot, "Systematic Oscillations in Tyrosine Transaminase and Other Metabolic Functions in Liver of Normal and Adrenalectomized Rats on Controlled Feeding Schedules," *J. Nutr.* **95**:207–227, 1968.

31. E. D. Whittle, and V. R. Potter, "Systematic Oscillations in the Metabolism of Orotic Acid in the Rat Adapted to a Controlled Feeding Schedule," *J. Nutr.* **95**:238–246, 1968.

CHAPTER ELEVEN

Science and Biological Man

Abstract Major advances in health are based on knowledge that can be applied to populations. Such knowledge is available to a vastly greater extent than it is being used; but if the knowledge were used without concomitant birth control, the results would be catastrophic, since the world population is already out of control. The question of whether mankind can be improved by biological evolution or by physiological and cultural adaptation is discussed and the latter two are favored.

Society and the Specialist

The great dilemma of modern society is the problem of how to harness the talents of the specialist, and the dilemma of the modern intellectual is how best to utilize his talents to promote the survival and improvement of mankind. It was not always so. Until quite recently the problem of society was assumed to be capable of solution by breaking up knowledge into disciplines, which by a kind of intellectual free enterprise system would obey the law of the marketplace and expand or contract according to the laws of supply and demand. The product of the disciplines could be weighed and measured in terms of the public demand for their output, and the industrial, agricultural, medical, or political entrepreneurs could enter the knowledge supermarket with a reasonably clear shopping list.

I said that there are two dilemmas in the society: specialist relationship, the one as seen from the viewpoint of society and the other as seen by the intellectual. The switch in terminology must be explained because not all specialists are intellectuals and not all intellectuals are specialists. But while a specialist is frequently a craftsman or a technologist, an intellectual is not likely to be recognized as such unless he has received a Ph.D. in a discipline. In the course of his preparation and final effort, he is likely to become more and more specialized. Moreover, to receive recognition or just to have the personal satisfaction of nonredundant accomplishment, he is forced to specialize in an increasingly narrow front. Thus, I began as a chemist, then chose biochemistry, then the biochemistry of cancer, then the biochemistry of one kind of cancer, and am presently interested in special aspects of that biochemistry. It is only recently—the last 10 years—that I have taken the time to look around me and to realize that there are problems more important than cancer research and that if the best minds in the world do not get busy on them, it will not matter whether the average life span is 68, 78, or 58.

Frankly, I'm worried about the fact that relatively few of our best minds are able to spend a significant fraction of their effort on the major problems of our time; and even though they might be able to agree on some things, they lack the ability to influence society in any profound way. Virtually every man of talent is occupied in a daily routine of detail, and the really major decisions are made by men whose main deficiency is that they do not have the time to consider all of the relevant information. Someone once said that much of the trouble in the world is caused by people who are convinced that they know the one true course for others to follow. As a scientist and a biologist, I am inclined to emphasize the fact that the future cannot be foretold and that no single path can be assured of success (1). If this view could be agreed upon, our course of action would not be bound to dogma; we would try to avoid positions of no-return, we would attempt to utilize existing knowledge on the nature of uncertainty, and we would hedge our bets on the future by encouraging pluralistic approaches to the problems of society. And of course we would attempt to set up some priorities based on existing knowledge. We would not assume that the future will take care of itself, and we would deal realistically with those products of technology whose rapid evolution could be reasonably delayed. There have been many symposia on Science and the Future of Man, and somehow they seem to end up in a glow of optimism in which the assembled scientists say in effect, "Give us the laboratories and we will give you the future." We hear talk about the Affluent Society (2) and are often led to believe that our problem is what to do with leisure. The problem is what *not* to do with leisure, and the problem is what to do with work that actually diminishes the likelihood that we can cope with the future. Optimism has recently been defined as a belief that the future is *un*certain, the other choice being certain disaster. What I am calling for is neither optimism nor pessimism, but an informed *realism* that includes *humility:* a humility in which we admit that not one of us knows how society should proceed, a humility that causes us to listen in order to utilize the thoughts of others. We need humility that is not merely a mask for incompetence but rather a humility that is willing to lay its measure of competence on the line, willing to step over the disciplinary boundary, willing to criticize and be criticized, and willing to modify and evolve a cherished personal insight into an effective working hypothesis or an action policy for a group. I am thus advocating interdisciplinary groups in which the members are competent in their discipline but not without humility. I am suggesting that the freedom of the isolated specialist or group of specialists to be unconcerned with the needs of society may become restricted because of the onrush of events. The problem has shifted to the nature, size, and orientation of the group in which the individual wishes to operate. Many individuals will, of course, operate in more than one group and play different roles in the various groups.

The Priority Problems of Our Time

There are certain problems that outweigh all others when we think about "Science and the Future of Man." These can be categorized alliteratively as population, peace, pollution, poverty, politics, and progress. We need to realize that because of various global changes, the first five may be a matter of survival and that survival is necessary for progress. In point of fact, we have done just the opposite. We have focussed on "progress" in terms of material goods and technological achievement as if they were ends in themselves. We are like the French empress who said "After us the deluge," and suddenly we wonder why we have student unrest in our universities. The fact is that we have some students who desperately want to believe in material progress in which the universities play a key role (3), and a few others who have said "to hell with it." Of course we have a few who are intellectual fakirs and some who opt for violence, but we also have a genuine group who place the priority problems of population, peace, pollution, poverty, and politics above personal material progress. They came to the university hoping to find an ecological niche in which they personally could find a way to live a life with a meaningful value system. I shall call them the *Survivalists,* and to them I dedicate this chapter.

The Survivalists do not necessarily look upon themselves as mission-oriented for the survival of mankind, but they consistently use the key-word "relevance." I think that, in most cases, relevance means relevance to one or more of the priority problems that I associate with the survival of the civilized world. There is a growing malaise not only among our students but among our faculty and among many thinking people throughout the world. This malaise is the reflection of a growing concern that maybe survival is not something to be taken for granted, a concern that maybe there is no one at the controls on the spaceship earth or even in the United States. There is a growing concern about the ability of governments to plan for the future while trying to cope with the present, whether the government is democratic, socialistic, or totalitarian. Even Père Teilhard de Chardin, the Roman Catholic thinker, who pleaded for a future-oriented philosophy, did not take for granted his mystical Omega point. In fact he said, "But there is another possibility, obeying a law from which nothing in the past has ever been exempt, evil may go on growing alongside good, and it too may attain its paroxysm at the end in some specifically new form. 'There are no summits without abysses' " [quoted in (1)].

The Role of Biology

I come now to the role of biology in the priority problems. I think that it may be assumed that a biologist speaking in a symposium on Science and the Future of Man will speak largely in terms of progress. He will quickly summarize the achievements of the past [cf. reports by the National Health Education Committee (4)] and then he will say, "and if you give us the laboratories and the money we will accomplish even greater things in the name of progress." And past accomplishments are such that expectations exceed reality. In some people the desire for immortality is so great that at the point of death they will pay to be placed in a deep freeze with liquid nitrogen at −170°C on the assumption that medical science will be able to thaw them out and restore their defective parts at a future date; and there are commercial establishments for this purpose, the freezing storage, that is. In my own field of cancer research we are honestly pushing as rapidly as we can to find methods for treatment and prevention of cancer; and although many awards have been given to members of our specialty and indeed to our laboratory, we do not have all the answers nor do we expect to be able to increase the average life span by very many years. What we do hope for is an alleviation of suffering and premature death in individuals and a large-scale prevention of cancer in terms of populations, for example, in terms of prevention of lung cancer by the elimination of cigarette smoking. In this case the knowledge is available, but vested interests and human perversity prevent the kind of action that would be effective.

Recently we have seen a flurry of organ transplants and have heard much talk and speculation about what amounts to gene transplants. The organ transplants represent medicine at the individual level and so far have required human donors. Even if the technique for using animal donors or mechanical pumps could be mastered, the procedures will always be enormously expensive and will leave society in a moral dilemma because it will be realized that it would be unjust to limit the procedures to the rich and impractical to extend them to the poor. We must regard these procedures as temporary and experimental and hope that they contribute to knowledge that can be applied to a wider scale.

The gene transplants are based on the knowledge that the genes have known chemical structures based on only four code units which can be sequenced in an almost infinite number of ways. [The sequences run into the thousands and a sequence of only 10 units can be put together in over a million ways (5).] Viruses are made from similar units, and some viruses can be inserted into a gene sequence to transform it into something different. Thus, it is reasonable to assume that we are approaching the time when so called "bad" genes might be replaced by "good" genes for medical purposes. There are so many constraints and reservations about the whole business that its discussion in public is premature for any other purpose than to warn the public about the possible future abuse of such dangerous knowledge, for that is what it would certainly be (6). Certainly public discussion with an eye toward congressional appropriations for research funds should be critically examined for conflict of interest.

Even more dangerous than gene transplants is the possibility that cells from a selected and presumably "successful" individual could be placed in a vat of the appropriate chemicals and developed into any number of replicate individuals, all as much alike as identical twins. Some believe that the maneuver would have a chance of success on the basis of present knowledge. Here again we are talking about dangerous knowledge inasmuch as we really do not know how to select the appropriate individuals or how to predict the outcome of such a project. The dilemma is the old one of nature versus nurture or heredity versus environment; and speaking as a moral philosopher, I would argue that the potentialities for improved nurture should be given a better trial before we try to seek a biological solution. This is what biology is all about. Its basic job is to teach us the relationship and significance of nature and nurture, that is to say, heredity and environment, evolution and adaptation, eugenics and acculturation (or education); but these matters require *interdisciplinary* approaches.

Biology for the Future

We should re-examine the role of science in dealing with biological man and realize three important points. The first is that the really great advances in human welfare have come in terms of knowledge that could be applied to populations and not in terms of individualized medicine. Second, the knowledge is presently available to alleviate sickness and suffering that is rampant in whole populations, but it is not being applied. Some of the world health problems are of enormous magnitude. A recent talk by Dr. Halfdan Mahler of the World Health Organization dealt with "the lack of scientific committment in solving the priority problems in tuberculosis immunization" (7). He dealt with "the human tendency to identify one's own professional microsystem with the immensely more complex macrosystem of mankind" which suggests that each specialist believes world problems would be solved if his specialty could only receive more financial support. Dr. Mahler spoke in favor of applying available knowledge to whole populations and stated that there are at present 1.5 billion people in the world who are infected with virulent tubercle bacilli; that there are 15 to 20 million people who are capable of transmitting tubercle bacilli; that 2 to 3 million new cases will occur in the next year; and that 1 to 2 million will die from the disease. Of course the point is that more than 90 percent of the tuberculosis problem is to be looked for in the underdeveloped countries.

Having said (a) that great medical advances come in terms of measures applied to populations and (b) that available knowledge of this type is not being applied to large segments of the population both abroad and within our own country, I must now make the third point (c) that the world population is out of control. A scientist who has thought about the subject extensively, Garrett Hardin, has concluded that "the population problem has no technical solution; it requires a fundamental extension in morality" (8). By morality he does not mean the morality of the official Catholic Church, but he hopes for a system of birth control that is effective and that is accomplished by "mutual coercion mutually agreed upon" by a majority, in which "Freedom is the recognition of necessity." For my part, I am inclined to believe that his idealistic approach will not work with any more likelihood than the present attempts are working in the places where they are most needed. But the present attempts are seriously hampered by certain church people in our own country and in Latin America and by their curious coalition with the communist representatives in the United Nations in matters pertaining to population problems.

It is clear that the application of available health measures under point (b) would only exacerbate the world population problem described in point (c). It is unlikely that the twin problems will be solved by moral persuasion, and it is almost inevitable that governments will be forced to use methods that are effective even though they may be morally offensive to some. It has been stated by Kingsley Davis (9) that planned parenthood does not and will not go as far as the situation demands and that some kind of additional constraint will be required to control the population explosion. Instead of individual choices to take or not to take the pill or to use some other method, we are rapidly approaching the day when various kinds of *broadly applied* measures will become mandatory (10). Proposals may be made to add the antifertility chemicals to certain foods or to water supplies in large cities (10) where these items could be controlled, just as vitamins are now used to fortify various foods. This kind of thinking can be predicted on the basis of the acceptance that has attended the addition of artificial sweeteners to foods, but I must say I am opposed to the latter and would be opposed to the former. I would not, however, oppose a broadly applied measure if its practicality could be demonstrated in a pilot program and shown to be effective. I will insist that to apply a practical measure will be moral, and not to apply it will be immoral. There are many possible ways to deal with the problem in terms of techniques that are already available and that have been widely tested, and it is my position that any move to institute broadly applied health measures under point (b) will have to be coupled with broadly applied effective birth control techniques because of point (c) if the world is to escape the dire consequences of present policies and attitudes.

There are many who feel that the dilemma of government inability to coordinate broad programs of health with fertility control is staggering enough in India, Latin America, Asia, and Africa but that the problem does not exist in the United States. I cannot agree with this attitude because I feel that the United States is the only country that has even a remote chance of leading the world out of its present combination of unlimited reproduction, malnutrition, disease, and political unrest. We have all of these things right here in the United States; and if we are to help others solve this combination of difficulties, we must do it by example and not by gratuitous and piecemeal suggestions to people in the other parts of the world. We must attempt to mount a coordinated attack on these problems at home and learn by a diversity of pilot projects how the difficulties are intermeshed and what course of action can solve the problems concomitantly. I take the position that the problems cannot be solved by individual intent and that technological solutions that can be broadly applied must be urgently and actively pursued in the United States. Such a technological search can be carried out only by interdisciplinary groups that include not only biological scientists but also a variety of other disciplines. A major question is whether individual freedom of choice can be maintained or whether the survival of society will require some kind of "mutual coercion mutually agreed upon."

Whether broadly applied measures "mutually agreed upon" is what Garrett Hardin had in mind as "a fundamental extension in morality" as opposed to a technical solution is not clear to me, but I am inclined to believe that a technical solution will have to be imposed even though it is not "mutually agreed upon" unless a process of increased enlightenment can be started immediately. Even with a maximum effort at public education, I am doubtful that this attempt will be made in the present political atmosphere in the United States and the world. The solution that Hardin hoped for is perfectly reasonable in a population that is homogeneous both racially and religiously, but an effective limitation of the birth rate that might be agreeable to a majority in this country now or in the near future is political dynamite in a country such as ours in which we have both racial and religious minorities. To me, the answer seems clear enough. We can never survive into the future if minorities feel that their only hope for justice is to become an emergent majority by outbreeding the present majority. In order to move toward a world that can survive, we have to make it no disadvantage for any individual to be a member of a minority group whether that group be ethnic or religious, and we have to arrange it so that controlled reproduction is for every group and also to the advantage of every group. This brings us back to the problem of *nature* versus *nurture,* mentioned earlier. When we look at biological man as a species for whom it is our responsibility to provide for survival and improvement, how do we look at race, religion, and the problem of heredity and environment? How do we look at biological man?

Nature or Nurture?

The question "Which is the more important, heredity or environment?" is as old as Darwin and in fact much older, for in the Old Testament we are told that "a bad tree cannot being forth good fruit." The science of eugenics has been discussed pro and con for many years and is still a favorite topic for some. However, the Nazi master-race ideas coupled with the more recent notions of white supremacy in many parts of this country and the world have been rejected as morally degrading by some and intellectually unsound by others. Speaking on science and biological man seems to place upon one the obligation to face this issue. The question is particularly timely because of a recent 123-page article by Dr. Arthur R. Jensen in the *Harvard Educational Review* (11), "How much can we boost I.Q. and intellectual achievement?" Jensen claimed that Negroes in general had significantly lower I.Q. than whites on nearly every type of intelligence test. He concluded that intelligence is determined largely by heredity and cannot be altered significantly by environment, although in an interview he indicated that he would not recommend widespread use of his ideas without further research and said, "I'm trying to stimulate more research." This statement recalls my earlier references to Dr. Mahler's comments about specialists and their own microsystems. In calling for more research we have to ask whether the tentative conclusions are true and what course of action we would take if the conclusions were true?

Several comments are in order. First, it is absolutely clear that there are tremendous variations in the intellectual capabilities of *individuals within* any so-called race, and these capabilities must be affected significantly by heredity, as Jensen (11), Hirsch (12), Dobzhansky (13), and others (14, 15, 16) have emphasized. This means that the hereditary potential of any *individual* cannot be predicted on the basis of skin color or any other physical attribute keyed to race. It cannot even be accurately predicted on the basis of knowledge about his parents, or about his brothers and sisters; and if we were to start a breeding program to improve the race, we would not know what psychological tests to make use of. As a corollary to this statement about individual variation, it is very clear that the wide variation between individual members of one so-called race overlaps by at least 85 percent the range of another so-called race, according to the available tests and statements (11).

Second, if we had all the proper psychological and physical tests and the know-how to use them, it would take several hundred years to begin to get significant numbers of the desired types. We do not have that much time.

Third, even if we could get the types desired, on the basis of present ideas we have no assurance that a population dominated by these types would increase the probability of man's survival in the world of tomorrow. On this line of thought I take a dim view of Jensen's suggestions for further research on racial differences since I think the research would do more harm than good at the present time (16). I do not dismiss it entirely, but I would like to postpone it until a better world has been achieved by other means. There is a point to be made for eugenics, but the world is not ready for it. It may never be ready, although individual couples may benefit from genetic counseling even today. I think most geneticists would favor many loosely segregated gene pools, with individual cross-breeding freely permitted.

Having adopted a negative view on the possibilities inherent in biological evolution through breeding programs, gene transplants, or personal replication and having nevertheless emphasized the great genetic variation between individuals, I would like to end this chapter with a plea for more consideration of the multiplicity of end results that are possible in every individual. Although we are born with a genetic capability that is different from that of any other person in the world (13), it is not a genetic capability that has only one outcome. As anthropologist Clifford Geertz put it, " . . . we all begin with the natural equipment to live a thousand kinds of life but end in the end having lived only one" (14). And as Geertz also commented, we are all desperately dependent upon the extra-genetic, outside-the-skin, environmental mechanisms by which the culture in which we live controls and programs our behavior (14). But our adaptability as individuals is not only behavioral, it is also physiological; and most of us are capable of far better health than we actually achieve. By improving living habits in terms of diet, exercise, and nonsmoking, it should be possible to either prevent or greatly delay the tremendous number of fatal heart attacks that now occur in men under the age of 60. The reason is that through physiological adaptation we are made stronger by carrying certain optimized loads and conversely made weaker by carrying no loads (3, 6, 15). We need to develop a culture that recognizes the differences between individuals and de-emphasizes the differences between races, and that permits individuals to develop in quality and diversity but not in quantity. If we admit that we do not know what single course to pursue, we have to choose a solution that will permit multiple paths to be followed. To permit an uncontrolled increase in population will not give us either the possibility of multiple solutions *or* the time to test them. Acquiescence to uncontrolled fertility will in my opinion lead to war, pollution, poverty, and pestilence beyond the point of no return. As a moral philosopher I therefore say such acquiesence is immoral.

Summary

I have approached the consideration of biological man in terms of his survival as a species and not in terms of the longevity of individuals, which I said was in any case affected more by broadly applicable techniques than by individuaiized treatments.

In terms of survival I emphasized the priority problems of our time as population, peace, pollution, and politics and suggested that to ignore these in favor of material and technological progress is to court disaster. I proposed to call those who have similar views *Sur-*

vivalists. I dismissed the long-range importance of organ transplants and individualized super techniques as unjust if applied only to the rich and impractical to apply to the poor, and valued them to the extent that they lead to more generally applicable knowledge.

The dilemma of biological man is that real advances in health are based on knowledge that can be applied to populations, that such knowledge is available to a vastly greater extent than it is being used, and that if the knowledge were used without concomitant birth control, the consequences would be catastrophic. The world population is already out of control.

I concluded that adequate birth control could not be accomplished on the basis of individualized medicine and that broadly applied methods would have to be instituted by governmental decision. But unless individuals could be treated fairly regardless of their race or religion, the organized minorities would object to birth control imposed by a majority. In fact, the present lack of government action is caused in part by a fear of political repercussions on the part of the minority groups who often exercise a balance of power.

The question of whether mankind can be improved by biological evolution or by physiological and cultural adaptation was discussed. The potentialities of the latter two were favored, and the limitations of biological evolution were regarded as overwhelming in the present state of the world.

With the above considerations in mind, to permit an uncontrolled increase in population anywhere was judged to be immoral.

REFERENCES AND NOTES

1. V. R. Potter, "Teilhard de Chardin and the Concept of Purpose," *Zygon, Journal of Religion and Science* **3**:367–76, 1968. (Chapter 2 of this volume, pp. 30–41.)

2. John K. Galbraith, *The Affluent Society* (Boston: Houghton Mifflin Company, 1958).

3. V. R. Potter, "Bridge to the Future: The Concept of Human Progress," *Land Economics* **38**:1–8, 1962. (Chapter 3 of this volume, pp. 42–54.)

4. The National Health Education Committee, Inc., *Facts on the Major Killing and Crippling Diseases in the United States Today,* 1957 and 1966 Editions, New York, N. Y. 10017.

5. V. R. Potter, *DNA Model Kit* (Minneapolis, Minn.: Burgess Publishing Co., 1959).

6. V. R. Potter, "Society and Science," *Science* **146:**1018–22, 1968. (Chapter 4 of this volume, pp. 55–68.)

7. Professor Donald Smith, University of Wisconsin, Madison. Personal communication, report on a conference at Airlie House, Nov. 19, 1966.

8. Garrett Hardin, "The Tragedy of the Commons," *Science* **162:**1243–48, 1968. (See also his reference section.)

9. Kingsley Davis, "Population Policy: Will Current Programs Succeed?" *Science* **158:**730–39, 1967.

10. B. Berelson, "Beyond Family Planning," *Science* **163:**533–43, 1969.

11. Arthur R. Jensen, "How much can we boost I.Q. and Intellectual Achievement?" *Harvard Ed. Rev.* **39:**1–123, 1969, Winter.

12. J. Hirsch, "Behavior Genetics and Individuality Understood," *Science* **142:**1436–42, 1963.

13. T. Dobzhansky, *Mankind Evolving* (New Haven: Yale University Press, 1962).

14. C. Geertz, "The Impact of the Concept of Culture on the Concept of Man," in John R. Platt, ed., *New Views on the Nature of Man* (Chicago: University of Chicago Press, 1965), pp. 92–118.

15. René Dubos, *Man Adapting* (New Haven: Yale University Press, 1965).

16. J. F. Crow, J. V. Neel, and C. Stern, "Racial Studies: Academy States Position on Call for New Research" (section on News and Views, National Academy of Sciences Statement "prepared with the assistance of" named authors), *Science* **158:**892–93, 1967.

CHAPTER TWELVE

Biocybernetics—The Key to Environmental Science

Abstract Biocybernetics is the science of feedback relations between the living and nonliving components of the ecological system. This science must be developed and mastered if a livable world is to survive. There is a divergence between the ecological viewpoint and the economic viewpoint, but this divergence must be resolved. Animal populations tend to oscillate because of feedback relationships, but the human population is increasing exponentially. Survival parameters should be identified and monitored, and zero population growth should be a world objective.

E-Day

Biocybernetics is a term that can be used to cover the whole range of biological interactions that occur between man and his environment. The term includes the various parts of the environment in the absence or the presence of man. It derives from the broader term *cybernetics*, coined by Norbert Wiener from a Greek word meaning steersman, in ancient usage the pilot of a ship (1). Today the term is used to cover the feedback relationships by which parts of a complex system affect the behavior of the overall system and, more specifically, the way the output from any part of the system ultimately affects the input to the same part (2). In a society that has tampered with the natural environment on a colossal scale with inadequate knowledge of the ramifications of biocybernetics, there are mixed feelings of guilt, frustration, and defensiveness in various segments of the population, when there should be a unified attempt to achieve a societal wisdom that will permit mankind to survive and improve the quality of life. The year 1969 may go down in history as the year in which a rising tide of individuals rather suddenly reached a conclusion that the world had changed. Prior to 1969 most college students, in the United States at least, had assumed that a college or university education constituted some kind of an escalator that would enable them *individually* to achieve the good life, or at least lift them above the problems that beset the average or below-average family in terms of their control over their own destiny. To the extent that they had altruistic motives, they assumed that by working at the level of their elevated competence in some suitable specialization, society would benefit, and reward them adequately. During a period of about 10 years, the decade of the 60's, there was a growing sense of *orphanization* among the entire upcoming college generation. (By this new word I mean to imply a *process,* rather than a single event.) No longer was the university to be their *alma mater* (nourishing mother); no longer were biological fathers and mothers standards for them to challenge; no longer was Mother Nature solid beneath their feet; no longer was their Heavenly Father "out there" to guide and administer. The state of disrepair in all these images and the sense of rage and betrayal in many of our young people justifies, in my opinion, the use of the term *orphanization* to describe what has happened to the generation that was coming of age in the 1960's. Suddenly in 1969 and 1970 the orphanized generation realized that they had no place to hide from technological by-products. Individual solutions such as a home in the suburbs or a second home at the lake had little meaning if an increasing haze of smog began to envelop it or a traffic jam with no by-pass intervened between home and work. Individuals suddenly became vulnerable to every kind of public emergency, seriously affected by water shortages, garbage collector's strikes, power failures, a heavy snowfall, an atmospheric "inversion," or by deliberately disseminated toxic chemicals (DDTC) entering their food, air, or water (3). April 22, 1970 was Earth Day, the Environmental Teach-in on nearly every campus in the country and a fitting climax to the decade of orphanization that had just passed. But what of the Future? If the concept of Frontier Freedom or Frontier Philosophy is now recognized as fundamentally antisocial (4), if the life of the Noble Savage is no longer accessible, if the lifeboat dilemma is Everyman's problem, if Earth really is a spaceship, if we must all hang together lest we hang separately, what must we do? Where can we turn for wisdom? How can we save the natural environment on which we all depend? Mankind no longer can afford the luxury of wars between nations, and must join hands in coming to terms with the environment. The problem is too big for individuals to solve alone, and too big for individual nations to solve alone. But a nation such as ours could save itself by leading the way toward the solution to every nation's problems by example, and individuals can and must help our nation find the way. Every local problem is a possible laboratory. Prototype solutions could be proposed, tested, and modified by small interdisciplinary groups with adequate feedback from an informed electorate.

The problem is basically one in biocybernetics complicated by the vagaries of human nature. Again, as so many times before, we have the problem of those who want to act on the basis of what they believe and feel they already know, and those who believe that no one knows the best "bridge to the future" and that what we are left with is a belief in process, a method that will buy time and remain open-ended along multiple courses of action. Already a dichotomy seems to have developed. It is by no means certain that the conventional wisdom referred to by Galbraith (5) will be able to choose for survival.

Ecology or Economics?

During the next three decades we are going to witness a fateful contest between two schools of thought, and it cannot be predicted whether they will be harmonized and integrated or whether they will become increasingly polarized, with eventual victory for one school or the other.

On the one side will be the *ecologist–conservationists* who stress two ideas: (a) a commitment to the maintenance of a satisfactory life for man into the long-range future and (b) a conviction that the first aim can be achieved only if technology is prevented from doing violent and irreparable damage to the multitude of other organisms that maintain organic variety in the total environment (6). Although the ecologists were historically not concerned with the human population explosion, they are inevitably being drawn into coalition with those who want to limit human reproduction and must, it would seem, soon favor "zero population growth."

On the other side of the contest for the direction of public policy are the technological economists who are disdainful of biological scientists and who assume that economic growth is not only the goal but the only reliable test of technology. They seem to deny that population control is necessary and to imply that zero population growth would be a catastrophe. Some of these contrasting views have been succinctly pointed out by George Macinko (6), whose earlier paper on the dissipation of open space by contemporary planning gradualism (7) first attracted my attention in 1965. More detailed expositions of the opposing views are found in the record of a memorable symposium entitled *Future Environments of North America*, edited by F. Fraser Darling and John P. Milton (8). This 767-page volume contains 34 prepared papers plus additional statements and discussion. From the record one has the impression that the biologists were on the defensive. It will be interesting to see a volume recording a similar confrontation on the same subject in the 1970's, since the outlook has changed so much since 1965. The short article by Macinko (6) is really a key to the understanding of the longer book (8) because it makes one aware of the dichotomy between the ecologists and the economists. The extended verbatim discussions by the participants (8) would be even more fascinating if one were to label each speaker economist, conservationist, ecologist or planner as might be deduced from the author footnotes accompanying each major presentation. The two references (6, 8) are top priorities for background reading in Biocybernetics. Future reference will be made to specific portions of the record of the symposium (8) which can only be understood in terms of its dichotomy. Kenneth Boulding presents the idea in a clever ditty including the words:

> Ecology's uneconomic,
> But with another kind of logic
> Economy's unecologic. [(8), p. 717]

One of the least sympathetic presentations, from the biological point of view was the paper, Technology, Resources, and Urbanism—The Long View," by Richard L. Meier [(8), p. 277]. His paper concluded by recommending that " ... efforts should be encouraged toward penetrating the marine frontier leading to eventual settlement of the aquatic wilderness. The sea offers the most promising escape from overcrowding." He began by commenting that "Nature-centered adaptive policies of the kind which have been repeatedly advanced in the past ... are being philosophically undermined, statistically outflanked, and economically overwhelmed." Perhaps before becoming totally alienated we ought to inquire what past recommendations he had in mind. In any case it is high time that ecologists prepare a brief that cannot be philosophically undermined, statistically outflanked, or economically overwhelmed.

Technology Assessment

As pointed out earlier, statements written in 1965 might not have been written in 1970. In the interval technology has been brought under examination as never before. For example, The Harvard University Program on Technology and Society has issued a series of research reviews, abstracting books and articles with a commendable effort to integrate their content. Particularly relevant is Research Review Number 3 on Technology and Values (9) which, as indicated earlier, could be better understood in a simplistic separation into economic and ecologic viewpoints, with the next level being scientific versus humanistic viewpoints. We now have not one dichotomy but two and must plead for a technology that serves rather than dominates, and a humanism that proceeds from a knowledge of biocybernetics coupled with a sense of history rather than from history alone.

That times have changed can best be illustrated by reference to reports from the National Academy of Sciences to the Committee on Science and Astronautics, U .S. House of Representatives. The first report in 1965 was entitled "Basic Research and National Goals." The second, in 1967, was "Applied Science and Technological Progress," in which there was essentially no hint that progress and technology might not be almost synonymous. Thus Robert A. Charpie of Union Carbide Corporation [(10), p. 357] referred to "all of the important environmental factors which contribute to successful innovation: the entrepreneurs, the venture capitalists, the banks, the universities, and local, regional, and national governmental bodies." He recommended that "the Federal Government should take the opportunity to encourage in whatever way possible the already successful technology-oriented large companies to continue to take ever greater risks in the knowledge that therefrom will flow a stream of revolutionary innovation which will make it possible for this society to continue to grow apace of its social aspirations which are so important today."

In 1969 the third report asked the important questions of how technological decisions are arrived at, who decides, and on what basis? Thus, at long last we came to "Technology: Processes of Assessment and Choice" (11). This is undoubtedly the most succinct and perceptive analysis of the conflict between economics and ecology that is available, although this comment is a simplistic description of the 150-page report. This small volume is evidence that there are future-oriented intellects at work on the interface between the humanities and science, and it is one of the evidences that change has occurred since the 1965 symposium referred to earlier (8). Perhaps the clearest statement on the relationship between economics and ecology was as follows: "With few exceptions, the central question asked of a technology is what it would do (or is doing) to the economic or institutional interests of those who are deciding whether or how to exploit it" [(11), p. 26]. Earlier the report referred to the "tyranny of small decisions" and to decisions to develop technologies "without explicit attention to what all those decisions add up to for society as a whole and for people as human beings" [(11), p. 10.] In other words technology has been guided almost exclusively by the profit motive without reference to the long range effects on society, as we have pointed out earlier in this volume. What more need be said to show that the "philosophically undermined, statistically outflanked, and economically overwhelmed" biological views may now have to be weighed in the balance, with man's survival and improvement and attention to people as human beings the standards against which technology must be judged. Fortunately, the panel gave every evidence of turning their attention to this overriding issue (11). The kind of problems that arise and the processes of technological assessment and choice simply cannot be resolved in the absence of an adequate environmental science, and biocybernetics is the key to that science.

There need not be a dichotomy between economics and ecology. Biocybernetics can provide the link between the two fields since both lend themselves to analysis in terms of feedback. Kenneth Boulding's article, "Economics and Ecology" [(8), pp. 225–234], describes several common features or analogies that suggest the possibility of an overall system in which subsets in economics and ecology would interact with each other. McHarg [(8), p. 307] put it very nicely when he said, "It seems to me there is a unity of ecology and economics in terms of energy utilization and the adaptation of organisms to"the environment, including each other, and man." I would place survival as the key concept to effect a synthesis of ecology and economics. In meeting the economic arguments I would argue variety, not for variety's sake, but for survival; beauty, not for beauty's sake, but for survival; adaptability, not as an interesting phenomenon, but adaptability for survival. Technological decisions should not be made on the basis of profit alone, but should be examined in terms of survival. This is where ecology and economics must find a meeting ground.

Feedback Loops from Effect to Cause

Biocybernetics promises to provide an intellectual framework for elaborating the principles and actual mechanisms by which the natural environment operates. As such, it should provide a "bridge to the future," embracing larger and larger spheres of interaction including economic and sociologic systems. In previous chapters I have placed considerable emphasis on the random, the unpredictable, and the disordered event. I should therefore make it clear that the perspectives given in this chapter are not intended to offer the hope that disorder can be eliminated from the lives of future generations. Understanding biocybernetics is not for the purpose of establishing absolute control or eliminating all perturbations, but is instead a matter of understanding the difference between stable and unstable systems in relation to the perturbations that will inevitably occur.

The biocybernetic viewpoint differs from classic thinking by its downgrading of the simple notions of sequential *cause* and *effect*. For centuries philosophers have looked for ultimate causes. They appear to have thought in terms of sequences of consecutive events in a kind of historical linearity as opposed to the concept of feedback *loops*, in which the result of an action (effect) acts back on its cause either to stimulate (by positive feedback) or to inhibit (by negative feedback) the process by which the effect is brought about. I have been unable to discover the feedback concept under any name in the writings of the great philosophers in the period from Descartes to Kant, when Locke, Hume, Kant, and others were struggling with the philosophy of the rational understanding of causes and effects (12). The feedback concept appeared on the scene after these classic philosophers were no longer living, and they could not be affected when James Watt (1736–1819) invented a governor to regulate the speed of steam engines (see Tustin, reference 2). Even with governors and thermostats in wide use, it was not until the 1950's (1, 2) that the feedback concept became generalized and linked to the word *cybernetics*, whereupon it inevitably would be compared to philosophical notions of purposefulness.

Atomic Reactors as Black Boxes

The feedback concept can be described most simply in terms of a "black box" (i.e., a mechanism whose interior details need not be specified at the outset) with an "input" and an "output" such that the output is used to modify the behavior of the "black box" so as to either increase or decrease the flow of energy or material from input to output. There are a number of terms used to describe cybernetic or biocybernetic systems or cybernetic instruments such as servo mechanisms, thermostats, chemostats, tracking mechanisms, adaptive control systems, automatic regulators, automation, self-regulating systems, and others. The essence of understanding the principle is that all of the regulatory devices *must* include *negative* (i.e., inhibitory) feedback in order to achieve stability and control. Any feedback system that contains *positive* (i.e., stimulating) feedback *alone* will be unstable. The rate of change in a purely positive feedback system will accelerate either until all the input material is used up or the system"explodes." A chain reaction, also called an autocatalytic system, is an example of positive feedback. In an atomic bomb or in an atomic energy generator a reaction proceeds in which *each individual atom* of a substance A hit by a smaller particle p is converted (decays) to a substance B plus energy plus n particles, n being greater than 1. In the form of an equation

$$A + p = B + \text{heat} + np$$

If only a spoonful of A is present, most atoms of A will be quiescent and only a few will be decaying to B atoms plus particles. The particles will be radiated in all directions, and only a few of them will hit quiescent A atoms and generate more particles. If larger and larges masses of A are brought into a "pile," eventually the mass will "go critical" and become "self-sustaining" as it begins to capture a higher percentage of the particles that convert A to B and still more particles. For example, if the number of particles given off at each decay is 2, the sequence of events in a pile of critical mass will be as follows in relation to time:

At t_0 $A + p = B + 2p +$ heat
$\downarrow$

t_1 $2A + 2p = 2B + 4p +$ heat
$\downarrow$

t_2 $4A + 4p = 4B + 8p +$ heat
$\downarrow$

t_3 $8A + 8p = 8B + 16p +$ heat

etc., to give 32, 64, 128, each time doubling the rate until explosion disperses the system.

Such a reaction will clearly go faster and faster until explosion or until nearly all A has been converted to B under the *positive feedback* of the particles on the process of converting A atoms to B atoms. In a bomb the whole process is complete in a fraction of a second with a destructive and, to date, wasteful explosion, in contrast to the process in a useful energy generator in which *negative feedback* is used to control the system. How can this be done? One way would be to gauge the amount of energy produced and use some of it to move particle absorbers into the pile to capture the particles in a nondecaying substance, instead of letting them hit the atoms that are reactive. These particle absorbers would act to slow down the reaction. The *output* of the pile would be gauged by a *sensor* and compared with a *standard*. If the output were too high, some of the energy would be used to increase negative feedback. If the output were too low, the negative feedback could be diminished permitting the autocatalytic process to increase. It should be emphasized that in the situation of too much negative feedback with energy too low (with reference to the standard), the properly designed system would still have enough energy to *decrease* the negative feedback. Only a small fraction of the total energy output is needed for purposes of regulation.

Living Systems as Black Boxes

Not only an atomic pile, but also a living cell, can be described as a model feedback system though still a black box as far as all the details are concerned (cf. Chapter 1). A living cell is a community of molecules in a black box in the sense that we can look at the input as a flow of molecules (and energy); and we can look at the output as a flow of molecules plus energy and as a periodic division into two cells in the case of the unicellular organisms, as mammalian cells in laboratory suspension cultures, or as special sites in higher organisms. Many of the interior details of this dynamic system are known, and the number of feedback loops must number in hundreds. Although we do not have information on all of these loops, we can specify the broad outlines of the cells' feedback requirements. In the presence of an adequate supply of essential nutrients, the cells have an input of nutrient molecules and an output of waste molecules and energy. In living cells or living multicellular organisms all of the molecules that are present are usually referred to as *metabolites*, a word for molecules undergoing change in the course of *metabolism* (the sum total of processes associated with life). In a cell that is not engaged in cell division there is still a need for a continual, if not continuous, input of nutrients, and there is an ongoing need for feedback (see Fig. 12.1). Internally, the cell must monitor the status of its energy reserves and its structural elements. As essential structures decay they must be replaced. Incoming molecules must be altered in one way to maintain energy reserves and in another way to replace structural elements. All of these decisions must be made according to standards that are built into the total hereditary substance (DNA) which, interestingly enough, appears to be uniquely stable and not to decay unless the cell dies. The cell is built in such a way that its actions are guided by the feedback loops that indicate whether the energy reserves and structural elements are being maintained. Within certain limits it can alter its behavior and composition and *adapt* to environmental conditions.

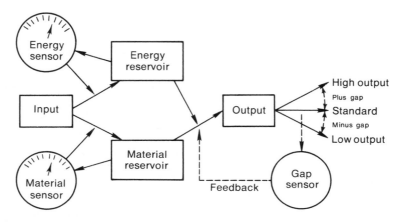

Fig. 12.1 Feedback controls in living systems give purposeful behavior: the purpose is to survive.

Whenever the environmental conditions exceed the ability of a cell to adapt we see *pathology*, the condition of a sick or a dying cell which at times can be recognized by either microscopic or chemical signs. The finding that all cells have built-in feedback controls that automatically tell them what to do to survive makes cells appear very purposeful, and indeed they are purposeful. Their purpose is to survive, and if they have an independent existence, their built-in purpose is to survive and multiply. Their adaptive stratagems to accomplish these ends are many and marvelous, especially in cases of starvation and lack of water. The usual tactic in single-cell organisms is to go into some kind of spore formation and "hibernate" until conditions are favorable again. Small wonder that early biologists could find *design* in every form of life they studied! Design is arrived at by trial and error, with death to the individual and curtailment of procreation the penalty for a faulty feedback design. If the cell survived for us to see, it can be shown to possess design features that are similar to the mechanisms in other successful life forms. In the laboratory we can produce by random methods and selection what I have referred to elsewhere as *idiot cells* (13). These cells survive and live under laboratory conditions because we can make up for the foolish things they do *in terms of their survival*. We can give them the special nutrition and conditions they need to survive and multiply, but what they do does not make sense. They will make vast amounts of an enzyme whose product they cannot use, and they will divert major amounts of their nutrition to making the enzyme and the product. Placed back in a natural environment, these cells would soon die, and only the few that could undergo mutation to correct the defect would survive for more than one generation.

When we move from single free-living cells to higher organisms, we find that cells no longer divide as rapidly as they are capable of dividing when not under negative-feedback control. Within each animal the internal feedback loops are still monitoring the energy supply and the structural elements, but now we find that the feedback loops extend from the output from each cell to the sensors of all the other cells. Cells in the liver are in molecular feedback communication with all the other liver cells; but, in addition, they are in molecular communication with heart cells, brain cells, kidney cells, and so on. All these cell types are organized into a higher organism by virtue of the built-in standards set by their hereditary material and their ability to adapt within limits to changes in their environment. Again, as in the single cells, when the organism encounters an environment that is too unfavorable for its adaptive powers, the result is pathology. We encounter sick cells and sick or dying animals or people, with pathology now visible to the unaided eye in many cases, in addition to the microscopic or chemical evidence. Again, we have the overwhelming feeling of *design* as we witness the repetition of successful feedback loops in species after species, with many modifications of the underlying theme: stimulus perturbs the system and response restores the system through feedback loops within the cell, within the organ, or within the organism. To anyone who examines the feedback systems of living organisms from an evolutionary standpoint, it is clear that the arguments between reductionist and holistic viewpoints are absurd, as noted in Chapter 1. The molecular communication within and among the simplest organisms has been amplified and extended to a community of cells of the organ or organism, transmitted no longer by environmental water or air but by blood, lymph, and nerves, and completing a feedback loop from the output of one cell to the sensor of another cell! In higher organisms we find dozens of instances of feedback between organs by means of hormones (messenger molecules), with a given hormone from one organ affecting receptors in cells of several organs. In the major loops it is quite usual to find organ A sending hormone A' to organ B, whereupon organ B sends hormone B' to a variety of other parts of the body but also closes a feedback loop to organ A where it inhibits the production of hormone A'.

As shown in Fig. 12.2, organ A produces hormone A', stimulates organ B to produce hormone B' which inhibits A' production but stimulates organs C and D to produce their specific products X and Y and so on. In this kind of multiple feedback system, the concentration of hormones A' and B' in blood will oscillate somewhat out of phase. These feedback loops are necessary for the survival and day to day function of the organism. They evolved from the molecular communication between cells of the simplest kinds, and they lead to the production of adaptive control systems (Chapter 1) that give the appearance of having been *designed* for a particular environment, just as a giraffe appears to be *designed* to eat leaves from tree tops. Darwinian evolution has constantly operated in terms of feedback systems to evolve characteristics in addition to form and color, and without effective feedback the design does not survive!

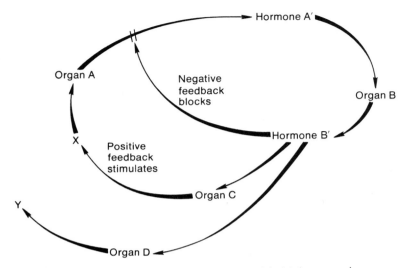

Fig. 12.2 Hormones exert feedback control in higher organisms.

Population, Feedback, and Ecosystems

When we look at a major ecosystem in terms of the plants and animals therein, it is frequently found that populations are not constant but tend to oscillate. The earliest attempts to understand the phenomenon were based on a common-sense observation that many species are preyed upon by other animals that are sufficiently dependent upon a single kind of prey to be influenced by the numbers available as a food supply. A classic example is the observable fluctuations in the number of lynxes in Canada (2), which could be judged by the volume of the fur trade. There was a maximum and a minimum fluctuation approximately every ten years, and this was attributed to the relative number of rabbits. A large rabbit population would lead to an increase in the number of lynxes, while a large lynx population would decimate the rabbits. As the rabbit population decreased, the lynx population would likewise decrease for lack of food. With fewer lynxes, the rabbit population would rise again, and so on (Figs. 12.3 and 12.4).

In addition, the vegetative food supply for the herbivorous animals could affect the number of herbivores in a cycle that would resemble the predator–prey relationship. Operating at another level,

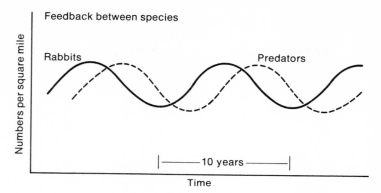

Fig. 12.3   Oscillating populations of rabbits and predators.

the cycles in rainfall would affect the vegetative abundance, and perhaps the rain cycles would be affected by sun spots or other planetary phenomena (Fig. 12.5).

The human population appears to have been increasing exponentially to what would seem to be a disaster level in the next three decades. In modern times we have increased the ability of people to have children and raise them to the age at which they in turn can have children of their own. Particularly during the last few centuries, neither war nor famine has been great enough to stem the explosive increase resulting from an interference in the birth and death rates that may necessarily have been in balance for survival of the species in prehistoric and primitive times. When we look at the exponential increase in the human population, it is usually drawn as a smooth curve emphasizing the phenomenon of positive feedback; but, of course, the curve would not be smooth if we had precise data for the past 5000 years. It seems quite likely that during much of man's history, the population curve may have had ups and downs that

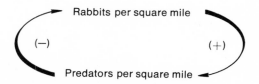

Fig. 12.4   A proposed feedback loop between predators and prey.

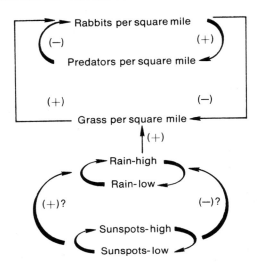

Fig. 12.5   Possible theories of factors relating to oscillating populations.

tended to cancel each other and prevent the emergence of what we now refer to as the "exponential rise" or population explosion. The shape of the human population curve is difficult to reconstruct even when the areas are islands and the time is comparatively recent as emphasized in a recent paper, "The Demography of Primitive Populations" (14). But in the last few decades the rise in the human population has indeed been so great that war, famine, and disease have not cancelled the overall increase, for which the data, though imperfect, are certainly adequate to establish the fact that even the rate of increase is increasing (15).

Studies on Populations of Small Mammals

A number of studies have attempted to understand the feedback factors that produce the oscillations seen in the numbers of animals in local areas of various sizes. The exponential rise in the human population has resulted from a relative increase in positive feedback factors (food supply, sanitation, antibiotics) over the negative feedback factors (famine, war, pestilence, and unknown factors). In human populations the unknown factors include cultural evolution, which can be very rapid in both individuals and in populations to produce marked changes in behavior (16). But in addition to cultural changes that result in a conscious desire to limit family size, there are physiological and genetic changes to be considered. These may be advantageously studied in populations of small animals under field conditions. A useful introduction to the literature is provided by the recent publications of C. J. Krebs, who is actively engaged in research in this field. His work will be emphasized here because it represents the new generation of ecologists for whom *an integration of field studies and molecular biology* now seems mandatory. In 1963 Krebs noted cycles in lemming populations in the arctic regions and commented that "periodic fluctuations in small mammal populations have not been explained" (17). In 1965 Krebs and De-Long (18) referred to the fact that a species of field mouse, the California vole (*Microtus californicus*), shows periodic fluctuations with peaks every 3–4 years. They commented that such fluctuations could be caused by variations in food supply but cited references to show that this explanation was still controversial. They therefore planned experiments "to show whether a superabundance of high quality food was sufficient to promote exponential growth in a low density small mammal population" or whether oscillations would still occur. They found that the population increased at first and then declined even in the presence of abundant food and favorable weather with no evidence of significant predation, disease, or emigration. In 1966 Krebs extended this report with the purpose of demonstrating "that there is a specific set of demographic changes which accompanies population fluctuations in this species, in the same way that there is a specific set of symptoms which characterize a pathological disease" (19). He concluded (19) "self-regulatory mechanisms [i.e., feedback or biocybernetic mechanisms] may be responsible for these demographic changes but no direct evidence of phenotypic or genotypic changes in fitness was obtained in this study." Following a period of study with Dennis Chitty (20) and a tentative suggestion that hostile behavior might be correlated with food supply, Krebs and his students embarked on a study of field mice (voles) at the University of Indiana, in which field studies were combined with the techniques of molecular genetics (21). Two species were studied in terms of the fluctuating numbers of animals that could be counted by trapping techniques designed to count all the animals and avoid sampling difficulties inherent in capture–recapture methods. In addition to the classic methods, the authors obtained 2311 blood samples from a total of 3526 individuals trapped during the period between June 1965 and September 1967. They used the blood samples to characterize changes in the genetic makeup of the mouse population on a week to week basis, since they were able to use certain blood proteins as markers for genes that can be abbreviated as E, C, and F. The blood proteins occurred as variant forms that could be separated on an electrophoretic gel, and each variant form was known to be controlled by an allele at a single locus, i.e., by a single gene. Each of the two vole populations had two alleles, which were present in proportions that varied as a function of time.

Microtus ochrogaster populations were made up of a mixture of EE and EF individuals with EE's predominating when the population was increasing and EF's predominating when the population was declining. *Microtus pennsylvanicus* populations were a mixture of EE and EC populations also with shifting proportions during the increasing and decreasing phases of the population cycle. Although the results are still complicated by unexplained variation and the protein markers may be imperfect indicators of genetic changes that are much more relevant, the data represent a beginning in the possible correlation of genetic makeup, modulation of genetic expression, physiological adaptation, aggressive behavior, and reproduction behavior, in other words, the possible explanation of reproductive and aggressive behavior in molecular terms. Krebs has commented (personal communication) that Christian and Davis have emphasized physiological changes, especially endocrine stress (22), while Chitty has emphasized possible genetic changes (23, 24). Although the different views are still unresolved they are both in agreement that population decline can be the result of the interactions of individuals in crowded populations, in which an increase in aggressive behavior appears to lead to a decrease in reproductive success. Tamarin and Krebs (21) discuss their results in terms of the Chitty hypothesis, which proposes that during the phase of increasing and peak population, selection occurs for more aggressive animals. These selected types, though having increased fitness as far as aggressiveness is concerned, are then assumed to have lowered fitness through greater susceptibility to mortality factors, thus paving the way for population decline.

It may not be necessary to assume that the genetic makeup of the population shifts just because the ratio of EE, EC, and EF proteins in individuals shifts, in view of recent results in my own laboratory.

In our experience a gene in a transplantable hepatoma appeared to be "deleted" because the corresponding protein (a liver enzyme) seemed to be uninducible; but when the physiology of the animals was sufficiently altered, the protein was present in large amounts (25). It would be of great interest to determine whether or not the protein marker distribution in an individual vole could be altered over a period of hours or days by the experience of drastic over-crowding. Certainly if the animal studies are relevant to the human situation, it would seem that changes in reproductive behavior would have to occur in individuals by a modulation of their genetic expression (physiological or cultural) rather than by genetic selection.

Zero Population Growth

It appears essential to lower the birth rate by every possible educational and public health measure that can be instituted on a mass scale and to develop a worldwide political and economic situation in which large families are not looked upon as a solution to the problems of individual parents, minority groups, or large or small nations.

In the world situation the "demographic lag" is assumed to describe an inevitable decrease in birth rates when a primitive agricultural society becomes urbanized and attains a "higher" standard of living. The acceptance of this idea of inevitability may be very dangerous in a world that can scarcely afford the increased population that must occur in the interval that is required even under the most favorable conditions for the hypothesis. The increased crime, disease, illiteracy, and human degradation that is presently associated with urbanization in most parts of the world seems a high price to pay for any decrease in fertility that may result. We should be very critical of the motives and the professional and religious bias that may affect the judgment of world leaders who advocate more and more urbanization for *any* reason. Granted that the bias involved in the opposite view should also be subject to critical examination, it can be plainly stated that the bias in my own case is claimed to be a biological bias, an ecological bias, and a humanistic bias. We should look upon earth, man, plants and animals, sea, and atmosphere as a balanced ecological system. We should begin now to monitor all the parameters that may be relevant, and we should do this on a worldwide basis so that our efforts can be analyzed in terms of hypotheses that attempt to identify "survival parameters." In other words, we need to know whether we are losing or winning the game of survival. We need to aim for "zero population growth" on a worldwide basis, which suggests that on the average each family would be limited to only two children. Means should be found to effect a voluntary change in the birth rate on a year to year basis. Using economic rewards and the power of reason (16), this should be perfectly feasible in a literate world population. If the reproductive rate could be brought under control, it would be possible first to decrease the rate of population growth until a stable population was attained and then to lower it further until the "survival parameters" indicated a favorable balance in the total ecosystem. If the population could be *lowered* it could also be *increased*, and there seems to be no reason why a "managed" decrease in the world population should be regarded as a disaster. The aim should be to achieve an optimally functioning ecosystem with the human population at a level that could survive indefinitely, instead of blazing like a super nova that burns brightly for a short time and then fades to blackness. The science of *biocybernetics* is proposed as a guide for attaining an optimum human world population, and for defining the standard of living that would be possible at the various levels of population. With this information at hand, it would be possible to choose which "luxuries" could be produced to supplement the necessities of life. It would become apparent that many of the "luxuries" of life such as clean beaches, spacious parks, clean air, fine music, and variety in food, clothing, and home decorations were easily within the reach of all. But before we begin to think about improvement in the quality of life, we have to attain a world consensus that faces up to the necessity for zero population growth and an abandonment of the goal which had the American rate of material and energy consumption as its ideal. This is what the great debate of economics versus ecology is all about. *Ecology* says, first we should agree on survival as a goal, leading to population control, leading to an improvement in the standard of living. *Economics* says, first there should be an improvement in the standard of living, then an automatic control of population, then an automatic survival. The experiment is already in progress. All we need do is look around us, measure the parameters, and face the facts of life, spelled *biocybernetics*.

REFERENCES AND NOTES

1. Norbert Wiener, "Cybernetics," in Garrett Hardin, ed., *Science, Conflict and Society* (readings from *Scientific American*). (San Francisco: W. H. Freeman and Co., 1969), pp. 119–125.

2. Arnold Tustin, "Feedback," in Garrett Hardin, ed., *Science, Conflict and Society* (readings from *Scientific American*). (San Francisco: W. H. Freeman and Co., 1969), pp. 126–133.

3. Durward L. Allen, "Population, Resources and the Great Complexity," Population Reference Bureau, Selection No. 29, August 1969. Allen contrasts the life-style of a resident of a small town in the 1920's with that of an urbanized man of today to the disadvantage of the latter. R. L. Meier emphasizes a different view (reference 8, p. 277).

4. C. W. Griffin, Jr., *Frontier Freedoms and Space Age Cities* (New York: Pitman Publishing Corp., in press). Article in *Saturday Review*, February 7, 1970, p. 17.

5. John K. Galbraith, *The Affluent Society* (Boston: Houghton Mifflin Company, 1958).

6. George Macinko, "Conservation Trends and the Future American Environment," *The Biologist* 50:Nos. 1–2, 1–19, January 1968. A personal commentary on the symposium edited by Darling and Milton (See reference 8).

7. George Macinko, "Saturation: A Problem Evaded in Planning Land Use," *Science* 149:516–521, 1965.

8. F. Fraser Darling and John P. Milton, *Future Environments in North America* (Garden City, N.Y.: The Natural History Press, 1966). This book is a detailed record of an important symposium.

9. Irene Travis, *Technology and Values* (Harvard University Program on Technology and Society, Research Review No. 3) (Cambridge: Harvard University Press, Spring, 1969).

10. National Academy of Sciences, *Applied Science and Technological Progress* (Washington, D. C.: U. S. Government Printing Office, 1967).

11. National Academy of Sciences, *Technology: Processes of Assessment and Choice* (Washington, D. C.: U. S. Government Printing Office, 1969). It includes a professional biography of every one of the 18 distinguished panel members.

12. T. V. Smith and M. Grene, *From Descartes to Kant* (Chicago: University of Chicago Press, 1940). Readings from the original authors, with commentary.

13. V. R. Potter, "The Present Status of the Deletion Hypothesis," *U. Mich. Med. Bull.*, **23**:401–412, 1957.

14. Norma McArthur, "The Demography of Primitive Populations," *Science* **167**:1097–1101, 1970.

15. Paul Ehrlich, *The Population Bomb* (New York: Ballantine Books, Inc., 1969).

16. Margaret Mead, *Continuities in Cultural Evolution* (New Haven: Yale University Press, 1964).

17. C. J. Krebs, "Lemming Cycle at Baker Lake, Canada, during 1959–62," *Science* **140**:674–676, 1963.

18. C. J. Krebs and K. T. DeLong, "A *Microtus* Population with Supplemental Food," *J. of Mammology* **46**:566–573, 1965.

19. C. J. Krebs, "Demgraphic Changes in Fluctuating Populations of *Microtus Californicus*," *Ecological Monographs* **36**:239–273, 1966.

20. D. Chitty, D. Pimentel, and C. J. Krebs, "Food Supply of Overwintered Voles," *J. Anim. Ecol.* **37**:113–120, 1968.

21. R. H. Tamarin and C. J. Krebs, "*Microtus* Population Biology II: Genetic Changes at the Transferrin Locus in Fluctuating Populations of Two Vole Species," *Evolution* **23**:183–211, 1969.

22. John J. Christian and D. E. Davis, "Endocrines, Behavior and Population," *Science* **146**:1550–1560, 1964.

23. D. Chitty, "Population Processes in the Vole and Their Relevance to General Theory," *Canad. J. Zool.* **38**:99–113, 1960.

24. D. Chitty, "The Natural Selection of Self-Regulatory Behavior in Animal Populations," *Proc. Ecol. Soc. Australia* **2**:51–78, 1967.

25. V. R. Potter, R. D. Reynolds, M. Watanabe, H. C. Pitot, and H. P. Morris, "Induction of a Previously Non-inducible Enzyme in Hepatoma 9618A," in G. Weber, ed., *Advances in Enzyme Regulation* **8**:299–310 (London: Pergamon Press, 1970.)

CHAPTER THIRTEEN

Survival as a Goal for Wisdom

Abstract Wisdom may be defined as the knowledge of how to use knowledge for the social good. The search for wisdom should be organized and promoted in terms of the survival and improvement of the human species. Humanistic biologists should be organized into interdisciplinary scientific research and development groups with survival as their first goal. Societal competence may be defined as a function of wisdom and knowledge. The cyclic interplay of competence, environmental control, complex needs, and, finally, decreased competence is used to describe the problem of survival. Humanistic biologists need to develop a bioethical credo to encompass the significance of mortality, random suffering, and the future.

Wisdom: The Discipline for Action

As we approach the last three decades of the Twentieth Century, we become increasingly aware of the dilemma posed by the exponential increase in knowledge without an increase in the wisdom needed to manage it. Albert Schweitzer was keenly aware of the problem in 1948 when he said, "Our age has discovered how to divorce knowledge from thought, with the result that we have, indeed, a science which is free, but hardly any science left which reflects" (see p. 49). Today we are beginning to realize that somehow we must decide what proportion of our scientists shall be free to pursue pure science and what proportion shall be paid to look for solutions to the problems of society. Surely the search for wisdom cannot be undertaken without some agreement as to goals and common values, which many people seem to feel is an area outside the realm of science, and, indeed, to constitute metaphysics, philosophy, or religion. Doubt has arisen as to whether or not we can achieve a common set of values (1). We have elsewhere referred to the new wisdom that respects the delicate balance of Nature as a kind of humility that is equivalent to the ancient admonition "The Fear of the Lord is the beginning of wisdom" (Psalms 111:10), but neither the original version nor the paraphrasing seems accepted at this time. In seeking to advance a common value system for the future in which the test of wisdom is survival and improvement, we might do well to turn to Immanuel Kant (1724–1804) and his *Prolegomena to Any Future Metaphysics* and other excerpts reprinted by Smith and Grene (2). Kant was really concerned with *wisdom,* and his words make this quite clear. He fought a campaign for wisdom as a science and lost, which seems a pity; but time and the march of events seem to force us to ask the question again, "What is Wisdom?" in a scientific context. Speaking of metaphysics, Kant remarked [(2), p. 785], "It seems almost ridiculous, while every other science is continually advancing, that in this, which pretends to be Wisdom incarnate, for whose oracle everyone inquires, we should constantly move round the same spot, without gaining a single step. And so its followers having melted away, *we do not find men [who are] confident of their ability to shine in other sciences venturing their reputation here,* where everybody, however ignorant in other matters, may deliver a final verdict, as in this domain there is as yet *no standard weight and measure to distinguish sound knowledge from shallow talk"* (italics mine). It is the intent of this chapter to suggest that the issue of *survival* may provide a measuring stick that may attract the attention of reputable scientists. If as much effort were directed to global survival as to space exploration, scientists could be mobilized in a search for wisdom that might promote survival *and keep open the possibility* of improvement in the quality of life. I would like to quote Kant at greater length but offer merely one additional gem as an introduction to a very important issue in the matter of wisdom and survival. Kant observed [(2), p. 898], "Innocence is all very fine; only it is also most deplorable, that it doesn't keep well and is easily seduced. Therefore even *wisdom—which otherwise consists more in doing and letting be than in knowing—needs a discipline,* not to learn about it, but to afford its prescript admission and endurance" (italics mine). From the context Kant makes clear that by "prescript admission and endurance" he means the application of wisdom as an *action policy* based on reason and duty for either *doing* or *letting be.* Kant points out that men labor under opposing forces of duty and reason on the one hand and the satisfaction of those needs and inclinations comprehended under the name of happiness on the other. He seemed to have had an implicit recognition of man's long-range needs over many generations without explicitly commenting on the issue of survival. It would be interesting to see what Kant would do with today's issues, which really are concerned with the transient happiness of material convenience now posed against the question of our obligation to future generations. Boulding has argued that our own self-interest depends on our ability to identify with a community of men not only in space, but in time past and in the future (3).

That the issue is urgent is strongly stated by a contemporary scientist who has taken the option of going beyond his specialty to deal with the priority problems of our time. In an important paper, "What We Must Do," John Platt (4) suggests that "A large-scale mobilization of scientists may be the only way to solve our crisis problems." Platt points out that what makes our crises even more dangerous is that they are now coming one on top of the other. He insists that nothing less than the application of the full intelligence of our society is likely to be adequate. He grants the importance of nonscientists but concludes that scientific research and development groups are needed to convert new ideas into practical invention and action. His article is useful for its classification of our problems into degrees of intensity, and he estimates the time to crisis if no effort at solution is attempted. Platt concludes, "In the past, we have had science for intellectual pleasure, and science for the control of nature. We have had science for war. But today, the whole human experiment may hang on the question of how fast we now press *the development of science for survival"* (italics mine). As I have emphasized in Chapter 1, humanistic biology may be an appropriate discipline for the organization of a code of bioethics for survival.

Societal Competence as a Function of Wisdom and Knowledge

If wisdom is in reality an action policy for "doing or letting be," in the words of Kant, or the knowledge of how to use knowledge as we proposed earlier (Chapter 3), it can be seen that we are really concerned with competence or know-how at the societal level. The competence to do a job can be considered only in relation to the magnitude of the job, and the knowledge of how to use knowledge for the social good has to be considered in terms of the total organized and unorganized knowledge that has to be managed. Thus we might say that

$$\text{Societal competence} = \frac{\text{Wisdom} \times \text{organized knowledge}}{\text{Total available knowledge}} \tag{1}$$

The total amount of knowledge or factual information has increased exponentially, and it appears that the relative competence to manage the world may actually have decreased. Figure 13.1 is an oversimplified representation of the decline in philosophy and the increase in factual information, but it may have some interest. The graph was constructed by indicating the lifespans of various philosophers and scientists by blocks which represent the dates of birth and death on the abscissa. It is interesting to note how little science was available to Kant and the other philosophers of "The Enlightenment." They were so stimulated and encouraged by the advances made by Copernicus, Galileo, Kepler, and Newton that they felt confident that the workings of the whole world would soon be revealed. As experimental knowledge began to increase exponentially, however, it soon became too much for any single individual to comprehend, and there were no more attempts to visualize the Grand Design. In many respects biocybernetics may be the closest equivalent to Newton's discovery of gravity and the laws of planetary motion, but no comparable reference to a single individual is possible since so many have contributed to the structure, including Darwin, Mendel, and many whose names were not included in Fig. 13.1.

If we attempt to single out significant components in a kind of societal biocybernetics and try to think about problems of survival as well as the rise and fall of past civilizations, we are certain to greatly oversimplify and be subject to devastating criticism. Nevertheless an attempt must be made to develop a science of survival and

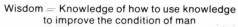

Wisdom = Knowledge of how to use knowledge
to improve the condition of man

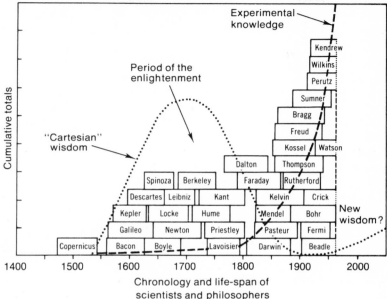

Fig. 13.1 Chronology and life-span of scientists and philosophers. The individual names represent no more than a sampling of prominent men in the period since 1900 and certainly should have included Einstein and the Curies, for example. Each block corresponds to the time of birth and the time of death for the individual represented and clearly indicates which men were contemporaries.

to describe models that are simple enough to serve as a means of communication and dialogue between interested persons, which is all any model can do.

I have focussed on feedback relations between three processes which occur in human populations and which I believe may be related to the problem of survival.

The first process is the search for order, which Anthony Wallace spoke of as an organizational instinct expressed both in religion and in science (Chapter 7). This search for order can be written as an equilibrium between ignorance and competence since the discernment of order ("organized knowledge" in equation 1) leads to the understanding of controlling factors in a system, and this in turn leads to the ability to predict, manipulate, and control the outcome. Thus we can write

$$\text{Societal ignorance} \rightleftarrows \text{Societal competence} \qquad (2)$$
$$\downarrow$$
$$\text{Control}$$

The concept of control is meaningless unless we specify what is being controlled. In every civilization the dominant issue is the control of the environment, which of course includes friends and enemies. As soon as we begin to control the environment, the need for control increases and we develop more and more complex needs. Thus we can write

$$\text{Control}$$
$$\downarrow$$
$$\text{Raw environment} \rightleftarrows \text{Controlled environment} \qquad (3)$$
$$\downarrow$$
$$\text{Complex needs}$$

As the needs of the population become more and more complex, specialization is increased and the individual becomes less self-sufficient and more and more dependent on the overall system, while the system becomes more dependent upon the reliable functioning of individual components. Meanwhile, there is a decreased individual responsibility for the design and function of the overall system. This leads to a decline in the competence of the overall system, that is, a tendency to increase the amount of ignorance. We are thus faced with a situation as follows:

$$\text{Complex needs}$$
$$\downarrow$$
$$\text{Individual independence} \rightleftarrows \text{Decreased individual responsibility} \qquad (4)$$
$$\downarrow$$
$$\text{Negative feedback on}$$
$$\text{societal competence}$$

These relationships have been combined into one diagram in Fig. 13.2, with additional positive and negative feedbacks suggested. A controlled environment can exert either positive or negative feedback on the development of societal competence. The balance depends on dominant value systems that determine the character and

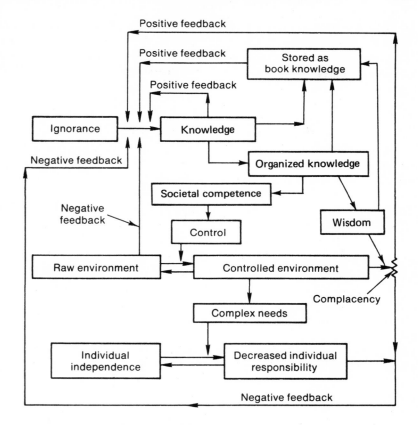

Fig. 13.2 Feedback relationships in human populations. Emphasis is on *societal competence* in generating *control,* on *control* in generating *complex needs,* and upon *complex needs* as ultimately leading to a breakdown in *competence.* The aim is to identify *survival parameters.* The word *wisdom* in connection with the symbol of a variable resistor labeled *complacency* is meant to indicate that societal wisdom is a special ingredient combining the character or mores of society into governmental policy to determine how the *controlled environment* will effect the negative feedback that will tend to optimize the balance between new knowledge, organized knowledge, and new wisdom needed for survival. **See equations 1–4 in text.**

mores of the people, as suggested by "wisdom" which determines the setting of the variable resistor in Fig. 13.2. This figure is admittedly a simplistic model, deliberately omitting the role of economics in determining the processes depicted.

There is little doubt that the profit motive has greatly speeded up the conversion of the raw environment to a controlled environment (equation 3) and to increased complexity of our civilization, without increasing its security. Any attempt to develop a science of survival will have to include the methodology for harnessing the profit system to reward individual initiative and responsibility when they are directed toward the enhancement of the viability and stability of the civilization. It appears that nations will have difficulty enough achieving a stable relationship with the natural environment without trying to dominate each other. The realization that survival requires cooperation may be hard to sell, but the idea must be delivered convincingly.

It is by no means established that the fall of past civilizations was the result of conquest (5). I suggest that the three processes with positive and negative feedback relationships described above can also be described in the form of three curves as in Fig. 13.3. These curves indicate that as "competence" increases, it is followed by a rise in "control" and that this in turn leads to an increase in "needs." As the needs become greater and greater, the "Golden

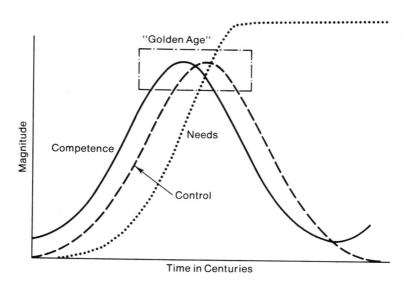

Fig. 13.3 Rise and fall of one civilization. A hypothetical construct based on the relationship between societal *competence*, societal *control*, and complex *needs* suggested in the previous figure. A civilization is postulated to be in a "Golden Age" when competence and control are maximal and not exceeded by needs.

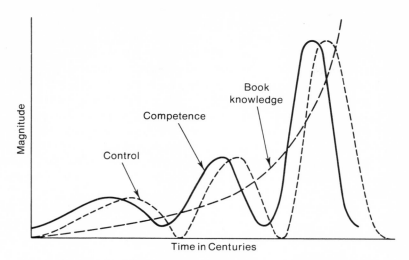

Fig. 13.4   Theory of history. A hypothetical construct based on the well-established fact of an exponential increase in the total amount of stored factual knowledge interacting with the postulated relationships in the two previous figures.

Age" of maximum competence and control is reached. The expanding needs eventually exceed the competence and control, negative feedback sets in, collapse occurs, and the Golden Age is ended.

If we think of this process superimposed on an exponentially rising curve of information or "book knowledge," we see a series of peaks that rise higher and fall harder (Fig. 13.4).This might be suggested as a theory of history, and it is by no means assured that civilization could be rebuilt after a worldwide collapse. There is no reason, however, why we must accept the inevitability of the fall of every civilization, although we may see many reasons why eventual collapse has occurred in every past civilization (5). If we realize that there is possibly a natural succession of events in the rise and fall of civilizations and that the problem is one in which the methods of systems research may be applicable, we may be able to see "what we must do" to survive. It seems doubtful whether any previous civilization had the means by which they could monitor the critical parameters of their survival, sense what was happening to them, and apply corrective measures soon enough to be effective. Even though our own situation, taking the world as a whole, may seem much more desperate than the previous world situations, we should realize that we have the means to monitor and chart the important "survival parameters" with the help of modern computers and data banks and to pick up danger signals long before the man in the street is aware of them. There were many who were aware of danger signals long before the present public clamor about a deteriorating environment, but they were not effective. There is no point in wondering why it took so long. It is important to agree on what the "survival parameters" are and to get busy with the monitoring systems. One of the things that is *not* a survival parameter is the GNP, or Gross National Product, which is highly misleading just because it is the gross product (6). We need to subdivide the GNP into components that promote survival, those that are possibly neutral, and those that decrease the chances of survival. Getting into the monitoring business is important because this is the only way we can apply a corrective measure and sense whether it is failing or succeeding without waiting for the results to become so obvious that the individual voter can smell or see the result. We need the voters to agree on the goals and technicians to tell us whether we are moving toward them or away from them.

Monitoring alone cannot solve our problems. There must be some competent interdisciplinary thinking on the subject of what to monitor and how to express the result. There must be some thought as to what short-range goals will contribute to the goal of survival, and there must be a major effort to convince the rest of the world that our record of the 1950's and 1960's may not represent the only possible solution to the problems of civilization. We have to convince the world that we are looking for new solutions to problems of disarmament and to problems of survival that go far beyond the issue of disarmament. We have to convince the world that when we argue for zero population growth and for conservation of natural resources, we are advocating a policy not only for them but for us. This will be hard to do, but we must do it by convincing example. It is no longer possible to say one thing and do another and get away with it.

The survival of world civilization will be impossible unless there is some agreement on a common value system, especially on the concept of an obligation to future generations of man. Many people in the United States regard people who differ in both nationality and religion as something to be either killed or converted. Yet there are many in the world community who hold strikingly similar views about the nature of man and of the world, but these views have not been clearly articulated. Perhaps the stress of the times could lead to a revitalization of the religious impulse in terms that could bring a unifying movement into the world community. In order to contribute to survival, such an articulation must clearly identify the obligation to future generations and must proceed on the assumption that this world is the only one we will ever have.

Toward a Common Value System

If the nations of the world are to find a "bridge to the future," they will have to realize that they must unite to preserve the fragile web of nonhuman life that sustains human society. From this moment on we are fighting a desperate war for survival, and we cannot indulge in fratricidal forays to uphold value systems that may no longer be relevant.

Science, particularly biological science, can offer guidelines for the development of value judgements based on the concept of survival (7). Scientific guidelines will not be identical with existing religious statements of belief, and they should be compatible with the paradigms of the worldwide network of biological scientists, many of whom are more deeply religious in their reverence for life than many of the religious devotees of "holy wars." In thinking about biological science as a source of value judgements for humanistic biologists, I recalled the concept of the paradigm in the sense employed by T. S. Kuhn in *The Scientific Revolution* (see Chapter 1). As pointed out earlier, a paradigm is in essence a statement of a theory that no one expects to be disproved, yet is open-ended enough to provide for further action. I asked myself what paradigms might be formulated in the case of issues usually considered outside the realm of science. In my opinion there are three main areas in which some existing religions have failed to revise their beliefs in accord with the advance of science. These are (a) an unwillingness to accept the idea of mortality (cf. Wallace's comments in Chapter 7, (b) an inability to understand the meaning of random suffering, and an inability to understand novelty in biological and cultural evolution as historically conditioned rather than as arising *de novo* as creations or revelations.

In agreement with Kant's idea that wisdom is a guide for action and not merely *possession* of knowledge, I attempted to state acceptable courses of action based on the proposed paradigms of accepted belief. The result is the Bioethical Creed on page 196, which presents five statements each beginning with a statement of *belief* followed by a statement of commitment to proposed *action,* to provide a future-oriented system of morality that is based on the hopes that all races and creeds have for their children and grandchildren. The attempt to construct a creed is based on a strong feeling that beliefs are important, because they determine what men do. They provide the emotional drives that energize both learning and action. It is hoped that the statements of belief and commitment on page 196 might be accepted by students and leaders of all races and nationalities.

Future Action

If the Bioethical Creed as *individual* belief were acceptable to a substantial fraction of influential scientists in different parts of the world, others would perhaps gain the courage to join in a worldwide movement. The more immediate issues of war and peace, population control, and conservation of natural resources could be taken up in *legislative* terms. A new kind of student publication entitled *Bioethics Review,* patterned after the existing *Law Review,* might be started with the objective of converting the proposed mores into rational action. The United States of America should begin to change its way of life to better express a concern for the future and for the rest of the world by providing an example of Bioethics in action. Statements of creed should not be considered as finished products but should undergo continual reexamination and refinement, and new statements should be added.

If our goal is the survival and improvement in the quality of life for the human species in keeping with the potentialities that can already be seen to exist, and in keeping with the constraints imposed by the total ecosystem, we must be able to carry on a humanistic biology that is truly multidisciplinary. We must maintain our idealism and we must be aware of the imperfection and disorder that are the natural components of the biological and physical worlds. We must also study the natural rhythms of all biological hierarchies and interlocking feedback systems and their components. With better understanding of the basic mysteries and an appreciation of the idea that "ordered disorder" is built into biological systems (Chapter 7) and that "disorder is the raw material from which order is conceived and selected" (Chapter 4), we may be able to monitor the "survival parameters" and to make open-ended decisions that can avoid positions of no return. Whether the survival of the human species in an acceptable form of civilization can be accomplished without the revision of many ancient and diverse beliefs is purely conjectural, but it would be surprising if survival could be based on erroneous beliefs. It seems likely that survival is possible only when the system of beliefs is compatible with the world situation. In earlier times the results of erroneous superstitions were local and the disasters were local. Now the whole world is influenced by events in any part of it. Change in outlook is needed, but will change come in time?

REFERENCES AND NOTES

1. Beryl Crowe, "Tragedy of the Commons Revisited," *Science* **166**:1103–1107, 1969.

2. T. V. Smith and M. Grene, *From Descartes to Kant* (Chicago: University of Chicago Press, 1940), pp. 784–899.

3. Kenneth Boulding, "The Economics of the Coming Spaceship Earth," in Garrett De Bell, ed., *The Environmental Handbook* (New York: Ballantine Books, 1970), pp. 96–101.

4. John Platt, "What We Must Do," *Science* **166**:1115–1121, 1969.

5. Shepard B. Clough, *The Rise and Fall of Civilization, An Inquiry into the Relationship between Economic Development and Civilization* (New York: Columbia University Press, 1957).

6. John K. Galbraith, *The Affluent Society* (Boston: Houghton Mifflin Co., 1958).

7. Ralph W. Burhoe, "Values Via Science," *Zygon, Journal Of Religion and Science,* **4**:65–99, 1969. Professor Burhoe provides an extensive bibliography in addition to his thought-provoking discussion. The same issue contained six other papers on the general subject of human values and natural science with many additional references.

A Bioethical Creed for Individuals

1. Belief: *I accept the need for prompt remedial action in a world beset with crises.*

   Commitment: I will work with others to improve the formulation of my beliefs, to evolve additional credos, and to unite in a worldwide movement that will make possible the survival and improved development of the human species in harmony with the natural environment.

2. Belief: *I accept the fact that the future survival and development of mankind, both culturally and biologically, is strongly conditioned by man's present activities and plans.*

   Commitment: I will try to live my own life and to influence the lives of others so as to promote the evolution of a better world for future generations of mankind, and I will try to avoid actions that would jeopardize their future.

3. Belief: *I accept the uniqueness of each individual and his instinctive need to contribute to the betterment of some larger unit of society in a way that is compatible with the long-range needs of society.*

   Commitment: I will try to listen to the reasoned viewpoint of others whether from a minority or a majority, and I will recognize the role of emotional commitment in producing effective action.

4. Belief: *I accept the inevitability of some human suffering that must result from the natural disorder in biological creatures and in the physical world, but I do not passively accept the suffering that results from man's inhumanity to man.*

   Commitment: I will try to face my own problems with dignity and courage, I will try to assist my fellow men when they are afflicted, and I will work toward the goal of eliminating needless suffering among mankind as a whole.

5. Belief: *I accept the finality of death as a necessary part of life. I affirm my veneration for life, my belief in the brotherhood of man, and my belief that I have an obligation to future generations of man.*

   Commitment: I will try to live in a way that will benefit the lives of my fellow men now and in time to come and be remembered favorably by those who survive me.

Author Index*

Abelson, P. H. 62(68)
Aldous, E. 62(68)
Allen, Durward L. 3(27)163(181)
Allen, G. E. – (29)
Arbib, Michael A. – (102)
Ashby, W. Ross 98(101)
Ashmore, J. 142(146)
Auerbach, Victor 51(54)122(132)

Baerreis, D. A. 6, 26(27)
Balliah, T. 138(148)
Baril, E. F. 127–129(132)140, 142
    (148)
Barnett, S. A. 46, 47(53)57(67)

Barricot, N. A. 26(28)
Barry, J. M. 17, 19(28)
Beadle, George 32(40)
Bellman, R. – (102)
Berelson, B. 155(161)
Berg, B. N. 143(146)
Berlyne, D. E. – (102)
Berrill, N. J. 3(27)
Beveridge, W. I. B. 108(117)
Bolton, E. T. 62(68)
Boulding, Kenneth 165, 167(181)185
    (195)
Brasch, R. 141(146)
Bryson, R. A. 6, 26(27)

* Pages where citations occur are shown without parentheses; pages where bibliographic references are given are shown in parentheses. A dash preceding a page number indicates that the name listed appears in the bibliographical references but is not mentioned in the text; a dash following a page number indicates that the name listed appears in the text but is not listed in the bibliographical references.

Burhoe, Ralph W. 193(195)
Burtt, E. A. 43(53)

Cahill, G. F., Jr. 141(146)
Cannon, Walter B. 118–120(131)
Carson, R. 3(27)59(68)
Charpie, Robert A. 166(181)
Chitty, D. 177, 178(182)
Christian, John J. 178(182)
Clough, Shepard B. 190, 191(195)
Cohn, C. 129(132)
Conney, A. H. 137(146)
Crick, F. H. C. 7, 17(28) 10(28)
Crowe, Beryl 184(195)
Crowe, Beryl 184(196)
Curvin, J. W. 6, 26(27)

Darling, F. Fraser 165(181)
Davis, D. E. 178(182)
Davis, Kingsley 155(161)
Delisle, B. B. – (102)
DeLong, K. T. 177(182)
Dill, D. B. 134–136, 139(146)
Dobzhansky, T. 31(40)48(53)158, 159(161)
Docter, R. F. 142(147)
Dodds, E. R. 90–92(101)
Driver, P. M. 94–96(101)
Dubos, R. 73(74)137, 141, 144(146) 158, 159(161)

Eddy, E. D. 44, 48(53)
Ehrlich, Paul 176(182)
Ernster, L. 137(146)

Furst, P. T. 86(101)

Galbraith, J. K. 86(101)109(117)151 (160) 164(181) 191(195)
Gebert, R. A. 139, 142, 143(147)
Geertz, C. 36(40)106(116)135(146) 158, 159(161)
Gilkey, L. – (101)
Glass, B. 144(147)
Goldman, A. 122(131)
Greene, John C. 18, 25(28)
Greenstein, J. G. 122(131)
Grene, M. 57(67) 168(181) 184(195)
Griffin, C. W., Jr. 164(181)

Hadamard, Jacques 108(116)
Hafner, E. M. 6(27)
Handlin, O. 79(79)
Hardin, G. 155–156(161)
Harrison, G. A. 26(28)

Haselden, K. 32(40)
Heidelberger, C. 14, 15(28)
Hickey, Joseph J. 4, 22(27)
Hirsch, J. 158(161)
Hollifield, G. 142, 143(147)
Humphries, D. A. 94–96(101)
Huxley, Julian 26(29)

Iberall, A. – (102)

James, William 135(146)
Jensen, Arthur 157–159(161)
Johansen, G. 6, 26(27)
Joseph, D. 129(132)
Jukes, T. H. 87, 89(101)

Kahn, Roy M. – (102)
Kallen, Horace M. 90(101)
Kant, I. 184–186(–)
Kavanau, J. L. 96–97(101)
King, J. L. 87, 89(101)
Kleinman, A. 120–121(131)
Knox, W. E. 122(132)
Koestler, Arthur 89, 97(101)
Kollar, E. J. 142(147)
Krebs, C. J. 177–179(182)
Kuhn, T. S. 6, 7, 13(27)

Lamar, C., Jr. 139, 142(147)
Langmuir, I. 66(68) 85(101)
Leong, J. L. 130(132)138(148)
Lesher, S. 139, 142(147)
Levine, George 25(28)
Levine, S. 105(116)
Levy, G. 138(148)
Lightbody, H. D. 120–121(131)
Lilienthal, David 50(54)
Lin, E. C. C. 122(132)
Lipman, F. 64(68)
Livingston, Robert B. 108(116)
Lowery, G. H., Jr. 4, 22(27)

Macinko, George 165(181)
MacKay, D. M. 63(68)
Mahler, Halfdan 154(–)
Mandel, A. J. 142(147)
Matsuzawa, T. 138(148)
Mayer, J. 140(147)
Mayr, Ernst 31, 32(40)
McArthur, Norma 176(182)
McCulloch, W. S. – (102)
McElroy, W. D. 13(28)71(74)
McHarg, Ian 167(181)
McKeon, R. 66(68)
McLeod, J. 6, 26(27)

McShan, W. H. 122(131)
Mead, Margaret 82(77)177, 180(182)
Meier, R. L. 165(181)
Mendelson, E. – (29)
Meyer, R. K. 122(132)
Miller, E. C. 130(132)137(146)
Miller, J. A. 130(132)137(146)
Miller, James G. 38(40)133(147)
Milton, John P. 165(181)
Morris, H. P. 139, 142(147)179(182)
Mullins, R. F., Jr. 105(116)

National Academy of Sciences 167 (181)
National Health Education Committee, Inc. 152(160)
Neel, J. V. 158(161)
Neutra, R. S. 145(147)
Nichol, C. A. 142(147)
Nogar, Raymond 20, 25(28)

O'Connor, C. M. 51(54)
Ono, T. 139–140(147)
Orrenius, S. 137(146)

Paddock, William and Paul 3(27)
Palmer, J. O. 142(147)
Pardee, A. B. 62(68)
Parkinson, C. N. 47(53)
Parson, W. 142, 143(147)
Pelton, R. B. 65(68)
Peraino, C. 139, 142(147)
Pimentel, D. 177(182)
Pitot, H. C. 125–129(132)139, 142, 143(147)179(182)
Plato 56(67)
Platt, John R. 6, 8(27)(40)88(101) (146)185(195)
Potter, V. R. 6, 26(27) 10, 12, 13, 14, 15, 17(28)36(40)51(54)60(68)107 (116)113–114(117)121, 122, 125–131(132)139(147)142, 143, 145 (148)153(161)172, 179(182)
Presswood, S. 6(27)

Rankin, J. 6, 26(27)
Raushenbush, Stephen (53)
Reiner, J. M. 10, 12, 13, 19(28)
Reynolds, R. D. 179(182)
Rosen, F. 142(147)
Rous, P. 37(–)
Rudd, R. L. 58(68)

Schimke, R. T. (131)
Schlesinger, Arthur 93(101)

Schmitt, F. O. 108(116)
Schweitzer, A. 49(53)
Scotch, N. A. 65(68)
Shapere, D. – (29)
Shipley, E. G. 122(131)
Siegel, F. L. 65(68)
Simpson, George Gaylord 31(40)
Siperstein, M. D. 138(147)
Slater, G. R. 142(147)
Smith, Donald – (161)
Smith, T. V. 57(67) 168(181) 184(195)
Spengler, O. 47(53)
Stern, C. 158(161)
Swanson, C. P. 20(28)
Symon, K. R. 6, 26(27)

Tamarin, R. H. 177(182)
Tanner, J. M. 26(28)
Teilhard de Chardin, P. 26, 30–39, 46(39)85, 87–88(100)
Tepperman, H. M. 140, 142(148)
Tepperman, J. 140, 142(148)
Thoday, J. M. 47(53) 57(68)
Thomas, Owen 25(28)
Time, The Weekly Newsmagazine 93 (101)
Toffler, A. 133(148)
Toynbee, A. J. 47(53)
Travis, Irene 166(181)
Tustin, Arnold 163, 169, 174(181)

Ute, T. 142(146)

Virchow, R. L. K. 57(68)

Wagle, S. R. 142(146)
Wald, George 88(101)
Wallace, A. F. C. 24, 56(67)83–84 (100)
Watanabe, M. 125–129(132)140, 142 (148)179(182)
Watson, J. D. 7, 17(27)16(28)
Wattenberg, L. W. 130(132)138(148)
Weiner, J. S. 26(28)
White, E. H. 13(28)
Whittle, E. D. 127–129(132)140, 142 (148)
Wiener, Norbert 162, 169(181)
Williams, R. J. 65(68)
Wolstenholme, G. E. W. 51(54)
World Council of Churches 73(74)

Yaffe, S. J. 138(148)
Yates, R. A. 62(68)
Young, J. Z. 98–100(101)

Subject Index

Adaptation, not equivalent to conformity, 112

Adaptation, cultural: impinges on evolutionary and physiological adaptations, 24; in individuals and in populations, 124

Adaptation, enzymatic: in animals, 122; to toxic hazards, 137; to daily regimens, 139; to fasting, 140

Adaptation, evolutionary: in populations, 124; delimits physiological adaptation, 23

Adaptation, physiological: limited by genotype, 21; key to biology, 22; in individuals, 124; defined by Prosser, 136; related to positive health by Dubos, 137

Adaptation, three kinds of, 122–124

Aflatoxin, production of hepatomas by, 138

Alternative metabolic pathways, determined by competition among enzymes, 15

Bats, as predators, confused by protean behavior, 94

Biocybernetics, as key to environmental problems, 162–182

Bioethical creed, proposed for individuals, 195

Bioethical Review, proposal for, 194

Bioethics, as a science of survival based on biology and wisdom in action, 1; as biological knowledge plus human values, 2; based on realistic knowledge of man, 5, 26; should seek biological agreements at international level, 26; humanistic biology, the discipline for, 185

Biological science, criticized by Koestler, 89

Biology, component disciplines in, 2–3; knowledge of, still incomplete, 9; role in priority problems, 152; for the future, 154; humanistic, 185

Black box, concept of: to describe

Black box (*Cont.*)
    atomic reactor with feedback, 169; to describe living system with feedback, 170
Breeding programs, doubtful utility of, 158
Bridge to the future, new public policies could provide, 2; through combining science and humanities, 53; for nations of the world, 193

Cancer, in man, analogy with man on earth (Berrill), 3
Catalysis, needed for life processes, 14
Cause and effect, no longer a simple sequence, 168
Central Dogma (F. H. C. Crick) as a paradigm in molecular biology, 7
Chance, fingers of, dream of mastery by human research (Teilhard), 33
Civilizations, fall of, as a function of "competence, control, and needs," 190
Computer, inventive, 63
Conservatives, as pragmatists, 78
Control, chemical, of life processes, generates dangerous knowledge, 63
Copy-error, in genetic system, 18
Creed, bioethical, as a set of commitments based on beliefs and biological realities, 196
Cybernetics, from Greek word for pilot, 162
Cycles, metabolic, of life, of death (Fig. 9.1), 123
Culture, as environment, 135

Death, decisions involving, 72–74
Decision-making, in a free society (Fig. 8.2), 111–112
Demographic lag, dangerous to assume inevitable decrease in birth rates due to, 179
Design, arrived at by trial and error, 172
Dilemma, in society/specialist relationship, 150; of biological man, seen as public health without birth control, 160
Disciplines and intellectual free enterprise system, 149

Disorder, built into biological and cultural systems, 24; source of novelty, 36; science needed to perceive the relation between order and, 56; religion and science both attempt to explain, 56; in human activity and thought, 83–102; chaos, randomicity, chance and, 85–87; and Teilhard de Chardin, 87–88; in human affairs, 90; seen in Book of Job as suffering of innocent, 90; as the raw material from which order is conceived and selected, 90; in Greek literature, 90–92; confusion theory versus conspiracy theory, 93; seen as protean behavior, 94; ordered by natural selection, 94; described as variable behavior, 96–97; seen in human behavior, 98–100; built-in, in mental processes, 107
DNA, deoxyribonucleic acid, role specified by Central Dogma, 8; and information storage, 16; and information replication, 17; double helix, model of, 17; and mutuation, 18; transcription to RNA, 61

Ecology, in conflict with economics, 164
Economics, in conflict with ecology, 164
Ecosystems, cycles of predators and prey in, 174; many components in, 175
E-day, Earth Day, Environmental Teach-in, 163
Energy storage, gauging, and replenishment, 16
Environment, optimum (table), 105; optimum, requires adaptation, 114, 129; optimum, 133–148; optimum, seen by physiologist, 144
Enzyme, amount, changes in, 120; induction, clinical application of, 138
Enzymes, as proteinaceous catalysts essential for life, 14
Error, in genetic system, 18
Essential metabolites, defined, 13; in bacteria, 62
Essential nutrients, defined, 14

Ethical revolution, six ways in which science can contribute (Lilienthal), 50

Euphoria, accompanying new idea, 108

Evolution, Darwinian, and copy-errors in DNA, 18; supported by Teilhard, 31; and views of Darwin and Spencer, 45; cultural, 109

Extinction, fate of most species, 47

Fasting, adaptation to, 140–142

Feedback, concept of, most important biological idea since Mendelian heredity, 19; and intelligence, 62; effect seen to act back on cause, 168; concept of, traced to governors and thermostats, 169; selected elements of, in human populations, 187

Feeding schedules, controlled, 125–129

Fossils, studied by Teilhard, 30

Free will, problem of, 62

Future, Council on the, 75–82

Future, impossible to foretell, 150

Garden of Eden, Adam and tree of knowledge, 70

Genotype, 17

Golden Age, in feedback terms, 191

Happiness, 8

Hazards, environmental, 20

Holism, defined as a concern with the whole animal or the whole ecosystem, 7

Homeostasis, Cannon's six postulates, 119

Homogenate technique, for enzyme quantitation, 121

Hormones, as components of feedback loops, 173

Humanism, contrasted with science, 25; Christian, combined with science, goal for Teilhard, 31

Humility, in face of dangerous knowledge, 12; as necessary ingredient, 151

Ideas, analogy with DNA molecules (Fig. 8.1), 107–108; Galbraith's test, 109

Idiot cells, certain mutants as poor design, 172

Imperfection, in biological information system, 18

Infant mortality, decreasing, 71

Information, replication, related to Mendelian genetics, 17; storage, in genotype, 16; overload, producing future shock, 133

Instinct, not infallible guide to optimum environment, 112–113

Instincts, sum of individual, inadequate for world survival without help from bioethics, 4

I.Q., racial differences seen by A. R. Jensen, 157

Journal for Mankind, proposed, 81

Knowers and doers, as scientists and technologists, respectively, 76

Knowledge, eight ideas about, 49; unmanageable, rise of, 58; image of dangerous, first seen in relation to scientific warfare, 58; dangerous, described as knowledge without wisdom, 33; dangerous, and specialization, 69; dangerous, the answer to (Rockefeller report), 70, 75

Land-grant colleges, related to concepts of more and better, 44

Leisure, as health hazard, 133–134

Liberals, as pragmatists, 78

Life, origin of, 79

Living systems, as black boxes with feedback, 170

Longevity, and caloric restriction, 143

Machine, the living, coming to terms with environment, 61

Man, seen as error-prone cybernetic machine, 12; as information-processing, decision-making, cybernetic machine, 36; as infinite reservoir of possibilities, 78; as limited animal, 78; nature of, 106; as cybernetic machine, 110; biological, and science, 149–161

Materialism, as credo of American life (Eddy), 44

Matrix, of perceived human experience (Wallace), 56

Mechanism, new version of, defines man as an adaptive control system (Reiner), 10

Mechanistic biology, twelve categories and paradigms in, 13–21
Mendelian genetics, 17
Metaphysics, pretense of wisdom decried by Kant, 184
Milieu intèrieur, dictum of Claude Bernard, 120
Molecular structure, 13
Monitoring, as early warning system, 191
Moths, exhibiting protean behavior, 94–95
Mutation, as copy-error in genetic system, 18

Nature, and nurture, 157

Omega Point, mystical goal of evolution as seen by Teilhard, 31; as a scientifically and philosophically oriented ideal society, 33; a cultural concept, 34
Orphanization, coined word implying process, 163
Oscillations, metabolic, 125–129

Pandora's Box, analogy with new knowledge, 70
Paradigm (T. S. Kuhn), more than a hypothesis, 7
Paleontology, human, studied by Teilhard, 30
Pathology, as failure in adaptation, 172
Philosophy, part of cultural adaptation, 24
Poliomyelitis, success in conquering, raised hopes for research, 60
Population, studies with small mammals suggest unknown factors in regulation of, 176; zero growth of, as goal, 179
Population problem, and morality, 155
Problems, priority, keyed to survival, 151
Progress, human, as the goal of the universe, as seen by Teilhard, 31; an American tradition, 42; religious concept of, 43; materialistic concept of, in terms of *more* and *better,* 44; scientific-philosophic concept of, 45; towards perfection, Darwin's view of man, 46; not an accident, but a

Progress (*Cont.*)
necessity (Spencer), 46; not inevitable (Spengler, Toynbee), 47; scientific-philosophic concept of, seen as realistic, 49
Protean behavior as unpredictable, 94
Public health, and population explosion, 71

Realism, as proper substitute for liberalism or conservatism, 78; coupled with humility, 151
Reductionism, the method of molecular biology, 7
Religion, as a process of maximizing the quantity of organization in the human experience (Wallace), 84; primitive, defined, 85; humanistic, 85
Religion and science as direct expressions of organizational instinct (Wallace), 84
Replication, of individuals, undesirable, 154

Science, responsible for impact of new knowledge on society, 64; no consolatory alternatives from (Handlin), 80
Scientific approach, distinguished from nonscientific approach by objective verification, 6
Scientific revolution, biological science a part of, 5
Shock, physiological (Fig. 9.1), 123; cultural, as failure in adaptation, 124; future, a failure in cultural adaptation, 133
Silent Spring (Carson), as pinpointing the end of the growthmanship era, 3
Specialist, best use of by society, 149
Stress, optimum, as optimum stressor level, 134
Structure, cellular and organismic, permit classical characteristics of life to be functional, 19
Survival, a science for, proposed by Platt, 185; of world civilization, requires some common values, 192
Survivalists, as name for concerned youth, 152
Survival parameters, need to agree on, need to monitor, 191

Tampering, with man and nature, inevitable, needs humility, 11; to do nothing now is a form of, 17

Technology, control of, 77; now subject to value judgements, 166; processes of assessment and choice regarding (report), 167

Thalidomide, disaster of, speeded change in abortion laws, 59

Tranquilizers, induction of detoxifying enzymes by, 138

Transplants, gene, organ, 153

Trinity, new, of molecular biology (DNA, RNA, protein), 61

United States, as a society confused as to values, 80

Utilitarianism, a product of materialism, 44

Values, further evolution of, 38; in peril, 80

Value systems, need for some agreement on, 193

Vitalism, as opposed to mechanism, 10

War gases, devices, seen as dangerous knowledge, 58

Welfare, human, must build adaptive capacity, 115

World problems, ten areas in need of solutions, to lessen world tension, 52

Wisdom, as moral knowledge, 49; of the body, book by Walter Cannon, 118; instinctive, breakdown of, 143; survival as a test of, 183–196; as action policy for doing or letting be (Kant), 185; societal competence a function of, 186; as knowledge of how to use knowledge for the social good, required for survival, 186